THE ART OF
BEING FREE

THE ART OF BEING FREE

How Alexis de Tocqueville Can Save Us from Ourselves

JAMES POULOS

ST. MARTIN'S PRESS ✥ NEW YORK

www.stmartins.com

Design by Meryl Sussman Levavi

Cataloging-in-Publication Data is available at the Library of Congress

ISBN 9781250077189 (hardcover)
ISBN 9781250134042 (e-book)

Our books may be purchased in bulk for promotional, educational, or business use. Please contact your local bookseller or the Macmillan Corporate and Premium Sales Department at 1-800-221-7945, extension 5442, or by e-mail at MacmillanSpecialMarkets@macmillan.com.

First Edition: January 2017

10 9 8 7 6 5 4 3 2 1

With love to N.J.P.

These are the spells by which to reassume
An empire o'er the disentangled doom

Contents

THE ART OF BEING FREE

Introduction

This is a weird book for people who feel like they might be a little crazy.

Maybe more than a little.

It is weird in that it utilizes a concept familiar from the internet's junkier precincts: *this one simple trick will solve your stubborn problem!* But instead of a trick, it offers another book, written by a young French aristocrat practically two hundred years ago. Huh? And instead of a single problem, it swaps in the entirety of life itself! Your life, my life, all our lives (if we're American, anyway). Yeah. And, finally, instead of proposing to resolve the strange situation of democracy in America, as that book does, *this* book proposes that our situation can really only be ameliorated. Ours is a crazy predicament that can't be hoped, prayed, distracted, worked, or played out of existence. It's so maddening because it can't be solved. But what if that was okay? Maybe, just maybe, our predicament won't break us if we choose—in an unexpected way—to give ourselves a break.

If no part of this wager or its assumptions ring intuitively true to you, this book is probably not going to work for you. Of course, you should try it out anyway. (What are you, a slave to probabilities or something?)

But if it does ring true, you probably do feel pretty crazy. You probably have a sense—vague as it may be—that the weirdness of American life and the intractability of its predicaments, large and small, are intimately, inexorably bound up with the craziness of everyday life. It's entirely possible that the motto on our coinage, IN GOD WE TRUST, still captures the most popular response to that. But, increasingly, a more useful motto for us might be "DEAL WITH IT."

This book is my attempt to DEAL WITH IT. One of its themes is that books, ironically, can only get us so far in dealing with it. That's not just because reading a conversation is like talking to a painting, a saying Plato attributes to Socrates.* It's because we Americans have a *specific* problem—our craziness—that's baked into the fabric of our lives and the fiber of our being. *That* problem is *especially* poorly suited

---

*Socrates says he "cannot help feeling" that "writing is unfortunately like painting; for the creations of the painter have the attitude of life, and yet if you ask them a question they preserve a solemn silence. And the same may be said of speeches. You would imagine that they had intelligence, but if you want to know anything and put a question to one of them, the speaker always gives one unvarying answer. And when they have been once written down they are tumbled about anywhere among those who may or may not understand them, and know not to whom they should reply, to whom not: and, if they are maltreated or abused, they have no parent to protect them; and they cannot protect or defend themselves." Plato, *Phaedrus, The Dialogues of Plato*, Vol. 1, trans. Benjamin Jowett (New York: Random House, 1937), 278–79.

to "answers" you can think up, write down, and read in a book. Nevertheless, it would be truly insane to look upon books as devilish garbage that can only confuse and fail us. In fact, one unsettling way our craziness manifests is in our temptation to take a bipolar view of books. So many of them let us down, or wind up irrelevant on arrival, that our cynicism and disillusionment grow as fast as our quietly desperate hope that the *next* book, somewhere out there, will finally deliver the goods. Imagine how reassuringly more sane we could be if we spent a little time with a book that did manage to address our specific problem more directly and fruitfully than any other.

I would like you to consider that Alexis de Tocqueville's *Democracy in America* is that book, and it is the reason I have bothered to write the book you are reading now. After all, instead of writing this book, I could have hiked to the top of Griffith Park. I could have eaten a salad on the Malibu pier. I could have recorded a full-length LP with my band, or played baseball with my son, or worked part-time as an Uber driver to send my parents on a Greek vacation without putting a painful dent in my salad budget. But here I am, the author, and here you are, the reader. This experience is what we make of it. Let's make the most.

TUTORIAL

In order to do that, before we get into the genius that is Tocqueville, I'd like to give you a kind of how-to guide: namely, how to read this book. To be frank, this is likely not much like other books you have read. Although it concerns heavy, intense, and very "intellectual" issues—what some philosophers call "matters of ultimate concern"—it is written for *you*, not philosophers. This is not even a book "just" for Tocqueville nerds. Many nettlesome debates underlying philosophy and political theory will simply be danced over, sometimes with questionable dance moves and unconvincingly sexy glances. In part, that's because I've chosen to focus on capturing your imagination. In larger part, however, it's because I found myself, several years ago, unwilling and unable to become a full-on expert in academic thought manipulation. Confronted with a choice of completing a doctorate in political theory or talking with "real Americans" about what the hell is happening to us in our crazy, mixed-up world, I opted for the latter. Some professors out there don't have to make that kind of choice—which is nice for them, probably. For me, it's paramount that the way I talk with you about our crazy, inescapable predicaments comes from a recognizably human place, and the best way I can do that is by living and writing as someone who doesn't have to strain to convince you that we're both blundering along in the same real world.

Nevertheless, although this is the kind of book where you will be invited to contemplate bad sex, having it all, and other canonical concerns of the age, this also is a book that is teeming with big words, sweeping concepts, and a perspective on our human past, present, and future, such that its scope can seem jarringly out of proportion to its ostensibly casual attitude. But if you can handle it in Shakespeare, who took that vertiginous contrast to amazingly dizzying heights, you can certainly handle it here. This ain't Shakespeare. In fact, crazy combinations of high and low are more than just a reflection of real life. They *are* real life.

And here is my first and last trigger warning: even if you are a typical postmodernist, you might be taken aback a few times by the shifts in tone. Not only do the highbrow and the lowbrow mix in this book; the middlebrow jumps in too. Even worse (for some people), the profane and the sacred intermingle. This is a book that deliberately follows Tocqueville's lead by taking religion and spirituality as seriously as it does theory and practice. If this makes you nervous, or fills you with dread that I am going to smuggle in an *ideological agenda*, I invite you to DEAL WITH IT and read on.

Seriously: what is the worst that could happen? I am not going to hypnotize away your commitments or principles. You will not be brainwashed or traumatized. This book is for souls mature enough to function in an interesting, productive, and, yes, *risky* conversational environment. Despite what you may have heard or sensed, the bar for entry here is actually pretty low. From beginning to end, I ask, with all the solicitousness of an online dating profile, that you be tall enough to ride this ride.

So here is your how-to guide for reading *The Art of Being Free*. First, do not read it as a political book. It isn't one. There are lots of great political books about Alexis de Tocqueville and his globe-straddling masterpiece.* Some of them

---

*For me, some of the most influential include Joshua Mitchell, *The Fragility of Freedom* (Chicago: University of Chicago Press, 1995) and *Plato's Fable* (Princeton, NJ: Princeton University Press, 2006); Peter Augustine Lawler, *The Restless Mind* (New York: Rowman & Littlefield, 1993); and Patrick Deneen, *Democratic Faith* (Princeton, NJ: Princeton University Press, 2005). For a richly Tocquevillean approach to contemporary problems at the intersection of policy and politics, see Yuval Levin, *The Fractured Republic* (New York: Basic Books, 2016). In various ways, these

are even called *The Art of Being Free!* Mark Reinhardt's *The Art of Being Free*, for instance, examines how Tocqueville, Marx, and Hannah Arendt can help us learn how to access the direct practice of democratic politics.[1] Wendy McElroy's *Art of Being Free* shares a bit more with mine; hers is designed to help people imagine ways of building and sharing free lives regardless of how little space there is for democratic politics.[2] But McElroy makes zero reference to Alexis de Tocqueville, even though this book's title is found verbatim in *Democracy in America*:

> It cannot be repeated too often: nothing is more fertile in marvels than the art of being free, but nothing is harder than freedom's apprenticeship.[3]

---

works illustrate how Tocqueville helps us fruitfully question judgments and assumptions about social life that have become all too axiomatic, whether more closely associated with the political "left" or "right." Though intellectually and spiritually indebted to all, this book is a decidedly more *Californian* endeavor than any. Tocqueville understood that the South nourished a considerably different type of American than the North. I invite you to confirm through your personal experience that the West Coast has added another twist to the story. It's true, per Tocqueville, that our common American character *does* prevail sociologically over our sectional differences—and that Californian society, especially around Los Angeles, *does* open an especially habitual kind of access to experiencing the superabundance of equal identity even amid abundant unequal difference. As we'll see, Tocqueville sensed this too, connecting Americans' westward journey through the physical world with their spiritual journey toward ultimate visions of equal identity. Logically, that quest reaches *not* its end or apotheosis but its most *characteristic* quality in a place like Los Angeles. It's a voyage that still "has its pluses and minuses," in the parlance of our times. Much of my intentionality for writing this book comes from a sense that Tocqueville's view at the midpoint of our spiritual history and identity can come into unprecedented focus from the viewpoint available, here and now, right in my midst.

Unlike Reinhardt's or McElroy's books, mine foregrounds Tocqueville and backgrounds politics. That's because—important theme alert!—Tocqueville is worth spending our life force on since he talks about things more fundamental than politics. Yes, the assumption here is that politics, including inequalities of power, are not what matter most in life. You should read this book with an awareness that both Tocqueville and I want you to consider setting politics aside while pondering these more basic, important matters—and if you can, when you think about it again, it will work for you in possibly surprising ways.

In fact, you're even going to have to set aside the idea that inequality is the most important aspect of American life, even though doing so is a stumbling block for many people who ostensibly aren't even concerned with politics. Sociology (Tocqueville's discipline, and the one practiced in this book), for instance, has been largely captured by the view that inequalities are the most prevalent and most consequential things around. That view is so forcefully held and so apparently beyond criticism that it has become not only virtually *synonymous* with the dominant vision of what politics is for but virtually *sacrosanct*, too. For many sociologists, there just isn't anything else to care about more than inequality, and there just isn't anything else to do but to combat it politically. Consider the "theme statement" from a recent annual meeting of the American Sociological Association:

> No set of questions is more fundamental to sociology than those about inequality—what is it, why is it, how does it come about, and what can we do to change it? ... Through what processes does this

work? How can we intervene in those processes? How do these processes interact to create the intersectionality that people experience in their everyday lives? . . . Our task at these meetings is to locate the key junctures among these multilevel processes that provide the levers by which different sorts of inequalities among people and groups are systematically made or unmade in the contemporary context. This is the essential first step towards changing those inequalities.[4]

From a standpoint like Tocqueville's, it's certainly essential to attend to real-life everyday experience—not just as a social theorist, but as a human being. But when you do, as Tocqueville helps us understand, you can discover that wherever inequalities are dancing, *underlying equalities* are calling the tune. In this book, along with Tocqueville, we will completely dismiss the notion that the only valid (or possible) purpose of social thought is to identify, discredit, combat, and eventually destroy inequality.

But not because we will take a celebratory or Pollyanna-ish attitude toward inequality. Even if American society is often an inscrutable hodgepodge of shifting fortunes, status, and degrees of sanity, it often produces very clear winners and losers. However, Tocqueville and I both seek to emphasize the unique way American society produces such a widespread, shared experience of living life *losingly*—that the myriad social, cultural, economic, and political differences among us are worthy of analysis for (many) reasons other than inequality.

Second of all, be aware that this book is going to cover a

lot of ground. Much as Tocqueville had to write *Democracy in America* based on a necessarily finite tour around America, we will be taking a moderately whirlwind tour of Tocqueville's book. Although the thoughts therein open, I believe, onto potentially infinite vistas, I also believe there's just no way to get access to that experience without adopting what Friedrich Nietzsche called a "Napoleonic tempo."* Although this is not an overtly warlike book, we will be on the march, we will be expecting a certain degree of fitness, and we will be shooting at moving targets.

To keep up and keep your bearings, you'll want to stay mindful of my big, basic claims about who we are. For instance, one of Tocqueville's central claims is that our identity (how and how much we're freely interchangeable) is way more important to our experience of life than our differences (how and how much we're not). Even where it *appears* that our differences overwhelmingly define some aspect of life, Tocqueville wants us to attend fully to the underlying equality that in fact makes those differences manifest, relevant, and, often, incredibly annoying.

In this book, I want you to envision three basic characteristics of our underlying equality—but not by using

---

*See Friedrich Nietzsche, *Beyond Good and Evil* (New York: Vintage, 1989), pt. 8, sec. 254. Nietzsche uses the phrase to praise the novelist Stendhal, a contemporary of Tocqueville's, as "France's last great psychologist"; Stendhal, says Nietzsche, encompassed "several centuries of the European soul, as an explorer and discoverer of this soul: it required two generations to *catch up* with him in any way, to figure out again a few of the riddles that tormented and enchanted him." Less of a psychologist than Stendhal, Tocqueville is much more of a sociologist. But this book presumes to romp through the territory of the American soul in a similarly expansive fashion, for much the same purpose.

adjectives, the way we so often do. I want us to use adverbs. Fear not, there's a method to the madness here. Throughout this book we'll be consciously rejecting today's prevailing obsession with identity in the sense of *whoness*. Rather than focusing on *who* or *what* we are, we're going to focus on *how* we are—because our *howness* tells us more of what we need to know about being than our whoness does. While we reflexively hear adjectives to declare what we are—*I'm rich, I'm bored, I'm fine, I'm awesome*—we can train our ears to hear adverbs announce how we are, even though it sounds odd or outlandish at first: *I am, richly; I am, boredly,* and so on. See the difference? So picture with me the following three elements of our equal howness. First, we are *crazily*. Second, we are *selfishly*. Third, we are *melodramatically*. Again, don't worry: we won't be taking at face value these three characteristic *ways of how we all are*. This whole book is a sort of extended inquiry into what the hell these defining adverbs mean, a query that can only be answered in reference to *how* they show up for us in our everyday lives.

After taking a quick look at the sources of our American predicament, I'll close with an even quicker word about how different from Tocqueville we should occur to ourselves as being. And then we'll be good to go.

Oh, yeah—one last thing. Read the footnotes. They were baked with love. Just for you.

LIVING CRAZILY

So: you are probably mildly annoyed by a lot of things every day, including the fact that so many of them annoy you. But relatively high on your list of irritations is likely the crazy way that we talk about the craziness of American life. From one perspective, we have a good working knowledge of what we really mean. When we hear Patsy Cline or Aerosmith sing about being crazy, we know exactly what they're saying. When people on the internet talk about their favorite friends or enemies or celebrities being "cray cray" (or just "cray," or whatever neologism is currently on top in the competition for our imagination), we get it. They're not talking about being clinically ill, although that might be a more or less incidental part of the "problem." They're talking about a kind of internal motion that feels beyond our power to control, not just because our relationships often have that effect on us but also because, deep down, we know that not really being in charge of ourselves is part and parcel of the life we live. Compound craziness: life has this fundamentally unworkable, ridiculous character, yet we ridiculously try to make it work, fighting fire with fire.

But while some of us—the most and least envied of us, I suspect—might be considered *extremely* crazy, most of us settle into a mid-tier equilibrium of crazily manageable unmanageability. Like sadism and masochism, full-on manic and depressive experiences are the exception. Most of the time we're moving toward or away from one of the two poles of the human psyche or spirit: a lively-to-frenetic state of outwardness at one end, and a restful-to-paralytic state of inwardness at the other.

You would think that, in a world where autism is increasingly recognized as a spectrum of disorders with varying degrees of severity, our more formal talk about the craziness of American life would take on the same practical tone as the pop culture conversation. But if we shift our perspective, we suddenly don't seem nearly as culturally self-aware as we pretend to be. On the one hand, we don't take mental illness as seriously as we should. We laugh at endless news stories about people flipping out and acting bizarrely, nodding along in a creepy conspiracy of silence about how drugs or disease have driven them to distraction. Yet at the same time we take mental illness *too* seriously. We leap at the chance to label ourselves and others with this or that disorder—to our own detriment. However superficially hobbling, many of the "problems" we reflexively medicate today could in fact offer us the kind of lodestars in too-short supply in contemporary life—if we could just sit still with them for a moment. Instead of confronting us with the unsolvability of life, throwing our spread-thin selves back on our stretched-thin resources, disorders give us concrete problems that we can wrap our minds around—and that science, in the form of prescriptions, can throw its massive resources into. Instead of leaving us alone with the quiddity of life—the baffling mystery of how we can all be unique, yet our uniqueness can be so irrelevant—disorders give us an identity and a community. Instead of turning us loose on the chaos of life without a reliable rule book—or turning the chaos of life loose upon hapless and vulnerable us—disorders can actually *order* our existence, supplying us with the routines that arrange our horizontal movements and with steps that vertically structure our aspirations. Through sickness, health.

Wait a minute. In a social or cultural order that breeds disorder, disorder becomes a strategy for creating order? That massive paradox is characteristic of American life. And it is super annoying. We have enough paradoxes as it is! Our country is exceptionally strong yet powerfully gripped by fear, insecurity, paranoia, and occasional outright panic. In the land of the free and the home of the brave, our potent aversion to risk has made us dependent on institutions that are "too big to fail" and has wired us into a system where structural change, or even significant reform, is more or less impossible. What is happening at the level of society is also happening at the level of the individual. Allegedly, we Americans are more autonomous than ever. Many of us intuit that, in other ways, we're more tethered than ever to our debt, our baggage, our issues—to sum it all up, our fate. Why would we want to pile on another paradox?

LIVING SELFISHLY

Unlike Taylor Swift, we can hardly just shake it off. It shouldn't necessarily be a *problem* that there's a huge gray area between mental health and mental illness, but for us it is a problem because, in spite of ourselves, we're so bad at coming to terms with it. Neither our professional experts nor our public opinion is able tell us the *whole* of what we sense the story to be—despite the fact that "self-help" is as ubiquitous as the air we collectively breathe. The self-help industry is great at giving us perspectives on the whole, or slices of it, even as its many niches and particularities make claims to a level of transcendence, completeness, or universality that's forcefully compelling. Movements, memes, gurus, cults, and *New York Times* bestsellers—you know, *crazes*—rise and fall, flare and fade away. But we're still here. And, as usual, we're left holding the bag.

What's in the bag? The self! In an era when money

represents the total adaptability and limitless movement we all aspire to, we tell ourselves that selfishness is a big problem in American life. Greed, narcissism, solipsism, addiction—you name it, we blame it. Yet when we ask "the self" to bear the burdens of our crazy life and world, the self lets us down like a bad boyfriend or girlfriend. You might see this as evidence that the self is actually a pretty horrible person. I see it as an important indication that a lot of our craziness results from imagining that the self is a person at all, or even a thing.

Think of it this way. We all develop a decent feel, somewhere along the way, for what "personhood" means. When our feel is not so good, or becomes a point of contention, controversies crop up. For instance, are human fetuses persons? (If so, starting when?) Are dolphins? Personhood isn't an inherently legal category—it's much more organic and subtle than that—but it feels weird for us, as humans, to agree that someone is a person yet allow the law to disagree. From that standpoint it seems completely crazy to consider whether "the self" that we talk about should be ascribed legal personhood. Although obviously we are beholding a person when we behold *ourselves*, our instincts rebel at the notion that we're reckoning with a person when we reckon with our *selves*.

The self occurs to us as something not just "inside" our person but something far shiftier, less reliable, more susceptible to manipulation. As a philosopher might say, we grasp that our selfhood is *contingent* in a way that our personhood is not. "I'm not feeling quite myself today," we might say in a silly English accent, trying to distract a friend or family member from how we think we're really feeling. As you might recall, Hamlet put himself into a version of this situation. "Hamlet is of the faction that is wronged," he says of his meddlesome, meddled-with self. "His madness is poor Hamlet's enemy."[5]

But we never joke about whether or not we're a person. No matter how "off" we are, no matter how sweeping an internal or external transfiguration we experience, we're always a human person—specifically, the same one we were yesterday and the same one we'll be tomorrow. If we let others know we disagree with that proposition, we will be seen as not just crazy but actually insane.

As you may have noticed, the imprecision of language is a problem. A worse problem, however, is that we *like* it that way. We sort of *want* it to be imprecise, and where it is, we, like Hamlet, exploit it to our advantage.* It's devilishly hard to determine where the self we construct ends and where the "real" self begins. It's almost as if we dreamed up this thing called the self in order to focus our chaotic energies on a single dysfunctional relationship.

So although the literature of self-help is well-intentioned,

---

*A fragment comes down to us from Gorgias, a sophist rhetorician whom Plato has Socrates contend with in a dialogue bearing Gorgias's name. In the fragment Gorgias claims that tragedy "creates a deception in which the deceiver is more honest than the non-deceiver and the deceived is wiser than the non-deceived." Quoted in Simon Critchley and Jamieson Webster, *Stay, Illusion! The Hamlet Doctrine* (New York: Pantheon Books, 2013), 16. When we consciously make a theater of the self, the better to believe our own lies, we become, like Hamlet, "but mad north-north-west" (act 2, scene 2). "When the wind is southerly," Hamlet continues, "I know a hawk from a handsaw." *What* "wind"?

it tends to disappoint in two important ways. First, it's unclear what it's designed to help us do. The best spin we can put on self-help is that its goal is to help us *succeed*, to win at whatever game we happen to play. That includes, of course, the game of choosing *what* game to play. Yet not all of us get to make that choice. In fact, to be more precise, that kind of unfettered selfish autonomy is a myth, a fable, even a lie.

For those of us who think a lot about the mid-twentieth century, the fable of autonomy probably ushers in a whole field of memories, feelings, and fears about the so-called death of the American Dream.* For those of us who think more about the mid-seventeenth century, the artifice of autonomy will likely summon up philosopher Rene Descartes, with his incredibly abstract and quintessentially modern

---

*Trying to write a book on the subject, Hunter Thompson observed what Tocqueville, as we'll see, surmised: the morbidity of the American Dream hinges on how the quest for autonomy decays into the quest for money. Intent on honoring Faulkner's admonition to see the world in a grain of sand, Thompson "finally found the American Dream" at the Circus-Circus, which occupies a pivotal role in what eventually fulfilled Thompson's contract for the American Dream book—*Fear and Loathing in Las Vegas*. As he explained to editor Jim Silberman in a letter meant to soften the trauma of his expense report, "you can't send a man out in a fucking Pinto or a VW to seek out the American Dream in Las Vegas."

> You want to be able to come roaring into the Circus-Circus in a huge Coupe de Ville and *know* the insanity of watching people jump and run and salute and all that crap . . . which is crazy, of course, but the insane truth is that the difference between $15 a day for a Mustang and $20 a day for a white Cadillac convertible is *massive* in LA or Las Vegas. That extra $5 is a ticket to Their World—that and constantly giving dollar bills to "boys" for quick unctuous service. (Which comes hard when the driver of the Cadillac is a huge gross drunken Chicano wearing a yellow fishnet shirt with a long hunting knife & a bottle of rum in his hand; but even that kind of culture shock disappears with a $2 tip, instead of just $1.) (Thompson, *Fear and Loathing in America* [New York: Simon & Schuster, 2000], 383.)

supposition that only the knowledge of the isolated, independent mind can shake us loose from doubt. Remember "I think, therefore I am?" That's Descartes. Rather than merely assuring us we can "just do it," Descartes's wager tells us that we *already are* a self, which others can allegedly help do whatever it is selves do. From his standpoint, the relationship between our personhood and our selfhood isn't a problem. In fact, the fact that they're pretty much identical is the *solution* to all our problems. But even if we decided that the self was also a lie, the better to be debunked and disbelieved like some of us have done with God, the brute fact of our personhood would make his kind of radical autonomy impossible and unliveable. We're just too interrelated. Our personhood is inseparable from our biological function, as creatures who are constantly imitating and remembering people and things. Descartes's notion cuts against the grain of our everyday experience in a way that makes it seem not just naive but perniciously so. Today we know that trying to "pull a Descartes"—that is, seeking certainty in the isolation of our rational mind—will only make us crazier. It's why a guy like G. K. Chesterton could say things like "the madman is the man who has lost everything but his reason."[6] Reason crazily tells us that, in the absence of everything else, the self exists.

Yet reason is not to blame for our dysfunctional relationship with the self. In real life, we know that the self is, like Hamlet's crazy alter ego, too clever a creation by half. We can *use* it in all kinds of sneaky, abusive, enabling, wicked, and cowardly ways—perhaps most commonly as an excuse not to confront *how* we and others are actually being. Turns out we're not really selfish in the predictable, superficial sense—that we want our way and to hell with everyone else. We're selfish in that we covet the self, our precious creation that's always on hand to enable our fears and give us excuses for doing whatever bad stuff seems like a good way to protect and improve its fortunes most quickly.

Herein lies another one of our big, annoying problems. After all, we don't like the idea that we have to muddle through life the long way, especially when it comes to what aggrieves us. We want foolproof shortcuts, and we want them now. Even if we suspect that our *ontological status*, as a philosopher might say, immerses us in a kind of doubt that is exacerbated by dwelling on it, our propensity is to grapple with that problem through *reason*—our own, our friends', or that of the experts we pay.

Our problem is that American life is more than any of our rational minds can handle. Not only do we ride our rationality like a bad motorcycle tough, pushing it to the limit, but after we blow out our engine, we *keep going*. We're not going to let a breakdown stop us. We want what we want! Confronted by the failure of so-called Cartesian thinking, our "will resists," sighs Tocqueville, even when our "reason frequently gives way."[7]

LIVING MELODRAMATICALLY

This is crazy. So why do we do it? Because we lack confidence about both the *why* of our human being and the *how*. Despite our propensity to whine, cower, and enable our own disempowerment through stupidly clever excuses, it really is exceedingly difficult for us to distinguish between *being* a certain way and *acting* a certain way. *Not to seem,* *but to be*—a maxim from the ancient tragedian Aeschylus[8] that once appealed to so many learned Americans—is now another one of our frustrating, irritating, paradoxical problems. As Nietzsche noticed in the late nineteenth century, we are all actors now.* Not only does self-help still struggle to show us *that we are* but it also struggles to show us *how to be*, as an authentic alternative to "seeming" or "acting."

If indeed you feel crazy enough to be comfortable considering the weird, you are probably open to the idea that focusing on *how* to be can clear the space for seeing the *whole* story about American craziness—not just some misleadingly incomplete slice or disconnected segment of our crazy lives. If so, that's a nice indication that this book is going to work for you.

In fact, a central contention of this book is that *Democracy in America* is *therefore* also for you. That's because Tocqueville somehow understood better than anyone how the dramatic craziness of life was a *constitutive*, baked-in part of Americans. We can't find reliable refuge by trying to become superindependent or superdependent people. Neither our autonomy nor our interchangeability can save us. Rather than seeing ourselves, above all, as autonomously unique

---

*In "really democratic ages," a "cocky faith" possessed by "the Americans today" comes to the fore: "the individual becomes convinced that he can do just about everything and *can manage almost every role* . . . and whenever a human being begins to discover how he is playing a role and how he *can* be an actor, he *becomes* an actor." Friedrich Nietzsche, *The Gay Science* (New York: Vintage, 1974), bk. 5, sec. 356.

or interchangeably equal, Tocqueville suggests, we need to see ourselves as *being*, in a way that's superficially easy to grasp but surprisingly nuanced and subtle. We need to see ourselves as we actually are: free.

In order to see ourselves accurately as free, Tocqueville counsels, we can't just place our trust in the abstract concept of free selfhood that a brain in a vat might conceive of. Nor can we simply take "their" word for it—whether "they" are our designated experts or the aggregate self, otherwise known as public opinion. Instead of receiving our belief in our freedom from knowledge or authority, we have to experience it—"for ourselves," as we Americans reflexively, redundantly, and self-soothingly add.

But wait, there's more. Once we achieve an experienced awareness of freedom as the characteristic of our being, we can't stop there. We can never "just be" because the craziness of life is constitutive. We can no more opt out of using and being used by life than we can opt out of breathing other people's exhaled air. As Tocqueville makes clear, we are *not* free to just be. Instead, we are *stuck* being free!

If you suppose that means we're stuck living lives of continually exploring *how* to be free, congratulations. You're on the right track. Although we may occasionally wonder *why* we are stuck being free, our characteristic American predicaments arise from taking our freedom as a given. Rather than simply "sacred" or "undeniable," as Thomas Jefferson dubbed it, our freedom is more precisely "self-evident"—to quote Benjamin Franklin instead.[9] We understand this, not because we have learned it as fact, but because we live it every day.

What's more, we don't live it in a narrowly personal

way—though, sometimes, a radically personal experience with freedom can upend our lives. Day in and day out, our free being is self-evident in the sense that it's *not* personal. It's neither friendly nor malevolent; not God and not the Devil. Unfortunately, that weirdly impersonal experience doesn't give us the easy out of becoming depersonalized and inert. We humans can't just *be free* for the same reason that we can't *just be*. Being a being isn't like being a rock. Here's where the distinction between *whoness* and *howness* figures in so powerfully. The life of our being is defined by adverbs. "How are you?" we wisely ask—only to answer unwisely, with adjectives. "Great! Fine. Terrible. . . ." We'd be able to make a lot more sense of our being if we answered adverbially. How are we? We *are* anxiously or calmly, firmly or irresolutely, enviously or pridefully, by turns.

Though we understand through experience that, in some ineffable sense, we always *are* freely, we also sense that freedom—that is, *being freely*—is something we're often bad at.

Ladies and gentlemen, here comes the melodrama. Even though you've asked people how they are hundreds or thousands of times, probably nobody has ever replied by confiding in you that they were being freely pretty badly. But that's the truth, isn't it? Millions of Americans, feeling their way through life, not always doing so well at freely being.

No wonder we're all so crazy. We grasp, right down to the marrow of our bones, that it's not easy being free. There's an inescapable, all-important *how* to it—a process, a practice, and an experience wherein our amazing abilities to think rationally and want irrationally can only get us so far. The same goes for our even greater talents of imitation and memorization. Well before we gain fluency, literacy, or even language, we knit our experiences together by imitating and remembering those around us. But there's a rotten catch. So many of us have remembered so well how to imitate people who are *inartful* at being freely that, as a matter of habit, we make the same mistakes. Although we grasp that freedom inheres in our being, we just keep making each other miss the mark.

That's why inequalities of power make us so upset, even though staggering equality is to be found almost everywhere we look, if only we look through the surface of our fears and grievances. In a recent issue of *The Chronicle of Higher Education*, professor and critic Laura Kipnis helpfully draws our attention to "the melodramatic imagination's obsession with helpless victims and powerful predators."[10] Guess what happens when you hang out in that headspace for a while—or, better yet, in the company of people caught in the grip of their own melodramatic imaginations? You catch on to a massive fear that we're so bad at being freely that we must constantly attend to how others pay the price for our failures, and we for theirs.

That brutal verdict is hardly confined to a single ideology. Although its believers often reach for a supernatural degree of certitude, it has Christian and secular proponents alike. In the melodramatic imagination, our pathetic, accursed inability to be freely makes a mockery of our hopes and dreams. At rock bottom, life itself is a litany of cruel, unfunny jokes. (And we wonder why so much of comedy is now mere mockery.) Not only are we fated to make a mess of our free being but we're also fated to mess up the lives of others as a result. And, crucially, we're fated to *know* that we're doing it, deep in the fibers of our being. Already raised by society as actors, we then realize that we're trapped on stages and in roles not of our choosing. It's like Macbeth, that drama king, says: life is full of sound and fury.[11] But instead of safely signifying nothing, it shows us how doomed we are to always hurt others or be hurt. Poor us!

So could it be that the ultimate melodramatic philosopher, Jean-Jacques Rousseau, from whom Tocqueville learned much, famously groaned that we humans are born free, but are everywhere in chains.[12] And so it is that, much to our frustration, there is still no *Dummies' Guide to Being Free*. There is no owner's manual, no textbook, not even a Freedom Bible. We cannot get a professional degree in being freely. The *particular* kind of how that pertains to being freely is not, I regret to inform you, part of this or any other how-to.

TOCQUEVILLE'S GHOST

One reason for Macbeth's melodrama is what a therapist might call his *very negative experience* with *guilt issues* surrounding the death of good old Banquo. Of course, Macbeth himself planned Banquo's murder.[13] Even in life, Macbeth was afraid of his friend—no wonder he later sees his ghost. For a while now, certain philosophers have pondered the problem of melodrama as a function of violence, debt, shame, and mourning. Karl Marx, for instance, kicked off *The Communist Manifesto* by warning that "a specter is haunting Europe"—a "specter of communism" that declared "the history of all hitherto existing society" to be "the history of class struggles."[14] Later, after Marx's ideas had fallen into disrepute, Jacques Derrida suggested that, now, a specter of

Marx was haunting philosophy.[15] But please keep in mind, as you read this book, that I don't want you feeling guilty about your relationship with Tocqueville's ghost.

We know that Tocqueville did not leave us with a free-be-er's handbook. What's more, according to varying accounts, Tocqueville's own concerns about how we'd fare in the inevitable absence of such a reference manual left him anywhere from mildly bummed to existentially depressed. One near-contemporary of Tocqueville's said his attitude toward democracy was of "sad belief, almost one of despair."

> On every page, reading him, we think again of [Blaise] Pascal's melancholy words, [which Tocqueville] more than anyone would have had the right to make his slogan: "I blame all equally, those who take the side of praising humanity, those who take the side of blaming it, and those who take the side of entertaining it; and I can only approve those who seek while wailing."[16]

One of my biggest objectives in this book is to dispel this sense of fated despair. Although the particular sort of *how* that pertains to being freely isn't a science, it *is*, Tocqueville tells us, an art. In fact, recall that, once you come into your own, "nothing is more fertile in marvels."

So that's it then, right? Practice the art of being free and say goodbye to not only Tocqueville's brooding ghost but the whole craziness of life?

Not exactly. *Democracy in America* isn't an infomercial and neither is this book. Remember, there's a second half to Tocqueville's beautiful insight into the art of being free. It's true that nothing's more wonderful, *and* it's true that nothing is harder to learn how to use, than freedom.

That's right. Being freely is about the adverb, not the noun. You can't use it up, like a treatment, in the knowledge that what you're using it to get rid of will eventually go away. You can't use it like a tool either, applying it to an unfinished situation until it's finished. Freedom can't be used to *finish things off*—whether they're problems, jobs, stories, or, well, ghosts. What it *can* do is mitigate life's craziness at its extremes. We won't ameliorate the madness by *performing our autonomy*, turning relationships with things (and people) that vex us into contracts we can terminate. We'll do it by *experiencing our freedom*, which is always already a part of all our relationships, chosen and unchosen, including with any of our supposed selves.

That's the story this book sets out to tell. I think that, ultimately, it's the story *Democracy in America* set out to tell as well. Nearly two hundred years later, my telling will ultimately differ, in some hopefully intriguing ways, from the story that Tocqueville told. Both books are written out of a sense that the turmoil around and within us is (still) indicative of a new world that's (still) going to last a long time. But because Tocqueville achieved so much penetrating, persistent insight into our American predicament—and because that insight introduces into our presence a quality of freedom that conditions us for more imaginative retellings— this book is first a fresh telling of his story, and only then a telling of my own.

Change

We Americans have a relationship problem. And we can't stop talking about it. In fact, much like the stereotypical romantic relationship, our ambivalence extends to *talking* about it. We can't live with it. We can't live without it. And we can't shut up about it.

What's got us so muddled is deceptively simple: *change*.

It's "the one constant" in a world where "the only rule is that there are no rules." We love it so much that we use it interchangeably with *progress* or *improvement*, two of our favorite things. We hate it so much that we're terrified it'll make *us* its prey next. We worry which privileged person is about to move our cheese—or worse, which capriciously convenienced schmuck is going to do so.* Always every-

---

*See Spencer Johnson, *Who Moved My Cheese? An Amazing Way to Deal with Change in Your Work and in Your Life* (New York: G. P. Putnam's Sons,

where yet never in one place, change is the perfect summation of our fascination with the possibility of everything and our fear of the certainty of nothing.

BETWEEN TWO FERNS

If you're not a complete loser, you probably know all about Zach Galifianakis's hit web series. Crouched, like so many of us, in a defensive posture of emotional unavailability, the celebrity actor's interview show protects itself, and us, by completely scrambling the distinction between mocking and celebrating our culture's self-consciously amateur awkwardness. *Between Two Ferns* is "really funny" in the way so much of comedy is today: when there are jokes, they don't make you laugh, and when you laugh, it's not because there are jokes. It's "really cool." President Barack Obama has appeared on it.

Putatively, *Between Two Ferns* is named *Between Two Ferns* because the title describes the physical location of Galifianakis and his on-set interview guests. But on a deeper level that Galifianakis may or may not have intended, there's a good reason to frame manufactured awkwardness with ferns. As Adam and Eve can tell you, the first articles of clothing were sewn shamefully from the leaves of bushes. Even today, as our better cartoons attest, when nothing else is there for you, when you find yourself awkwardly naked,

---

1998)—the book that announced our current era of obsessing over the science and spirituality of coping comprehensively with change. Later in this book you'll recall that the first edition of *Who Moved My Cheese?* was published in *September* 1998—a more culturally important month than you might now imagine.

you can usually count on a fern to duck behind. Sometimes, you've got ferns to the left of you, ferns to the right, but you're stuck in the middle, unable to dive for shelter.

In addition to being a metaphor for awkwardness, the fern is a great visualization of change. In fact, if you've ever experienced it, you know just how closely awkwardness and change are related. One minute, as Heidi Klum tells the weeping losers on *Project Runway*, you're on top. The next, you're *out*. Above all, for us, change means changing *status*. When our status has suddenly changed for the worse, the last place we want to be caught is between two ferns. We don't want to stand out from the foliage—we want to vanish behind it, the way Homer Simpson, in one of the internet's more meaningful gifs, backs unblinkingly into a hedgerow until he disappears.

Yes, yes, we know: sometimes it seems like the jerks at the top of the social food chain *never* lose out when awkward change strikes. They were "born on third base," or they "gamed the system," or they slept their way to the top, or hacked their lives, or whatever excuse we prefer to make for their enviably secure prosperity. But we also know how unenviably precarious it really is, especially after just a generation or two. In old Europe, aristocratic families persisted at an unreachable social height for century after century; in America, our mighty routinely fall, and our wealthy go broke, in the space of a generation or two—or less! American craziness makes crackheads out of celebrities, convicted criminals out of leading professionals, and casualties out of heirs and heiresses. "The actual moment completely occupies and absorbs them," says Tocqueville of the rich, the well-positioned, and the rest of us no less. "They are much more in love with success than with glory." The manners of our so-called elites *mirror* those of the rest of us, "almost always" lagging "behind the rise in their social position. As a result," he says, "very vulgar tastes often go with their enjoyment of extraordinary prosperity, and it would seem that their only object in rising to supreme power was to gratify trivial and coarse appetites more easily."[1] We know that even at the pinnacle, people focus way more on living large than on grandiose schemes, and ruination and humiliation are never completely at bay.

That's why, in the back of our minds, our constant anxiety about change boils down to a weird oxymoron. Turns out being "change's bitch," as we would and Tocqueville wouldn't say, isn't the worst fate. That's being *ignored* by change, so to speak—being simply irrelevant. There's another gif that's probably still twirling away somewhere in your feed, a knowingly outdated 3D-text image reading *lol nothing matters*, rotating brightly and briskly like an old customizable screensaver. Meant to mockingly signify the futility of people's feelings and opinions—possibly to the point of *all* feelings and opinions—it reflects back the ultimate in awkward loserdom imposed by change. Change? Yeah, no, it's too cool for you. Sorry not sorry! Stay FOMO!

It is not an accident that we talk this way about change on the internet—and increasingly, as I'm doing now, in real life. A keen observer of American life could see this coming a sociohistorical mile away. In fact, Alexis de Tocqueville *did* see it coming and painstakingly transcribed a soulful account of *how* and *why* it would come. His awareness of the way change occurs to us is the reason he wrote *Democracy in America*. It's the reason why we should care—a lot—that he did. It's the reason you're reading this book.

To uncover the art of being free in all realms of our lives—from religion to money to entertainment, from sex to death to love—we can begin with a simple task: taking account of where we exist in historical time. Tocqueville tells us something we're ready to hear: we're not just living at some random moment in human existence. But he also offers a provocation: we're at a crossroads. Our experience has been prepared for centuries, and how it turns out will impact human beings for centuries to come.

Naturally, that sends us into internal-monologue overdrive. *Oh, great. No wonder we're all so crazy.*

Yes, but hang on! You can do that, right? Americans are great at hanging on.

Let's forgive ourselves for our hair-trigger sarcasm, whipped out, as so often it is, to channel our frustration at being passive objects into a passionate performance as active subjects. Let's take a moment of Zen to soak into Tocqueville's cosmic vision. Life is pretty disorienting. Many of our worries stem from feeling lost in the shuffle of life. Much of what we argue about is how to orient ourselves in space and time. We find it equally hard to just shrug, on the one hand, as to surrender ourselves over to grandiose, all-consuming missions, on the other. Tocqueville offers us a different path, toward a different horizon. We can prime ourselves to embrace his logic just by considering that his *provocation* is actually an *invitation* to become extraordinarily (but not ridiculously) more chill. Then we can allow him to coach us through the realms of life step by step.

Ready? Here we go.

We like to think the present age is radically different and distant from the time of the American Revolution, to say nothing of the Puritans. Even though the uncertainties of contemporary life stress us out, we're more afraid of a world where nothing is new under the sun. For us, novelty is a compliment—of course, as Tocqueville would say. The very first words of his author's introduction confess that "no novelty in the United States struck me more vividly during my stay there than the equality of conditions."[2] The definitive aspect of American society, "the creative element from which each particular fact" about us, in Tocqueville's eyes, "derived," was a novelty! The goodness of novelty is in our bones.* For us, you can't turn back the clock, and it often seems not just vain but morally wrong to try.

The truth, says Tocqueville, is more complicated. We're so close to our newness, we often can't see it. Lost in the minutiae of small novelties, we forget that we're still fresh fish in a cosmic sea change that began hundreds of years ago. And, ironically, because the patterns laid down at our American origins are far more persistent than we care to imagine,† we're extra prone to downplay how much of the craziness of our lives is rooted in what Tocqueville saw were

---

* "The American lives in a land of wonders; everything around him is in constant movement, and every movement seems an advance. Consequently, in his mind the idea of newness is closely linked with that of improvement." Alexis de Tocqueville, *Democracy in America*, ed. J. P. Mayer, trans. George Lawrence (New York: Harper, 2006), 404.

† Nietzsche makes pregnant reference to "the democratic prejudice in the modern world toward all questions of origin." Friedrich Nietzsche, *Genealogy of Morals* (New York: Vintage, 1989), first essay, sec. 4.

new patterns established and spread by the people whose origins as new Americans traced to Plymouth Rock.

We're still at the very beginning of humanity's journey out of one era and into another. True, our experience tells us that we're in a world hugely unlike that of our ancestors. But we're also so focused on what's right in front of our noses that we struggle to create a long-term vision of our future. We intuit only dimly "what can be hoped or feared"; with "much curiosity and little leisure," we live out lives "so practical, complicated, agitated, and active" that we have but "little time for thinking"—and little ability to *project* creative intentionality deep into the future.* Too stressed out to master the centuries ahead, we console ourselves by at least feeling free of the past.

Were we less encumbered, we could begin to see just how close we still are in our habits, our feelings, and our mores to American life at its origins. We'd glimpse that the strange new kind of change we're going through now has more in common than we think with the kind of change at work in Tocqueville's time—just as fresh, important, and recognizable as it was back then. It's because Tocqueville has enough of the aristocratic mind-set to lounge around, pondering humanity's long-term future, that he envisions what we, as time travelers dumped in the mid-nineteenth century, could not: our own predicament.

By thinking about who we Americans could still be in this and future centuries, Tocqueville tries to warn our predecessors—and their descendants—how *not* to descend

---

*Nietzsche, *Genealogy of Morals*, 440. We *act* like our individuality is the source of our creativity; *actually*, it's our equality.

into social and individual madness. That's why he pays such close attention, in *Democracy in America*, to the way we live out our collective and personal journeys between past and future. He wraps the book around the idea that we can't make sense of our world except *as an experience of change*.

Not one for overindulging abstract ideas—a vice *we* are particularly vulnerable to—Tocqueville takes care to detail what kind of "change experience" defines our perplexing, problematic age. This long moment we entered into a few hundred years ago isn't a nonjudgmental mushball of random alterations. It isn't change for change's sake. But it also isn't change in the way that the ancient Greeks and Romans, right up through Niccolò Machiavelli, imagined: as a cyclical, natural process—fickle in its dispensations of fate, perhaps, but, on a cosmic level, locked in a loop.* Instead of hurtling forward on the rapids of history, we rose and fell like empires, seasons, or tides. For Tocqueville, the unprecedented moment he sees dawning in America—the one we're still living in now—is the Great Transition: out of what he calls the "aristocratic" age that had begun to die, into the

---

*Machiavelli had no patience for the apocalyptic Christianity of the End Times, and no knowledge of the more circumspect vision of history's Providential outworking that gained currency in later centuries. Both types of Christian vision set history on a course, not a loop, however many oscillations or setbacks there may be in the storied disjunction between human errancy and what Tocqueville called "God's object." Unlike the view of the ancients, Tocqueville's vision of change is a Christian one, even though it doesn't culminate in Armageddon. "To force all men to march in step toward the same goal—that is a human idea. To encourage an endless variety of actions but to bring them about so that in a thousand different ways all tend toward the fulfillment of one great design—that is a God-given idea" (Tocqueville, *Democracy*, 735). For Tocqueville, the kind of change we're going through *promises* unity, but *risks* uniformity.

"democratic" age now coming to life. One era, one world, one way of life is ending *forever*, and another one, a new one, is coming to replace it. The old, ancient age is *not* over and done with, mind you. And we assuredly haven't yet disappeared into the new one. Instead, we are beginning a long, strange trip through the slow fade-out of the first and the slow fade-in of the second. No matter how terrifyingly rapid *particular* big changes feel—whether personal ones, like death and divorce, or social ones, like the rise of robots and Donald Trump and other threatening cheese-movers—the truth is that a larger slowness transcends, unifies, and defines them all. In fact, from that higher perspective our pace may move even *more* slowly in the future, not less, the "irresistible" outworking of "the most continuous, ancient, and permanent tendency known to history."* This strange combination of surface speed and deeper slowness is a hallmark of today's Great Transition.†

---

*Tocqueville, *Democracy*, 9. Or, as Nietzsche put it, "The progress of this poison through the entire body of mankind seems irresistible, its pace and tempo may from now on even grow slower, subtler, less audible, more cautious—there is plenty of time." *Genealogy of Morals*, first essay, sec. 9. Nietzsche is always a good comparison with Tocqueville. The two saw the same great transition, felt opposite ways, and drew opposite conclusions.

†The social theorist Philip Rieff, much like Nietzsche and Tocqueville, succeeded in addressing "those troubled readers in whose minds and hearts one culture is dying while no other gains enough power to be born." Rieff, *Triumph of the Therapeutic* (New York: Harper & Row, 1968), 2. Rieff's interest in the displacement and possible replacement of Christian culture stemmed from his determination that "the dissolution of a unitary system of common belief" was "accompanied, as it must be, by a certain disorganization of personality" (2). Surmising that *this* great transition had "all but ended," he presumed that "the psychologizers"

Our first opportunity to chill, then, has to do with *responsibility* and *speed*—two things we stress out about all the (ahem) time. Even at our crucial historical crossroads, the pace of the change that defines us most isn't *up to us*. It's not our burden. "Just let go," as Tyler Durden would say; "Jesus, take the wheel," as Carrie Underwood would. We long for this kind of release from *adaptive responsibility* in lots of different, distinctly American ways. Here it is.

Indeed, says Tocqueville, we are granted access to this release *because* the tempo of that dominating, defining change is *moderate* enough not to terrify us. Not everyone was so

---

were "now fully established as the pacesetters of cultural change" (2–3). But Rieff warned that sociological theory, including Tocqueville's, had called their "individualist conceptions of the self" into question from the very beginning (3n1). While, on the one hand, Rieff claimed that "going over to the side of the latest, and most original, individualist" marked "the complete democratization of our culture," he also insisted that Freudian psychology had been hijacked by successors for whom that democratization was indistinguishable from a "talented hostility to culture" (9). Rieff raised these issues more than a century after Tocqueville. But in the ensuing half century, while the triumph of the therapeutic brought an alleged end to the post-Christian transition, the slow unfolding of equalization has still hardly come close to the end of Tocqueville's Great Transition. The march of equality through imitation and memory in everyday experience has been great news for the persistence of Christianity, not just for the persistence of Christian patterns of thought in secular life, which Nietzsche described as the "shadow" of the "dead" God on the "cave" of human culture. *The Gay Science* (New York: Vintage, 1974), bk. 3, sec. 108. With its deep emphasis on both equality and forbearance, American Christianity for Tocqueville is a graceful indication that conceptual frameworks still exist for us to keep on democratizing without growing ever more hostile to culture, the indispensable social mechanism for helping prevent us from driving ourselves and each other crazy.

lucky. As Tocqueville noted, Europe's experience of the Great Transition was traumatically accelerated. Sure enough, its blitzkrieg speed—from the French Revolution to the Napoleonic Wars to the nationalistic revolutions of 1848 to the Franco-Prussian War and the World Wars beyond—made the change from one era to another one big reign of terror. "Carried away by a rapid current," he laments, "we obstinately keep our eyes fixed on the ruins still in sight on the bank, while the stream whirls us backward—facing toward the abyss."[3] However potent that kind of analogy to nature, the terrifying tempo of Europe's transition made change a fearsomely unnatural experience, increasingly manufactured and mechanistic, outside of human proportions and exceeding our capacity to cope.* In America, by contrast, the speed of change *seems* blistering at the level of our petty affairs and competitive scrambles. But that we can even engross ourselves in such economies of small differences is a testament to how peaceably, sanely moderate the pace of our change really is. Instead of a Great Transition marked by endless, escalating, exhausting revolutions, ours is

---

*For Paul Virilio, the urban theorist who grew up amid the Nazi occupation of France, the enthusiasm for progress that characterizes democratic life begat a "propaganda of progress" that breeds terror by worshipping speed. See Virilio, *The Administration of Fear* (Los Angeles: Semiotext(e), 2012). The imperatives that grow up around this dark faith threaten, in Virilio's vision, to make further leaps of technological development hostile to life. Tocqueville wagers that, for us, at least, the stakes are lower. The art of being free entails the art of moving through our space and time with moderation well understood. Fortunately, we possess enough shared experiential resources to practice and share that art without capitulating to the fear that doing so makes us too inattentive to adaptively survive change at increasingly destructive speeds.

marked out in cosmic measurements that human beings, and human generations, can safely reconcile with their real-life experience.

The more cosmic a perspective on our craziness we key into, the more we can chill in its midst. Tocqueville, more a product of the aristocratic than the democratic age, looked upon the implications of this insight with the kind of awe we always get from beholding sublime vistas. When we think about it, the inexorable progress of the Great Transition is pretty much a given, part of the scenery, like water for fish. But for Tocqueville, it inspired reverent astonishment. "This whole book," he says, "has been written under the impulse of a kind of religious dread"[4]; but while any old aristocrat can feel that way watching millennia-old social arrangements disintegrate in the Old World, Tocqueville focuses on America in the New World, where even the most sweeping kind of change plays out in a charmed idyll when compared to the nightmarish panorama of European change. Tocqueville takes pains to observe that race slavery in America is a unique scourge, portending an uncharacteristic degree of blood and misery.* But even that sharpest of inequalities cannot accelerate the tempo of change to Europe's terrifying levels.

Of course, human beings have problems, however

---

*"The South has a large slave population, which is a menace now and will be a greater menace in the future" (Tocqueville, *Democracy in America*, 327). But rather than menacing "directly, through interests," slavery does so "indirectly, through mores" (376), creating a habit of pride destined to go down to violent defeat amid the patient, unshakeable advance of change away from inequality. Bloody as the Civil War was, it failed to efface the habit of pride that race slavery instilled, or to accelerate change into perpetual revolution.

fortunate they are, and one of our foremost problems develops naturally out of the otherwise blessedly slow pace of the Great Transformation. The risk that looms over us is not of sudden destruction but, as we say, arrested development. As Britney Spears fans might put it, the representative American is not an aristocrat, not yet a democrat—not in Tocqueville's sense, anyway. There is no surprise that ours is an age of mass awkwardness and socioeconomic teen worship. By Tocqueville's lights, we are the tweens of history, working self-consciously to grow up faster, nervous that we can't pull it off. "They see a multitude of little intermediate obstacles, all of which have to be negotiated slowly, between them and the great object of their ultimate desires. The very anticipation of this prospect tires ambition and discourages it. They therefore discard such distant and doubtful hopes," he says of us, "preferring to seek delights less lofty but easier to reach. No law limits their horizon, but they do so for themselves."[5] No wonder Katy Perry's escapist motivational pop, where we're all fireworks and teenage dreams, is such a moneymaker.

How predictable, too, that ours is a quintessentially tween-age era of both overexposure and a fear of missing out, a time of deep ambivalence about privacy and home. Although we miss sheltering ourselves from danger and doubt behind the canopy of the settled past, and we yearn to repose in the durable comforts of more than a shifting, mirage-like sense of the future, we are pulled by compulsion and competition out into what cleric Richard John Neuhaus once chastisingly called the "naked public square."[6] Zach de la Rocha, a man who would seem to share nothing in common with Richard John Neuhaus, strangely agrees.

"The front line is everywhere," he sang on "No Shelter," Rage Against the Machine's contribution to the soundtrack for *Godzilla* (1998). Without the fig leaves of the past or the garlands of the future, much more literally than we imagine, we live out our crazy lives between two ferns.

THE GREAT EQUALIZER

The colossal scope of our Great Transition* is not hard to set at eye level. Consider Horace Mann, another of Tocqueville's American contemporaries. For him, education was "a great equalizer" of social conditions "beyond all other devices of human origin."[7] For Tocqueville, both the good news and the bad news is that Mann's very American view of things is wrong. No purposive social project can be the real engine of equality. Instead, "the gradual progress of equality is something fated"—a "universal and permanent" type of progress "daily passing beyond human control," where everyone and everything "helps it along."[8] Our great equalizer is the Great Transition itself.

At first glance, this central proposition looks to drive us even crazier than we already are. We're deeply biased in favor of Horace Mann's proposition. Even if we agree with Tocqueville that social conditions are changing in more powerful ways than we can manufacture, we like Mann's

---

*In the wake of World War II, Hannah Arendt shared some similar worries in *Between Past and Future* (New York: Viking, 1968). Her concerns, however, centered on Europe—still caught, as Tocqueville feared, between a reactionary longing to re-enchant the past and a radical longing for permanent revolution. As you'll see, America is such a huge deal for Tocqueville because our origins outside of that trap set a pattern that can last as long as we do.

notion that, for us, equality is the soul of change. Tocqueville goes a step further. Although it's true that change in our moment is dominated and defined by equalization, he wants us to be aware that *the thing we have most in common is that change.* True, our equally shared humanity is our *deepest* commonality. But unlike billions of other people throughout history, and billions more in the future, we're under the special power of a special predicament, shaping our lives in a way we just have to deal with. Although we will have to take recourse to a good understanding of what it means to be human in order to fend off the craziness that arises when we deal with our predicament poorly, that's a reactive position to be in. It would be nice if we could think that the Great Transition is one of increased autonomy for everybody, where we can all march forward in equal proactivity. Turns out, our equal need for *reactivity* is much more powerful.

Yes, something is happening to all of us, something that defines who we are—like it or not. What's more, it's something all of us are pretty much aware of, because it's part of the fabric of everyday life. It's not something, like your favorite hot-button issue, that we need to raise awareness about. It's not something that affects us differently depending on who we are. In fact, it doesn't concern *who* we are, but *how* we are, and though, to be sure, we're "very different people" in some respects, this isn't one of them. When it comes to the Great Transition, we really are all in this together. But unlike oh so many "causes" that we rally for and against, there's no enemy here, no problem to be solved, no injustice or grievance for some perfected policy to erase or redeem. Rather than raising *awareness* of a *problem*, Tocqueville is out to cultivate *receptivity* to an *answer*. He doesn't want to set an ambitious agenda to advance us all, in the way that Horace Mann and countless other Americans would do. He wants to remind us of what relief awaits us, beyond our proactive efforts, from the burdens of ambition, agenda, and advancement—as well as the burdens of their evil twins, resentment, fixation, and compulsion.

Tocqueville is not a monk. His counsel is not to walk away from the world or practice the art of noble detachment. Ultimately, he's more concerned that we'll imprison ourselves in our own hearts, minds, and souls than that we'll be sucked into the craziness too deep and completely. Nevertheless, his message does resemble a Zen koan, the oracular style of quip designed to derail our fast and furious trains of calculating thought. What do you mean, there's something unchosen that really unites us? What do you mean, it affects our identity? What do you mean, the way to deal with it doesn't involve doubling down on the identities we have *or* the ones we want? It can make us less crazy without solving any problems? It doesn't punish anyone? No money changes hands? What is this, a scam? A cult? A miracle drug?

The Great Transition and the reaction it calls forth are none of those things. The life we face afterward won't be dramatically simpler. Tocqueville knows as well as anyone how complex, busy, and challenging our lives are. But after the transition-reaction experience, life can be substantially more *straightforward*. Once the art of being free becomes common sense, dealing with the Great Transition and its attendant craziness becomes more a matter of receptivity to life's grace notes than working the zillions of competing levers crying out for our high-stakes investiture of time, emotion, and life force.

Still, we probably all share some inherent resistance to Tocqueville's vision. No matter how nice it sounds to gain a new clarity and focus, we're skeptical of claims that begin with the acceptance of one of our least favorite things—an unchosen constraint to which we can only passively react. Thanks to our baked-in doubt and anxiety, we have rational and not-so-rational mechanisms working overtime to turn us against unchosen constraints. We think of all the confinements of ascribed identity, all the fetters of family, place, and circumstance.

Sometimes it feels like the only way to redeem what we're stuck with is to assert "ownership" over it; convert the unchosen into the chosen. Even better, we try to create our own identities—treating ourselves like technical projects or works of art, accessing membership in voluntary associations, or pursuing some combination of both. Even when these strategies throw us back on our own often feeble resources of self-esteem and confidence, exacerbating instead of ameliorating the crazy, they make us feel free—or, really, safe—from unchosen constraints. And even though we often dream of crafting identities so richly interesting that our lives are filled with friends and admirers, we find ourselves oscillating constantly back into the unquiet repose of personal solitude. There, alone, we sometimes painfully feel that we're stuck with our "real" selves. Even more often, perhaps, we feel an unsettling sense that when it comes to our "real" selves, there's precious little "there" there. We invite a lot of crazy into our lives by fighting unchosen constraints. Reporting on a tense meeting of the president and congressional leaders over the so-called surge of troops during the Iraq War, the *New York Times* records: "Pressed on why he thought this strategy would succeed where previous efforts had failed, Mr. Bush shot back: 'Because it has to.' "[9] That's us, always surging against our unchosen constraints. We think it's worth it because, in some curious way, we feel we have no choice.

That's why Tocqueville is such a help. And that's why we should be ready to listen when he tells us to embrace the unchosen constraint of our equal reactivity in the face of life's inescapable craziness. We *already* routinely succumb to the feeling that we must fight what we haven't chosen. But not all unchosen constraints are as bad as they seem. Some, in fact, give us surprising access to varieties of freedom we wouldn't otherwise notice among the din of our craziness and the constant of our change. If, after all, the answer to our crazy predicament is a new receptivity to the art of being free, that ought to put us in a generous—even adventurous?—mood.

VE BELIEVE IN NOSSING

Hold on. (That might be what you're thinking right now.) Do we *need* to embrace an adventure? Just because we're at a cosmic crossroads of craziness doesn't mean we *have* to deal with it. After all, isn't the most enlightened way of dealing with something just . . . allowing it to transpire? Surely, if history is in motion, one way we can exercise freedom right away is by freely opting to get *out* of the way. By letting it go, our arrested development can come unfrozen! Isn't that the approach that's truly in tune with the tenor of the times? Don't worry, be happy, *hakuna matata*, the arc of the moral universe bends toward justice! Didn't our president say that? How can insignificant little me, or you, or anyone disagree? In fact, why would we bother? Eat, drink, and be merry, for tomorrow we're old! And even when we're old, America's retirement communities will be more flush, with better amenities and better sex lives than today's senior citizens can dream of. Every week is already Spring Break at The Villages.*

Call it hedonism, call it Epicureanism, call it nihilism with a happy face: what about *this* response to the Great Transition? If Tocqueville wants to show us how we can chill despite the crazy, why not do him one better and chill so much that the crazy just, like, fades into the background? Don't like it, don't watch, right? Great Transition, meet Big Chill.

Judging from *The Big Chill* (1983), it's not quite that easy. Never seen it? You don't have to. Just read the theatrical poster, where Columbia Pictures chose two taglines to sum up the movie. "In a cold world," one reads, "you need friends to keep you warm." Okay, okay. So we chill together, right? Well, here's tagline two: "How much love, sex, fun and friendship can a person take?" There's a Zen koan for you.

---

*"Boasting 100,000 residents over the age of 55, The Villages may be the fastest growing city in America. It's a notorious boomtown for boomers who want to spend their golden years with access to 11 a.m. happy hours, thousands of activities, and no-strings-attached sex, all lorded over by one elusive billionaire." Alex French, "Club Meds," *BuzzFeed*, August 28, 2014, https://www.buzzfeed.com/likethebreadorthedressing/seven-days -and-nights-in-the-worlds-largest-rowdiest-retirem.

Rather than asking one of Hunter Thompson's favorite questions—"Just how weird can you stand it, brother, before your love will crack?"—*The Big Chill*, just thirteen years after the 1960s got too weird for love, asks you the reverse: just how much *intimacy* can you stand before your *weird* will crack—before craziness stops being the problem, and safe, sensible pleasure takes its place? That question first entered the popular consciousness with the rise of the Yuppies in the 1980s, the first generation to get famous for going (as the kids say) "normcore." And despite craze after craze since then, it hasn't gone away. The safe, sensible pleasures of Yuppie normcore gave way to the even safer, *more* sensible pleasures of *Seinfeld*. As fans of its meandering, unending blather and atrocious 1990s fashions know, it took a "show about nothing" to reveal to us the ultimate in normcore. No doubt, in a year or two, we'll get an even more contentless series creating even greater breakthroughs in bland, edgeless normality.

Believe it or not, Tocqueville was very worried about Yuppies and *extremely* concerned about *Seinfeld*—precursors, he might say, of the democratic age. He knew that the craziness of life during the Great Transition would create a strangely ubiquitous pressure to seek refuge in sensible safety and safe sensibility—culminating, we might say, in a whole civilization of awkward singletons dressed in mom jeans and dad sneakers. "If the citizens continue to shut themselves up more and more narrowly in the little circle of petty domestic interests and keep themselves constantly busy therein," he whispers, "there is a danger that they may in the end become practically out of reach of those great and powerful public emotions which do indeed perturb peoples but which also make them grow and refresh them."

> The prospect really does frighten me that they may
> finally become so engrossed in a cowardly love of
> immediate pleasures that their interest in their own
> future and in that of their descendants may vanish,
> and that they will prefer tamely to follow the course
> of their destiny rather than make a sudden energetic
> effort necessary to set things right.[10]

That's not going to happen *now*. It won't happen *soon*. We're still a tween civilization, we New Worlders. But as Dr. Drew might observe, it's right around this age that people suddenly gain the ability to ruin their lives for the long run, especially if they steadfastly refuse to so much as consider the long run. If we freely give up on life and all its attendant craziness, we won't be living freely at all. We'll go right along with the flow of history into the cosmic dustbin. Behind the soothing face of normcore, Tocqueville prophesies, is the yawning abyss of nihilism. It's as if *The NeverEnding Story* (1984) ended with Bastian bringing the Nothing to Earth by choosing to live in his parents' basement.

We're assuming that movies are still a cool way to chill, right? If so, reading the word *nihilism* possibly called forth for you a mental image of the three Nihilists from *The Big Lebowski* (1998). You remember: Peter Stormare, Torsten Voges, and Red Hot Chili Peppers bassist Flea, giving the Dude, our hero, such a hard time? They're the malicious Germans who mistake him for Jeffrey Lebowski, the *real* Big Lebowski—the ones who threaten him with one of cinema's most terrifying intrusions into the inner sanctum of normcore's Big Chill. Looming over the Dude, caught in his own bathtub, one Nihilist informs him just who he's dealing with. "Ve believe in nossing, Lebowski," he hisses. "Nossing. And tomorrow ve come back and ve cut off your chonson." The Dude, acting pretty chill, tosses off a sarcastic "Excuse me?" But later, his dreams are invaded with a horrific vision: all three Nihilists coming for his *johnson*, flexing huge pairs of scissors. A persecution complex involving castrating nihilists is about as big a metaphor for our fear of death as we could ask for. Big Chill, meet *The Big Sleep* (1946)—not coincidentally, the Coen brothers' inspiration for their normcore noir.

Tocqueville's warning is just as stark as the Nihilists'. In his nightmare, the Dude wins, but the creepily wrong way—bending nihilism toward safety, not violence (or, metaphorically, sterility, not castration). Remember the spinning gif that reads *lol nothing matters*? Picture it chilling on your couch, sipping a White Russian, wearing the Dude's pink jelly sandals and admiring the Dude's rug. Mistake complete passivity for total freedom, says Tocqueville, and the Great Transition will lead us not into temptation but oblivion. Dare to become emotionally available to the art of being free, however, and, well—instead of finding that the world slowly grows colder in the company of your friends, you'll find that *The NeverEnding Story*'s tagline is closer to the mark: "A boy who needs a friend finds a world that needs a hero."

Asked if he and his brother had set out "to teach America what Nihilism means," a "bitterly sarcastic" Joel Coen told filmmaker Doug Stone that "everything's a lesson for America."[11] In spite of it all, beneath our protective layers of irony, we know we haven't given up on happy endings. "I can change," we constantly remind our disapproving friends and lovers. We never say we can *be* changed.

Tocqueville did not come right out and call it heroic if you dare to accept that, just by being differently, you can always change the future. But he sure did suggest it was cowardly not to. "I fear that the mind may keep folding itself up in a narrower compass forever without producing new ideas," he sighs—that we'll wear ourselves out "in trivial, lonely, futile activity, and that for all its constant agitation humanity will make no advance." Yes, what Tocqueville helps us see is that, if we miss out on the art of being free, the democratic age will be one big failed attempt to escape the craziness of life by becoming too boring to feel crazy. In that nonfuture he sees "an innumerable multitude" of interchangeable people, "alike and equal, constantly circling around in pursuit of the petty and banal pleasures with which they glut their souls. Each one of them" has become "almost unaware of the fate of the rest" but for, as Verizon Wireless says, their friends and family. "As for the rest of his fellow citizens," the representative normcore American— think of the most stereotypical sitcom dad imaginable— "they are near enough, but he does not notice them. He touches them but feels nothing. He exists in and for himself."[12] Even the safety and sensibility of intimacy finally fades away.

Tocqueville doesn't even have to contend with modern technology and its talent for personal isolation. But *we know*. We *already know* how crazy life is even with Netflix binges, and spare evenings spent solo in the gym, and mindless, insomniac scrolls through our own Instagram feeds, tallying likes. We can already sense, more strongly even than Tocqueville, what an awful mistake it would be to try to escape from life's craziness the way we can never escape from the zombies—by retreating deeper and deeper into the house.

Still want to trust the Great Transition to social autocorrect?

Jerry, George, Elaine, and Kramer can safely banter themselves ever deeper into the unchanging present. Here in real life, that's a choice we don't have. The future is calling, and despite being tweens, we actually are tall enough to ride this ride. As Raoul Duke says to the hitchhiker in *Fear and Loathing in Las Vegas* (1998), "Get in."

THE ARISTOCRATS!

There's a famous joke you've probably heard if you like your humor raunchy and raw. Taking its name from its punch line, it's called "The Aristocrats!," and the basis is a family of entertainers pitching an act to a producer. Long passed down from comic to comic, it has finally hit the public consciousness—a small but significant sign of where we are in the Great Transition. As a comedian telling the joke, your objective is twofold: make it as *long* as possible, and as *crude* as possible. Theoretically, this is easy; you simply pile on more and more gross and outlandish features to the family's proposed act. Practically, it's hard. It's now pretty tough to shock jaded audiences, what with their high tolerance for perverse and transgressive fantasies. All the more reason for ambitious, competitive comedians to try! Turns out, the punch line of the joke actually does have what obscenity law might concede is redeeming social value. At length, the comic recounts, the producer finally inquires as to what the family calls their improbable troupe. With a flourish, the father takes on a most proper and distinguished air. "The Aristocrats!"

It's funny because that kind of debauched exhibitionism is the last thing we ought to expect to issue forth from aristocratic mores. (Unlike us, *Downton Abbey*'s Dowager Countess would *not* be amused.) It's funnier because we now know how debauched aristocracies can get. "When the members of an aristocratic society," says Tocqueville, turn "exclusively to sensual pleasures," they quickly descend into "sumptuous depravity and startling corruption. They worship material things magnificently and seem eager to excel in the art of besotting themselves."[13] They just can't help it.

Notice, too, that the joke has a not-so-funny edge. As Tocqueville observes, "love of physical pleasures never leads democratic peoples to such excesses. Among them love of comfort appears as a tenacious, exclusive, and universal passion, but always a restrained one."[14] Now, on the one hand, you might object that today we're way more devoted to carnivals of delight than naive old Tocqueville could imagine. Sex! Drugs! EDM (or whatever)! What about our porn addiction? What about our society-wide failures of portion control? We want it all and we want it now!

Right?

Although it's true that our taste for indulgence is considerable, it all goes to show, in two separate ways, how acute Tocqueville is. First, that taste indicates we haven't departed as far from the aristocratic age as we might like to think. Even if we don't want to live aristocratic *lives*, we somehow retain a longing for the aristocratic *experience*. Second, paradoxically, it shows that we've moved farther away from the aristocratic age than we think! "There is no question of building vast palaces, of conquering or excelling nature, or sucking the world dry to satisfy one man's greed," Tocqueville says of us.[15] Sure, he hasn't met the Kardashians; then again, I've sat down over M&Ms and Tootsie Roll Pops with the Jenners, and I can tell you, their office is no Versailles.* Kim doesn't want to bankrupt the world with her app. She wants us to stay prosperous enough that she can use it to make a buck off of each of us for as long as she possibly can. Comfortable as we are with sampling quasi-aristocratic experiences, even our most ostentatious full-time celebrities come nowhere close to the true aristocratic soul.

These insights are typically Tocquevillean—crystal clear in hindsight, but elusive at first glance. Like the others we'll encounter, they remind us that it won't be easy to make

---

*Still mourning the epic novel I'd abandoned in the wake of September 11, I successfully pitched Kylie and Kendall on a young adult novel—potentially the first in a series!—about two California sisters whose lives are upended by the return from New York of a long lost, and now deeply mysterious, friend. My cheese, as luck would have it, was moved. About three years later their debut novel dropped. *Rebels: City of Indra: The Story of Lex and Livia* follows two superpowered girls in the far-flung future whose lives are upended in a divided, dystopian metropolis: "a beautiful paradise floating high in the sky" with "a nightmare world of poverty carved into tunnels beneath the surface of the earth." Usually, wringing melodramatic entertainment value out of our fears of inequality is a pretty good bet. As it so happens, without a free-being artist to power the project, even that formula can't win anymore. Sad!

sense of our place in the slipstream of the Great Transition. To help get our bearings, it's important to reflect on what we already sense: the craziness we have to contend with in life comes, like "The Aristocrats!," in several different layers. In Tocqueville's telling, the Great Transition situates us in a crazy context in at least two ways. First, the very experience of being in transition—unsettled, changing, anxious, and shortsighted—is enough to make us crazy. And second, when we feel too overwhelmed, happily inert nihilism starts to look like the biggest—indeed, the only—surefire release.

But that's just the beginning. Look closer, and you'll see that two more predicaments contribute to the craziness of everyday life. In addition to our nervous sense that not even increased autonomy can supply us with the comforts of agency, we also derive an intense, optimistic yearning from our strange and transitional times. It's human nature to form a vision of the future, however vague and abstract it might be. Thanks to our experience, we know that for *some* of us, the future can be a wide-open realm of breakthroughs and extraordinary results. It can be a place where the sky's the limit in "satisfying" our "slightest needs."[16] Surrounded by ever-refreshing fountains of youth, ambition, and accomplishment, "You Only Live Once" is a call to live it up, not give it up. In the Great Transition, it's not just *possible* to make super-sized everyday fantasies real. It's also the most *profitable* thing we can do. Although we realize that we're setting ourselves up to burn out so badly or crash so hard, we know in our collective gut that *being inspirationally* is one of the most reliable ways to get people on our side. And without other people on our side, we won't have much luck getting anything done in the brief course of our one life.

That's right: the crazy is baked right into the optimism. And the more we admit it, the more our awareness reflects back on itself in a crazily infinite loop. It's like gazing into a set of funhouse mirrors. We know that it's over the top to *be* so over the top in our expectations and desires. We don't just want it all—we want to *have* it all. We sense that the key to accomplishing even little things is to set unreasonable or irrational goals—and the key to setting those goals is to have almost unjustifiable or ridiculous visions of who (or how) we can be. That's why one of our greatest challenges is staying stable, centered, and savvy enough to maintain that default state of overeager hyperactivity, and it's why one of our nagging insights, reflected back through experience, is that even with every possible choice at our feet, there's still something missing. It's still not enough.

Part of the problem is that it's so weird for us to possess such outsized visions of incredibleness and intensity. In a way, they're seriously out of sync with the other main themes of our everyday life: massive boredom, insignificance, directionlessness. It's almost as if our crazy love of dreaming big is a last-ditch survival mechanism to cope with our day-in, day-out awareness of how small, pointless, and ineffectual we turn out to be. For all but a minuscule few, life is about recognizing just how little change you can effect, from politics and economics to public opinion and popular tastes. It often seems so impossible to change even *one* person's mind, especially a partner or relative. We indulge our big fantasies despite what appears to be endless, intimate evidence to the contrary. Why do we do this? What are we, crazy?

Peel back another layer of the Great Transition. Remember, we're transitioning *out* of the aristocratic age, an era far longer than the present blip in time. "The surface of American society is covered with a layer of democratic paint," as Tocqueville puts it, "but from time to time one can see the old aristocratic colors breaking through."[17] We're crazy for our outsized dreams because we *inherited* the habit of dreaming big. For centuries, people powerfully remembered and imitated the kinds of individual greatness that are now extinct. Yet, through imitation and memory, they echo on, shaping our feelings, coloring our dreams, and adding a strange sharpness to our experience of everyday life.

INSIDE THE ACTOR'S STUDIO

This isn't a complicated concept, but it is incredibly profound. For a quick idea of what's at work here, consider the different ways we think of mimes and memes. For most Americans, mimes are a fairly preposterous Old World form of entertainment that's so self-serious it can't be taken seriously. But memes—those highly sharable, often captioned images that create fleeting crazes on social media—are a lot of self-conscious fun.

Both mimes and memes, of course, derive their name from the Greek word *mimeisthai*, meaning "to imitate." Recall from the introduction the idea that, "in a very real sense," we're "all actors now." It's no surprise that imitation is such a big deal for us. It's also no surprise that we tend to favor some sorts of imitation over others. But to get our bearings, we need, so to speak, to go "inside the actor's studio"—much like James Lipton, the famously dry and self-serious host of the show of the same name.

What we'll see isn't anything like the bland, sparse galleries where so much contemporary art is presented. To learn the truth about why the Great Transition occurs to us how it does, we want to get beyond that realm of appearance, into the inner sanctum of our crazy, selfish, and melodramatic psyche. Note that "studio" comes from *studium*, the Latin word that combines our sense of zealousness and focus into what our most respected and successful brands would translate today as "obsession." What's lurking around our inner storehouses of actorly obsession?

Breaking news: it's a hot mess in there. Tocqueville knows: our "national character" is stuffed with "incoherent opinions" and habits "that hang like the broken chains still occasionally dangling from the ceiling of an old building but carrying nothing." Dangling chains and broken links make an even better metaphor than aristocratic paint poking through democratic cover. In an aristocratic age, the most important thing about people is who they're superior and inferior to. In a democratic age, the opposite is true: the most important thing about each person is how similar, how equal, he or she is to everyone else. As we transition from one to the next, it makes sense that we would be confused about that transition and our place in it: after all, we're blundering through two very different organizing principles, or standards of value. Today, we would presume that a society of superiors and inferiors would be fragmented and at odds with itself—but we would be wrong: "aristocracy links everybody, from peasant to king, in one long chain," whereas democracy "breaks the chain and frees each link."[18] In our time, in the Great Transition, the breaking of the aristocratic chain is *unfinished*. It's a partial, messy, halting process susceptible to fits and starts. Our aristocratic inheritance,

Tocqueville tells us—our "baggage," to mix metaphors—is incomplete. To be specific, it's incompletely *remembered* and incompletely *imitated*.

And that's why, although Tocqueville isn't the only big-time thinker to weigh in on the importance of imitation and memory, he is the one who squares the best with how we process reality today.

For an illuminating contrast, let's consider Plato. In the *Republic*, he has Socrates present a much different picture of how mimicry and remembrance play out over historical time. A brief glance helps explain why Tocqueville's presentation works so much better for us.

Plato's Socrates tells a shocking secret. Not only do the things that rule our hearts determine who rules over us but the things that rule our hearts also degenerate from generation to generation. As human beings, we're so flawed that we defectively imitate our elders, who defectively imitated their own. We're all so defective that our idea of brilliance is doing the least bad job at remembering what the hell happened even a few generations ago. We keep joining in an unenlightened contest—competing over honors for who can "observe the passing shadows" of everyday life and "remark which of them went before, and which followed after, and which were together."[19] We're prisoners of imitation and memory.

So, while we should love wisdom above all things, we start out loving honor instead. Honor is sort of like status, but unlike the modern concept of status it's rooted in the idea that some ways of being are actually objectively the best, and ought to be maintained that way in an unbroken line over time. For the descendants of the honor-lovers, unfortunately, it's all too easy to see what's wrong with that worldview. It doesn't really make us happy. It doesn't really make us safe. As ennobling as it may be, it's also really impoverishing.

So it happens, says Socrates, that we wind up loving money. Rather than a worldview dominated by a narrow hierarchy of bloodlines and battle valor, we put our faith in one that's still very narrow but focused around wealth and prosperity. Get enough money, and you can rest easy at night. No nightmares, no sleepless nights. Unfortunately, for the descendants of the money-lovers, the flaw in that vision is also self-evident.

Starting to glimpse the pattern?

Surely chasing after lucre isn't the path to happiness and peaceful repose. And neither is actually piling up wealth. Surely the love of money is just a flawed attempt to improve on the love of honor.

But as the next generation adopts a love of all things equal—what *Socrates* calls democracy—the truth gradually emerges that this, too, is just a misbegotten effort to improve on the love of money that came before. (After all, with money, in principle, anyone can access or own anything.) The love of all things equally, in turn, opens the way to the love of power, a tyrannical love that leads humanity to hit bottom.[20] Dogged by our memory of the flaws of the past, we absurdly rely on our mimicry to try to escape them.

What a stark contrast with Tocqueville's story about the segue to democracy! As we'll see, Tocqueville warns that our taste for autonomy is apt to decay into a love of money, not the other way around. It's true that both Plato and Tocqueville focus intently on the ineffable imperfection of our memorious mimesis. But for Tocqueville, it's not a fatal flaw. Equality isn't fated to be the gateway to ruin.

To understand why, let's look at how Tocqueville's point of departure differs from Plato's. Tocqueville doesn't start with the ideal love of wisdom, from which we fools (says Plato) have fallen away through the stubbornness of memory and the errancy of imitation. Instead, he walks us back to America's real-life origins—back before the Constitution, the Declaration, and the Revolution, all the way to our Puritan forebearers. His reason is simple: he wants us to see which aspects of the aristocratic age we inherited and which were left behind in the Old World the Puritans fled.

We all know that the Puritans fled a potent mix of political and religious persecution. But when we think of them today, we're probably most likely to think of the Puritans themselves as *puritanical*, foisting their own brand of oppressive rule onto their newly formed communities. Indeed, Tocqueville observes, "sometimes the passion for regulation which possessed them led them to interfere in matters completely unworthy of such attention"; yet, he warns, we "must not forget that these ridiculous and tyrannical laws were not imposed from outside—they were voted by the free agreement of all the interested parties themselves— and that their mores were even more austere and [*yep*] puritanical than their laws."[21] That is, a free, equal group of people imposed crazy harsh laws *on themselves*, starting from the moment they landed in a new world.

That's a pretty good snapshot of our (incomplete) aristocratic inheritance. While in Europe "political existence started in the higher ranks of society and has been gradually, but always incompletely," disseminated downward, among our Puritan founders, "the local community was organized before the county, the county before the state, and the state before the Union."[22] We're used to thinking of all kinds of oppression as the same and intimately interconnected. But the oppression the Puritans fled was aristocratic, not democratic. In Europe, political power had acquired religious authority, and religious institutions had obtained political power. Nobody got to deliberate together. Nobody got to choose how to worship together. In throwing off one part of the aristocratic inheritance, the Puritans gained the ability to *narrow* their field of religious practice while *broadening* their field of political practice.*

Tocqueville says we "should continually bear in mind this point of departure," which spawned "two perfectly distinct elements" that *conflict* in the Old World but *combine* in America: "the *spirit of religion* and the *spirit of freedom*."† Delinked from the aristocratic inheritance, religion and politics can flow into respective spheres of life, interacting with an ease and logic that aristocracy could hardly conceive of, much less permit. By letting go of the struggle for power, we can let "the free play of intelligence" run wild in the secular sphere of public life; without trying to impose mastery through the claims of authority, we can let our turbulent lives rest in the "free and powerful" sphere of the soul.[23]

---

*"The founders of New England were both ardent sectarians and fanatical innovators. While held within the narrowest bounds by fixed religious beliefs, they were free from all political prejudices. Hence two distinct but not contradictory tendencies plainly show their traces everywhere, in mores and laws." Tocqueville, *Democracy*, 47.

†Emphasis in original.

The pull of this dynamic works the kinks out of the Puritans' overzealous approach. Laws copied out of the Old Testament eventually faded. Established churches gave way to a multitude of denominations, sects, and cults. Instead of being so habituated to top-down organization that it seems self-evident, we've embraced bottom-up organization, through the kind of face-to-face gathering begun by the Puritans, as the most natural, suitable thing in the world. For us, since the beginning, the *logic* of equality—afforded by our incomplete inheritance—prevails over the inequalities with which it is sometimes expressed.*

Turns out the spirit of equality born by the Puritans matters more than the inequalities they manifested. Their egalitarian habit of gathering together has been mimicked through memory right up to the present, in a way that asserts a much different relationship between money and democracy than Socrates claimed. Rather than proceeding in a relationship of sequential decay, Tocqueville sees both the love of money *and* the love of equality as *probably maddening* urges made *potentially fruitful* by our inherited, meliorative habit of freely gathering face-to-face.

WE'RE UP ALL NIGHT TO GET LUCKY

So what aristocratic habits of mind and heart and soul *were* sustained through memory and imitation?

One clue can be found in how we talk to each other. As

---

* "Puritanism, as already remarked, was almost as much a political theory as a religious doctrine. No sooner had the immigrants landed on that inhospitable coast . . . than they made it their first care to organize themselves as a society." Tocqueville, *Democracy*, 38.

we know, the transition between aristocratic and democratic life can be "gradual, with infinite nuances," as it is in America. Amid a nuanced transition, experience is characterized by an immoderate level of moderate enjoyments. We're flush with the sense that the old obstacles to progress are gone, and our joy isn't curbed by any anxieties over new ones lurking around the bend. That feeling of unimpeded possibility has the flavor of greatness to it, even if it's much different from the kind of demigod status attained by aristocratic-era colossi like Caesar, Charlemagne, or Napoleon. Not only does it affect our attitude (as we'll see) toward seeking fortune and earning money, but it also dramatically shapes the way we communicate. As Tocqueville observes, in the Great Transition "there is almost always a stage when the literary genius of democratic nations clashes with that of aristocracies, and both seek to hold their sway jointly over the human mind. Such periods do not last long, but they are very brilliant; they are fertile without exuberance and animated without confusion."[24] (Hopefully you're starting to have that kind of awesome but not too mind-blowing experience just by reading this book.)

So what aristocratic literature is still vying to capture our imagination? Can we name some epic legends that have done okay in pop culture lately—stories presenting a bygone age inaccessible to us now, yet rich with outsized drama that can still seize our fantasies and swell our hearts? You're probably thinking *The Lord of the Rings*, *Game of Thrones*, or *Harry Potter*. But my dad's personal favorite is *Spartacus*. "Imagine how Spartacus would react," he likes to muse, "if you told him before he died that, *over two thousand years later*, he would be the hero of a three-season TV series—plus a miniseries!" We're a long way away from losing our sense of greatness, even if fewer and fewer of us are about to imitate aristocratic heroes through literal conquest or battle.

In spiritual, economic, and creative matters, the transition away from the aristocratic age bequeaths us resources and memories that might not rule our lives, but certainly bring vigor to our imaginations and a focus to our efforts. It's in that sense that we're fans of obsession. Today, instead of standing with Gordon Gekko, we're much more likely to say, "Obsession is good. Obsession works." Greed, we sense, breeds inequality. Everyone can be obsessed—and, indeed, it often seems that pretty much everyone already is. Of course, our obsessiveness manifests as a constant restlessness that makes us envy money itself, as the second installment of the *Wall Street* franchise points out in its subtitle, *Money Never Sleeps*. And, to be sure, our enthusiasm for obsession powerfully tempts us down the road to *self*-obsession. But as the full course of the Great Transition begins to take shape, let's focus on the big picture. Pulled toward democratic ideals, we work naturally to cast aristocratic concepts and values in the most democratic light possible. We "democratize" them, seeking to prove (to ourselves and everyone else) that the good things once the province of the privileged few are, in fact, accessible to everyone.

The "clash" of aristocratic and democratic sensibilities that Tocqueville describes is immensely fruitful. It begins by inspiring us, not confusing us. We share a vision of a grand, sweeping movement toward betterment. Everyone, no matter how insignificant, plays a role. Some do it through religion, art, or commerce. Others show forth in other fields of human endeavor, ranging from (yes) the military to medicine to engineering, technology, and beyond. We are united, but not uniform. Our infinite paths seem to proceed in the same direction, toward the same lodestar. That is why this transitional time creates great optimism and dynamism.

But as we begin to complete the transition, as we inevitably will, Tocqueville warns that we'll tend to become frighteningly lonely, isolated, exhausted, and depressed. At first, the Great Transition is an unprecedented, unparalleled engine for optimism. Our sky's-the-limit feeling of wide-open horizons is "generated by the combination of the destruction of old boundaries" and the survival of our "memory of nobility and achievement"; but then, "the competition of all against all" sets in, slowly disillusioning us with "new constraints—and a loss of a sense of the possibilities for human greatness."[25] Not just for some of us, mind you—for all of us. As our ambitions begin to fade under the pressure of equality, our unity gives way, with only uniformity left in its wake. Our optimism threatens to sour into fatalism. Our utopia threatens to become a dystopia. If we all can be heroes, to lift a line from the David Bowie song that puts voice to the fear, we're increasingly nervous that we can only access a sense of greatness "just for one day"—or hour, or moment, or instant.

To put it in terms Daft Punk and Pharrell could understand, at the onset of the Great Transition, we happily keep ourselves up all night for good fun. But the more it progresses, the more we find ourselves nervously up all night in a feverish quest to get lucky. Maybe our moment has already passed us by. Maybe, just now, we were too anxious, too busy, or too exhausted to seize it—or even see it. Maybe that horrible fate is closing itself around ever more of us with each passing moment.

It's from fears like these that today's huge but intangible sense of malaise has arisen. And it's from the radical root of these fears that the rest of this book springs forth.

Faith

I was cruising along pretty confidently until I had to start this chapter.

It was supposed to begin with the words *I am a Christian.*

One of my closest confidants had convinced me to start it this way, and I was hooked. The statement is true, and the certain ways in which it's likely to mislead a lot of people gave me a perfect entree into Tocqueville's writings about faith and why we need it to stave off our American crazy.

But I felt as if those same strengths led me straight into a brick wall.

BREAKING THE ICE

Faith has been "problematic" for millennia. Today, the word is a magnet for a certain kind of melodrama. Not only are many melodramatic word warriors apt to perform outrage when someone problematically starts blathering about religion but many more of us are also apt to perform "in-rage"—punishing ourselves—when we so much as sense that we're about to advance (or fall back on) religious claims. Many of us believe that religion is a conversation stopper, as the postmodern liberal theorist Richard Rorty insisted. In a democracy, Rorty says, we "should try to put off invoking conversation-stoppers as long as possible. We should do our best to keep the conversation going without citing unarguable first principles, either philosophical or religious. If we are sometimes driven to such citation, we should see ourselves as having failed, not as having triumphed."[1] For people like Rorty, you should see yourself as having done yourself and your interlocutor a disrespectful disservice. You've violated the rules of democracy—not just in a political sense, but in the much deeper sense of mores and habits, the sense that Tocqueville uses.

Yet Tocqueville disagrees. And he shows us why.

Amid the Great Transition, our democratic instincts link language closely to progress. Americans' faith in direct experience as the only trusty source of knowledge creates a "general distaste for accepting any man's word as proof of anything" and a reliance "on the witness of their own eyes"—touching off endless arguments where each of us fights for authority by citing our own personal experiences.* Those who try to win these competitions by invoking reli-

---

* Alexis de Tocqueville, *Democracy in America*, ed. J. P. Mayer, trans. George Lawrence (New York: Harper, 2006), 430. "So, of all the countries in the world, America is the one in which the precepts of Descartes are the least studied and the best followed. No one should be surprised at that" (429).

gious authority only defeat themselves. Americans "are ready to deny everything which they cannot understand," with "little faith in anything extraordinary and an almost invincible distaste for the supernatural." (However, as we'll see, even outlandish and spectacular forms of spiritualism can take hold in a relative instant when rooted enough in direct experience.) Today, any appeal beyond experience encounters skepticism and suspicion—what's more, even personal offense, the prideful feeling we're not taken seriously as equals. We sense that being in democratic times does— and should!—mean speaking in democratic ways. Rorty, among others, tends to believe this means letting others make our business their business, by remaining proactively curious about whether their experiences yield knowledge ours do not. Tocqueville marvels: "If an American should be reduced to occupying himself with his own affairs, at that moment half his existence would be snatched from him."[2] Spend a minute or two on social media, and you'd guess that percentage has crept up over time.

Start off a conversation—or a chapter in a book about being free—by announcing, "I am a Christian," and you'll find yourself preaching to icy glares, heated shouts, or an empty room, if not, at best, the choir.

But that's just the start of the trouble. Compoundingly, nearly all of us use religion as one of the fastest, most convenient ways to safely identify others. That checked box saves us a lot of uncertainty in unpacking who and how someone really is—an awkward and risky procedure we don't often have the time or the energy for. With individuals as well as with life, we want to cut to the chase, and when somebody signals their adherence to this or that faith, we think we've got a handle on them. We're now supposedly sure about what makes them tick, and how similar or different they are from ourselves; we confidently calculate how much we like or loathe them, and how much we'd like to draw them closer or push them far, far away.

So I feared that the minute I led with what was in fact my surest and strongest step, I'd be betrayed by the culture around us, the virtual air we breathe.

Today, Christianity is typically seen as an all-consuming "fundamentalist" doctrine even more tyrannical than most secular ideologies, which routinely derive so much of their charm from the noncommittal or incomplete adherence they permit to their frequently vague and abstracted sense of the world. Although many intelligent practicing Christians, including my friend Ross Douthat, argue that Christianity itself is getting squishier from all the pressure,* the prevailing narrative still casts Christians as slaves to a narrow, exacting dogma. They're seen to share a specific set of enumerated judgments that encompass everything, from the minute details of our personal lives to the structure and destiny of the universe. As a condition of membership, they embrace tightly interwoven and comprehensive claims—not just supernatural ones but also ones about human nature, and how society *must* be shaped to measure up to reality.

This not-totally-crazy portrayal of Christians seems to

---

*"Pushing Christianity to one extreme or another is what Americans have always done," Ross writes about the "heretics" defining today's religious landscape. "We've been making idols of our country, our pocketbooks, and our sacred selves for hundreds of years. What's changed today, though, is the weakness of the orthodox response." Ross Douthat, *Bad Religion: How We Became a Nation of Heretics* (New York: Free Press, 2012), 8.

confirm that we've got them all figured out—in a way that *should* make us more confident in asserting just who and how *we* are. But the more we pretend it's true, the more crazy we're likely to get.

Here's what's primed to madden us. Under the prevailing view, especially among non-Christians, we might *want* Ross to be right that there's "no single form of Christian civilization, in the same sense that there is no stereotypical Christian life."[3] We *hope* it's true that the Great Transition can "break down boundaries" at a social level, freeing us from uniformity at a personal level *without* leaving us so uncertain and isolated that we become easy prey for abusive domineers. But that's because we *fear*, along with Tocqueville, that "limitless independence" will actually intensify the "constant restlessness of everything," worrying us and wearing us out.[4] "With everything on the move in the realm of the mind," Tocqueville says of Americans absent commanding notions, "they want the material order at least to be firm and stable, and as they cannot accept their ancient beliefs again, they hand themselves over to a master." When pushed, we'd sooner be told what to do than be told what to believe.

Yet, at the same time we're worried too little will be expected of us amid the Great Transition, we're terrified too much will be expected.* We fear that Ross is *right* to say

*Tocqueville carefully observed the typical American's acute discomfort in European society, where ancient *cultural* authority beyond experience created the same awkward confrontation that invocations of age-old *religious* authority now so often produce. In Europe, "he is afraid of claiming too high a status and even more afraid of being ranked too low." Ancient authority causes him to be "bothered by this ghost from the past, and his fear of not receiving due attention is increased just because

that Christianity contains some inexpugnable, nonnegotiable core creed. It alarms us to contemplate the way such a creed will inevitably *invade* the noncommittal squishy space where we often stay in motion, dodging dogmatic obligations that would uncomfortably thrust us into *superficially* compromising positions—whose *uncompromising* stance on the ultimate human questions threatens to trap us in a more exposed or isolated reality than we might be willing to stand.* Our vocal insistence that we totally have a handle

---

he does not know exactly what that attention should be." Our pitiful Yankee "wants to do enough but is afraid of doing too much, and not knowing the limit of one or the other, falls back into an embarrassed and haughty reserve." See Tocqueville, *Democracy*, 570.

*Sure enough, Ross documents, a "therapeutic theology that Rieff had seen coming" has fostered an "immensely tolerant" spirit, one that dives out of the way of all commandments rather than offend anyone by commanding (Douthat, *Bad Religion*, 232). "Indeed," wrote Rieff, "the therapy of all therapies, the secret of all secrets, the interpretation of all interpretations, in Freud, is not to attach oneself exclusively or too passionately to any one particular meaning, or object." *Triumph of the Therapeutic* (New York: Harper & Row, 1968), 59. Each of our millions of initiates into that practical, open secret "may be going nowhere, but he aims to achieve a certain speed and certainty in going. Like his predecessor, the man of the market economy, he understands morality as that which is conducive to increased activity. The important thing is to keep going" (41). Or, as he later glossed the idea, "the terminal sin is immobility." Rieff, *Fellow Teachers* (New York: Harper & Row, 1973), 178. Rieff tends toward the Socratic judgment that oligarchy, the regime ruled by the love of money, decays inexorably into democracy, the regime ruled by the love of all things equally and interchangeably. To reiterate an earlier point, Tocqueville gives us a different conceptual framework. Amid the Great Transition, the love of equality and the love of money can and do coexist and reinforce one another—for an indeterminate length of historical time. Tocqueville guides us *away* from the fear that this out-of-joint time, as Hamlet would say, is a crisis—either in Hamlet's own sense (where choices, e.g., whether to right the wrong rule of Claudius, must be enacted at once), or in the ancient Greek sense of *krisis* (where the decisive moment arrived in the change from sickness to either recovery or death, or, as Socrates might

on people when we find out they're Christian in fact suggests that we lack such a handle on ourselves.

Christians themselves, of course, aren't magically immune to our democratic longing to understand everything, without bearing that tremendous burden unaided. Complicating the picture, as Ross cleverly notes, even many "heretical" Christians depart from the credal core *because they think it's inadequate* to spring us from the trap of too little expectation, on the one hand, and too much on the other. "Christian heresies vary wildly in their theological substance, but almost all have in common a desire to resolve Christianity's contradictions, untie its knotty paradoxes, and produce a cleaner and more coherent faith," he observes. "They tend to see themselves, not irrationally, as rescuers rather than enemies of Christianity—saving the faith from self-contradiction and cultural irrelevance."[5] Rather than giving up on the faith to escape unreasonable expectations, many enterprising Christians demand too much of it, seeking something at once more reinforcing and more relieving than a mere creed.*

---

say, from one regime to another). In both those senses, the personal and the social converge. Amid the open-ended Great Transition, we're tempted to *dream up* the sense of crisis that would *drum up* an "empowering" choice—putting our out-of-joint time to rights through either reactionary or revolutionary acts. Though "polar opposites" in one sort of way, both these stratagems imagine that our insignificant, interchangeable selves can only exercise agency in today's time by completely serving one comprehensive doctrine or another: as if, without a way of life, there's no way to live. For Tocqueville, this broken logic is a recipe for madness.

*In a recent editorial in the *New York Times*, Arthur Brooks recounts a line penned for the paper at the height of the 2003 Iraq crisis by Regis Debray—a French president's former advisor, onetime Che Guevara pal, and, here, an accidental Tocquevillean: "The United States compensates

The modern liberal philosopher John Rawls called that thing a comprehensive doctrine; in our lingo, it's what happens when we use a kind of faith-based ideology to fill in one of today's most familiar cultural mad libs: "More than a _____, it's a way of life!"

Like all sales pitches, however, this one makes us reach for our wallet as often to guard it as to open it. Hungry as we are to enfold the universe into one all-encompassing way of life, our ever-present prejudice in favor of experience comes back to haunt us again. But instead of pushing us forcefully in one way or the other, it leaves us awkwardly torn about how to feel around religion. On the one hand, professions of religious faith—"I am a Christian!"—tempt us not to engage. On the other, that skeptical, practical voice whispers, as it does of all would-be ways of life, "What are you *really* talking about? What does that mean? Be specific! You're a *what*?" Turned off, yet secretly attracted: there's a sensation so familiar that its influence on comedy and criticism can be found everywhere.

But neither the cheers nor the jeers address the dilemma, pervading how we are, that seems too touchy to talk about directly. In growing numbers, we find religion both alluring and ultimately intolerable. Falling back on a "spirituality of niceness"[6] saves us from confronting the problem in public, but not in the silent solitude of the heart.

Perhaps *we* can't resolve the dilemma at all, even in private. Perhaps *shutting up* is necessary but insufficient . . . and only *opening up* can get us where we really want to go. Cer-

---

for its shortsightedness, its tendency to improvise, with an altogether biblical self-assurance in its transcendent destiny."

tainly, it would help us to see in a new light what we already know about Tocqueville's counsel. Recall that Tocqueville doesn't want to characterize our crazy present as a problem or crisis that awareness-raising will help us to solve. Instead, he wants us to cultivate a certain kind of receptivity that will reveal why it's so crazy. Once it's well cultivated, that receptivity will not simply *change* the way we *think* about the constitutive craziness of our experience; it will *be* the way we *thrive* in its midst. We'll be better off—*meilleur*—not because we've improved ourselves, but because we've lessened the stress of our craziness, *ameliorating* it. What we *do* won't save us; at least, not until how we *are* will. So, returning to matters of faith, we can surmise that our divided conscience around religion calls us more toward *being in a receptive way* than toward being in a reactive way, a.k.a. *doing*.

Nevertheless, one practical question remains. If what happens in the silent stillness of receptivity is key to living freely *and* getting a handle on religion, how can we possibly *talk* about why that's so?

More to the point, how can I *write* about it?

LEFT BEHIND

Faced with this question, I told myself, my predicament was devilishly unique. I'd painted myself into some kind of corner. Not only was I deeply aware that Christians caught in the Great Transition are so apt to hope—yet despair—that their *own* faith predicaments are devilishly unique, but I also actually believed that mine *really* was.

I couldn't chalk up this paralyzing, hypnotizing suspicion to a simple pride spiral. Like the typical American predicament, this one was all about practicalities. Ego aside, I thought, none of those other anxiety-pinned Christians had to write a book that purported to show—in an accessible, even breezy way—how we can all key in on the kind of peaceful presence that anchors the art of being free. Theoretically, of course, my predicament was hardly insurmountable. I'd thought up the content to put in the book; I'd ginned up the ability to write it all out. It was all just a matter of time. Year after year of marinating in *Democracy in America*—a book written in two volumes conceived, researched, and written over the course of roughly a decade—taught me that.

Then again, Tocqueville was an aristocrat and a genius. So his whole experience of time was different—*radically* different—from mine. Although he would die just nineteen years after *Democracy*'s second volume was published, time was not of the essence to Tocqueville in "getting it out" and "moving units"—at least, not in the monetary sense so instinctive to me and my fellow Americans.

And Tocqueville knew it too. "Men living in democratic times have many passions," he conceded, "but most of these culminate in love of wealth or derive from it. That is not because their souls are narrower but because money really is more important at such times."[7] I won't get into the gory details of how this thought—this reality—harried me wherever I went, whatever I drank, however much I napped. There was no escape. Here I was, trying to write a book about keeping cool amid ubiquitous forces driving us bonkers . . . amid ubiquitous forces driving me bonkers.

It was worse than humbling. As Tocqueville explained, on one level, the situation stings because our pride is at

stake. "Distinction based on wealth is increased by the dis-
appearance or diminution of all other distinctions" as the
Great Transition rolls on.[8] But at a more basic level—the one
that takes ever-greater precedence over the lofty ambitions
we're ever more apt to let go—we correctly feel that losing
the race for resources mortally threatens our ability to make
even obscure and ordinary lives work. Say an author somehow manages to complete a manuscript while finding a way
to put their pride out with the trash. (Crazy, I know. Bear
with me.) Their trial still isn't over. Even the most expert
and disciplined author is a wild gambler, required to *bet*
that all of the effort disappearing into the book will *pencil
out* in the most mundanely economic sense possible: that of
household provisioning.

(*Help me!* You can read between the lines. *Read to the end!
Recommend me to your friends! Or I will "literally" disappear . . .*)

Of course, these manic-depressive realities are hardly
confined to the life of a writer. The same careworn distress
appears, Tocqueville noticed, wherever Americans live;
wherever they work. Even the "constant recurrence" of their
shared concern is stupendously "monotonous," he laments.*
After all, "the details of the methods used to satisfy it" im-
merse them in the same sort of drudgery. It's a catch-22: our
only workaday way to pursue a sense of security and contentment is to act out our discontented insecurity.†

---

*Nietzsche scorns "the breathless haste with which they work" as "the
distinctive vice of the new world. . . . Even now one is ashamed of resting,
and prolonged reflection almost gives people a bad conscience . . . ; one
lives as if one always 'might miss out on something.' " *The Gay Science*
(New York: Vintage, 1974), bk. 4, sec. 329.

† "It seemed to me that Babette and I, in the mass and variety of our pur-
chases, in the sheer plentitude those crowded bags suggested, the weight

Just as depression threatens to enclose us completely, however, we hit the panic button. As Tocqueville put it, our American minds are so tightly confined "to the search for physical comfort" by the bind of our social circumstances that "they feel imprisoned within limits from which they are apparently not allowed to escape"; yet, when our fearfully fantasizing imaginations do manage to break through, our "minds do not know where to settle down," and we "often rush without stopping far beyond the bounds of common sense."[9] Like the bad motorcycle gang we imagined in this book's first chapter, we'd rather break down than fail to break through the workaday monotony making us feel so unfree.

---

and size and number, the familiar package designs and vivid lettering, the giant sizes, the family bargain packs with Day-Glo sale stickers, in the sense of replenishment we felt, the sense of well-being, the security and contentment these products brought to some snug home in our souls—it seemed we had achieved a fullness of being that is not known to people who need less, expect less, who plan their lives around lonely walks in the evening." Don DeLillo, *White Noise* (NewYork: Penguin, 1984), 20. This passage is quoted in a book by Sheena Iyengar called *The Art of Choosing* (2010), advertised as a finalist for the *Financial Times* and Goldman Sachs business book of the year award. Its own epigram, however, is from Archibald MacLeish, proudly identified as a Pulitzer Prize–winning American poet: "What is freedom? Freedom is the right to choose: the right to create for oneself the alternatives of choice. Without the possibility of choice a man is not a man but a member, an instrument, a thing." (MacLeish's formula calls to mind that of William James, whose quip that "my experience is what I agree to attend to" forms the epigram for Winifred Gallagher's book-length case for attentiveness, *Rapt*.) Tocqueville helps us grasp that this pattern of thought is at once too political—restricting freedom to a right—and too economic—restricting it to a choice. *Free-dom* is not a property but a realm. Nor is it a realm where we're free to just be. Properly understood, through experience, it is where we *just are* stuck with *being freely*, no matter how much we convince us we're not. One handy name for this *where*, Tocqueville intimates, is *the soul*.

It wasn't always this way. Before the Great Transition, obstacles, toil, and inertia didn't occur to people as practical crises the way they did after it got going. Only in our current age does the prospect arise of being left behind: by "the times," "the crowd," or "public opinion," all of which increasingly converge into a single, domineering, one might say *rapturous* vector. And only in our age does the *behind* in which we're left occur to us as every bit as materially devastating as banishment, ostracism, or exile were in the old days.* Like those ordeals, being left behind isn't just terrible because we feel so rejected. Both kinds of experience actually put us in an untenable practical position, one in which building a life commensurate with our humanity becomes logistically impossible—barring some extraordinary intervention. It's not accurate enough to say we're just suffering from fear of missing out. We actually feel forsaken—not by God,[10] but by circumstance, or what Carl Sagan conceded[11] was an "indifferent universe."

---

*And yes: I'm thinking here of a secular version of *the* Rapture—the moment Christ's faithful are zapped into heaven as His second coming and, therefore, the End Times, get underway. The Rapture is the focus of *Left Behind*, a smash hit series in the market for Christian genre fiction. Between 1995 and 2014, the *Left Behind* series topped out at sixteen novels, four films (including one reboot), one computer game with three sequels, some graphic novels, and an album of songs, *People Get Ready: A Musical Collection Inspired by the Left Behind Series*. As Ross points out, the modern-day Rapture first gained currency around a century ago, when Cyrus Scofield's bestselling reference Bible "claimed to trace, with quasiscientific precision, a series of stages in salvation history that would soon culminate in the Second Coming of Christ" (Douthat, *Bad Religion*, 34). For present-day Americans desperate to evade the wrath of History, Obscurity, and Notoriety—the three horsemen of our round-the-clock apocalypse—each day, as in some Christian imaginations, might be the dreadful day of judgment.

My writer's paralysis horrendously rammed home the point. Thanks to the egalitarian era I lived in, I couldn't write *The Art of Being Free* under anything like the favorable conditions that had allowed Tocqueville to produce *Democracy in America*. The Great Transition had obliterated them. While he had the time and money to think through a grand predicament confronting all of humanity, I couldn't even afford to ponder my way out of my wee individual predicament. Suddenly, dispiritingly, Tocqueville's genius became a cruel, nihilistic curse.

NO WAY

Of course, this was typically American crazy talk. Starting out with the simple intention to proclaim the "good news," I ended up driven to preach the worst sort of everyday news: the ease with which even those of us bearing the best of intentions can be driven, in an instant, to utter distraction by an insecure frenzy for coin. Outrageously, I had fallen prey to Hunter Thompson's dark prophesy—the same one I'd warned you about, in my own words, in the very first chapter of *The Art of Being Free!* "The morbidity of the American Dream hinges on how the quest for autonomy decays into the quest for money." *Instant karma*, I groaned inwardly.

So back to Tocqueville I went.

A mustard seed–sized amount of faith redirected me to the fifth chapter of *Democracy*'s second volume, "How Religion in the United States Makes Use of Democratic Instincts"—a chapter I've already quoted from once in the chapter you're reading now. Right there, I recalled with a start, just five short paragraphs in, Tocqueville confessed something astounding.

He was at a disadvantage I was not.

Masterfully, he set up a cosmic punch line. "Only minds singularly free from the ordinary preoccupations of life, penetrating, subtle, and trained to think, can at the cost of much time and trouble sound the depths of these truths that are so necessary."[12] *Yes, yes*, I growled. *Lucky you.*

But there was a catch: "We see," he murmured, "that philosophers themselves are almost always surrounded by uncertainties, that at each pace the natural light which guides them"—a.k.a. reason—"grows dimmer and threatens to go out"; alas, "for all their efforts they have done no more than discover a small number of contradictory ideas on which the mind of man has been ceaselessly tossed for thousands of years without ever firmly grasping the truth or even finding mistakes that are new."[13]

Yes, Tocqueville lectured me back. *You may not have the time or even the brilliance to rationally unpack and undo your special predicament.*

But guess what?

My philosophy, my aristocracy, are but invitations to vanity—temptations to distract myself from the deeper reality religion reveals. Even if a sudden influx of billions freed you up to become as remarkable a philosopher as I, you'd find yourself in the same extremity as I!

The same extremity?!

"Which extremity," I hissed. "What is this, a joke?"

Deep breaths, said Tocqueville. *The extremity wherein we accept that no one will understand what we're saying, or care, unless we lay our own faith on the table.*

"Oh," I said.

The extremity in which we contend that, today, nobody's sanity holds by reason alone.

"Ohh."

The extremity, said Tocqueville, *that leads us to show how sanity unfolds when you don't view Christianity as a way of life—but a religion only.*

"No way!" I gasped.

Way.

Peculiar as my predicament was, Tocqueville had seen it all coming. He confirmed the general paradox: "Fixed ideas" about "primordial questions" are still "indispensable to men for the conduct of daily life," while, infuriatingly, "it is daily life that prevents them from acquiring them." Yet dogmatic doctrines that promise escape from this trap make us lonely prisoners in the very cosmos they purport to encompass in exhaustive, totalistic detail.

I returned to the trial of beginning this chapter.

Sentence one: "I am a Christian."

Sentence two: "My Christianity is not a way of life."

VE BELIEVE IN EVERYSSING

But what could I mean when I say that my Christianity is *mine?* In a book that questions the reality of the "self," saying "mine" might constitute a "speak-o"—our Hamlet-style neologism for a windbag's verbal typo, hot air blowing in what ends up a manipulatively unsuccessful direction.*

---

*Jonathan Gruber, the MIT economist who played key counselor in the drafting of the Affordable Care Act and its Massachusetts forerunner,

Does Tocqueville have an answer?

Of course he does.

Think back to Tocqueville's concern that our crazy times and our fevered minds would lead us to collapse into the comforts of normcore nihilism. Sure, we might spend an odd night "exploring" our "fantasies," climbing into black leather onesies and hissing "dangerously" in a German accent. But day in and day out, we'd be way more like Seinfeld than *The Big Lebowski*'s "scary" Nihilists. In fact, we'd make nihilism safe for ourselves and for sex, reproductive or otherwise. We'd chillax in the burbs or the city, having a kid or two, or a dog or two, or a drink or two, or ten, or whatever, until one day we'd go, gently medicated, into that all-encompassing night. ("A little poison now and then: that produces pleasant dreams. And a lot of poison at last, for a pleasant death."*)

But a lot of us still aren't into the whole nihilism thing. We're just too proud. We're early enough in the Great Transition—it's so long it's potentially open-ended, remember—that nihilism is mostly just one of many amus-

---

knows the value of a little calculated crazy in the competitive pressure cooker of court. When shocked observers pressed him on how he could once have suggested, contrary to expectation, that states without their own health exchanges would lose access to federal subsidies under the new law, Gruber shook it off: "My subsequent statement was just a speak-o—you know, like a typo." Give thy thoughts no tongue? To thine own self be true? What would Polonius do?

*"They have left the places where living was hard: for one needs warmth. One still loves one's neighbor and rubs oneself against him: for one needs warmth. . . . Nobody grows rich or poor any more: both are too much of a burden. Who still wants to rule? Who obey? Both are too much of a burden. No herdsman and one herd." Friedrich Nietzsche, *Thus Spoke Zarathustra* (New York and London: Macmillan, 1896), 46.

ing fantasies we play for laughs. On a more sober level, however, we also believe we lack the luxury for that type of nihilism. Life is work, especially if you have the ounce of pride that makes even ordinary people ambitious. We still would rather feel good *about ourselves* than actually feel good.

As a result, we all wind up conforming to the rules of life's big competition. When work—like working out—makes us feel bad, we often feel good about ourselves. *That means it's working!* Again: we'd much rather be told what to do than what to believe. We give in to the rat race because it seems like we have to in order to think well enough of ourselves.

Therein lies a problem worse than a catch, even a catch-22.

More than a survival mechanism, our competitive conformity is a way of life.

We know how this works. Although ownership in the material world can help cultivate an ethic of responsibility, it more often produces the opposite, "materialistic" effect: irresponsibly pretending we can impress ourselves about who we are by impressing ourselves with what is ours. We know this is more than a little ridiculous, but we're led to act so irrationally by the force of our own logical reasoning. At a time when the Great Transition's vast equalizing forces make no secret of how interchangeable and insignificant we are, we foolishly struggle to *distinguish* ourselves—as much in the uneasy quiet of our private conscience as amid the competitive clamor of public life—by *submitting* to doctrines that purport to offer universal knowledge. Think of some of the most enduring rap slogans, like Wu-Tang's "cash rules

everything around me" or Biggie's "fuck bitches get money."
Remember Tocqueville: "That is not because their souls
are narrower but because money really is more important at such times."* Our melodramatic spirit is always re-
enacting a selfish sticker shock over the price tag of high
performance—and good performances. But if we reject
money as the universal measure of value and meaning, presenting an identity to others, or even to ourselves, becomes
akin to withstanding a siege in solitude.

Unless, that is, you seek refuge in some other comprehensive doctrine?

Not exactly. Let's consider religion again. Scarily enough,
a pathological pattern reappears with a vengeance when it's
spiritualism, not materialism, that takes the mental benefits
of asserting ownership to crazy, distorting extremes.
Trying to define yourself by taking *ownership* of *your faith*
can quickly become an all-too-clever way to trick yourself
into using *membership* in *a way of life* to make your self seem
more special, more important, and considerably more real
than it is. Much like Hamlet made himself the star of his
own reality show by taking "ownership" of his "madness,"
Christians and non-Christians alike shut themselves off to
the art of being freely when they disappear into identities
mass-produced by worldviews purporting to explain it all.

Here's where Tocqueville demands that we elevate our
game. Unfortunately, none of the foregoing means I can

---

*Many of us should experience an unsettling moment of Zen recognizing
ourselves in Marilyn Manson's now suitably dated reference to the problem, in the bridge of the song "New Model No. 15" off *Mechanical Animals*
(1998): "Oh look, you're like a VCR / Stick something in to know just who
you are."

simply drop the idea that my faith is "mine." If I choose to stop trying to care about what my relationship to my faith really is, I'm instantly on the verge of convincing myself that I also don't need to care about what my relationship to my God really is. But at the same time, in an insidious way also creepily reminiscent of Hamlet, what *seems* like a choice to *avoid* a choice—feigning madness to manufacture courtroom drama instead of just righting what's wrong, in Hamlet's example—is *actually* a decision to merely pretend you avoided the choice you don't want to make. If I *don't* refer to "my Christianity," if I take the attitude that my faith just "is what it is," I cleverly evade the most important question of all that Christianity (or any religion) addresses: what, as a human, is my relationship to God?

Even more cleverly, however, Tocqueville says: *the very act of evading the question answers it.*

How? If I don't address my relationship to God, I fail to distinguish myself from God. But rather than therefore seeing myself as a god—an inherently laughable idea in our times—I start to see *everything* as God, and then, finally, I wind up believing that "God" is just a word we can use for "everything."

I'm primed by the Great Transition to seek refuge down that slippery slope. In our times, as "each individual becomes more like his fellows, weaker, and smaller," I focus inevitably on what defines us all; my "human mind seeks to embrace a multitude of different objects at once, and it constantly strives to link up a variety of consequences with a single cause. The concept of unity becomes an obsession." And what's the biggest obstacle to the fullest unity? The distinction between God and everything else. "Not content with the discovery that there is nothing in the world but one creation and one Creator," I wind up "embarrassed by the primary division of things," hell-bent on "including God and the universe in one great whole"—the most simple and expansive solution to, like, my whole worldview problem, man. It really ties the cosmos together.

Tocqueville's reaction to this very choosy nonchoice is one of the greatest run-on sentences ever written:

> If one finds a philosophical system which teaches that all things material and immaterial, visible and invisible, which the world contains are only to be considered as the several parts of an immense Being who alone remains eternal in the midst of the continual flux and transformation of all that composes Him, one may be sure that such a system, although it destroys human individuality, or rather just because it destroys it, will have secret charms for men living under democracies.

Pantheism, as he calls the above concept, throws out the psychological baby with the bathwater. Out goes the illusory self (good); out goes my identity; out goes God's (not so good). Even in a song called "Everything Is Everything," Lauryn Hill didn't go that far.* But today, pantheism is one of our most logical and appealing solutions to the thirst for one concept that explains it all. It promises to wipe out our nagging worry that we have to choose between the biggest

---

*"Now hear this mixture / where hip hop meets scripture," she still instructed, in 1998.

possible cosmic shrug and the biggest possible cosmic hug. "All their habits of mind prepare them to conceive it and put them on the way toward adopting it," Tocqueville said of us. "It naturally attracts their imagination and holds it fixed. It fosters the pride and soothes the laziness of their minds."[14] Burn.

Still, if it works . . . why not?

Because it isn't enough to keep us from giving in to the crazy.

BREAK ON THROUGH

The crazy returns by a very simple path. Conceptually, the distinction between Creator and created may have the highest stakes, but it doesn't seem to be the most stubborn. That award goes to the distinction between man and beast (as we used to say). Not for lack of trying, of course—we all now know that apes have feelings, people refer to their pets as children, and dolphins are people too. But nonhuman personhood effaces an *ethical* boundary perhaps less important, for the sake of our sanity, than the *practical* one distinguishing humans from animals. "Though man resembles the animals in many respects, one characteristic is peculiar to him alone: he improves himself, and they do not."[15] In fact, this peculiarity is "as old as the world," and so, too, then, is what arises from it: the idea that we're the only ones capable of stopping ourselves from solving all of our problems.

Tocqueville calls this notion "the indefinite perfectibility of man."

Perhaps this strikes you as an inherently maddening idea, setting the bar higher than sanity can leap. Perhaps you never were the practice-makes-perfect type. If so, the reasons go beyond personal idiosyncrasy. They go to the heart of the Great Transition.

Turn back the clock. In an aristocratic age, it's not that people deny we can elevate our station, but that they believe our problem-solving abilities are limited by the conditions of life itself. So they don't even think that whatever causes pain, suffering, frustration, or sadness necessarily *is* a problem. "They think in terms of amelioration, not change; they imagine that the conditions of the societies of the future will be better, but not really different."[16] Because their life is ordered in accordance with a society-wide order, rules, ranks, and habits seem so fixed and eternal that no mental market emerges for contending ways of life that could, as we say, "complete" us. Now jump forward. Remember Tocqueville's metaphor of the broken, dangling chains—the aristocratic leftovers that persist so much despite the spread of equality that we come to feel they're spiting *us*. When the old web of habitual thoughts, words, roles, and actions does come partly undone, hanging persistently out of joint, the ideal of completion rushes in. For the first time a newly abstract idea of our inherent brokenness can arise, from our reality-based experience of profound incompletion. "Every man sees changes continually taking place," in a world where all "are jumbled together and habits, customs, and laws are changing"; as "old conceptions vanish and new ones take their place, then the human mind imagines the possibility of an ideal but always fugitive perfection." A vaguely inescapable logic gnaws at us: *because* we know we need to be fixed, we *dream* we can be perfected.

But the fantasy of perfecting our broken selves is no idle

reverie. "The soul's chief effort goes in that direction. Imagination is not dead, but its chief function is to conceive what may be useful and to portray what is actual."[17] Translation? Just picture the athletic ideal worshipped in our beautifully grim sportswear ads. Always pushing a little harder, always shaving another fraction of a second, toil is good. At a high enough level, even just watching others toil allows us to partake in the experience of *chasing down* the ultimate kind of humanity. "Thus searching always, falling, picking himself up again, often disappointed, never discouraged," our archetypal hero (in a manner ever more uniformly applicable to our quintessential heroine) is "ever striving toward that immense grandeur glimpsed indistinctly at the end of the long track humanity must follow."* Try reading that in your best portentous voice over the next Nike mini-movie to pop up for you on YouTube. For us, this vision can't be boiled down to some cheap slogan pretending to encompass the universal essence of being. Quite the contrary. It's the fabric of our lives.

Paradoxically, however, the reason we're all so apt to celebrate athletes is the way that they're grounded by their escape from reality. Just one more set of reps. Just one more point on the board. These artificial goals keep them afloat; in the real world, hemmed in by practical necessities, we flounder. Everything—except us, it seems—is "making such quick progress" that even the best among us will be "almost

---

*Tocqueville, *Democracy*, 453. "They still work, for work is entertainment. But they take care the entertainment does not exhaust them." Nietzsche, *Zarathustra*, 46.

useless" in "more than a few years." The onset of equality in the Great Transition has sped everything up, and the devil take the hindmost. Facebook is where your grandparents hang out. The "youngs" want evanescence, not timelines—radical contemporaneity, not reactionary nostalgia. Who has time for memories? Novelty is progress, and no one with any life force inside them wants to fall behind. Athletes seem to reveal that the more game-like work becomes, the better we're able to make ourselves whole. Too insignificant and interchangeable to rely solely on *inspiration*, we try to find our salvation in *iteration*—surrendering ourselves to the kind of repetition our top pop social scientists say can deliver us perfect breakthroughs for our broken—and broke—selves. "I'm so damn close I can taste it," as Macklemore raps, "on some Malcolm Gladwell, David Bowie-meets-Kanye shit. This is dedication—a life lived for art is never a life wasted." Invoking Gladwell's magic rep goal, he avows that "ten thousand hours felt like ten thousand hands" leading him through the dark forest of life as "a statistic" and into deliverance.*

Animals don't suffer like this. But rather than bringing us together, the idea that we're infinitely perfectible also

---

*See "Ten Thousand Hours" on Macklemore's breakthrough 2012 album with Ryan Lewis, *The Heist*; on the ten thousand hours theory, see Malcolm Gladwell, *The Outliers* (New York: Little, Brown, 2008). One important corrective to Gladwellism comes from the insight that iteration only reliably promises a kind of secular salvation around the most scripted and rule-bound fields of endeavor, where the threat of having your cheese moved merely seems, as you iterate away, head down, to be the smallest. See Frans Johansson, *The Click Moment: Seizing Opportunity in an Unpredictable World* (New York: Portfolio/Penguin, 2012).

draws a merciless, unforgiving line through humankind. To our horror, the spread of equality in the Great Transition divides brokenness itself into two separate and very unequal experiences.

The winners break through.

The losers break down.

And the hidden cost of pantheism rushes in. For us, an *undifferentiated* universe becomes an *indifferent* one. Without the primary distinction between Creator and created, the sensation of being forsaken *by reality itself* becomes too frequent and too painful not to drive us deep into craziness (or worse). We'd like the undifferentiated universe to smile on us. But how could it? Why would it? It didn't create us. It can't love us. All it can do—blindly, idiotically, and above all rarely—is "give us a chance." A lonely wind blows through the hollow of that chance. However fortuitous, a chance bestowed by no one is not a gift.

GRATUITY ADDED

Hang in there. Tocqueville is about to lighten the load. Or, in truth, we're about to do so ourselves, by becoming fully receptive to this crazy divide between winning and losing. Watch what happens as we experience its practical underpinnings. The competition to create ever-faster improvements fosters a cult of the breakthrough—one we're all quite familiar with by now. It's not just sports culture. It's tech. It's science. It's business. It's pop psychology. When we do criticize any of these subcultures—and as they accelerate, they do tend to converge—it's for their unhealthy obsession with winning. Instead, we should question our obsession with obsession. Obsession, we believe, is essential for breakthroughs, and breakthroughs are essential to what Lexus called *the relentless pursuit of perfection* (or, in an even bolder, later slogan, *engineering the impossible*). Quite rationally, we take the notion of our own perfectibility and "stretch it beyond reason."[18] Because we are *humans*, not animals, *our* species being leads us from skepticism about supernatural notions to fanaticism about perpetual breakthroughs.

And fanaticism about perpetual breakthroughs leads us to mysticism, not materialism—another non–news flash. "You cannot maintain a true tradition of breakthroughs," wrote Philip Rieff back in 1972; " 'the tradition of the new' does not exist—no more than can a world of celibates."[19] Or a world of charismatics, no matter how many innovations there are to identify with. For decades we have ruefully acknowledged the empty promise of "spray-on charisma," as it was once depicted in a *New Yorker* cartoon.[20] But do we know the idol we bow to? If there's one thing we can't break out of—no matter how many Zenned-out "break rooms" or "breakaway sessions" fill the space-time continuum of businesses, brands, and corporations—it's our obsession with breakthroughs. In its craziness and ours, competition convinces us we have to be ready for anything, no matter how hard we train.[21] Our mystical master isn't merit but— yes—chance. Rather than a gift, chance becomes an invisible cage lowered around us by our experience of *apparent* freedom.

"Man is born free," some Tocquevillean prankster could rewrite Rousseau, "but he is everywhere in chance."

Peter Thiel calls Chance an "unjust tyranny."*

Max Weber, confirming that our pursuit of wealth "tends to become associated with purely mundane passions, which often actually give it the character of sport," wondered some hundred years ago "who will live in this cage in the future."[22]

Yes. That's right. Us.

We can't lift this cage by reason alone. In fact, we can't lift it by ourselves alone. It's baked in to our world. Increasing equality devilishly divides us so sharply into winners and losers that the unity we long for fades. Yet the inequality that results is, even more devilishly, *superficial*—nothing deep enough to seem authoritative or commanding. Win or lose, we're all playing the same game, a game that makes life feel like a lottery. Even the winners—among society's craziest, not coincidentally—routinely suffer sanity-snapping setbacks, losses, and self-imposed torments. Some of our most successful, of course, try to share a different experience. "You can have agency, not just over your own life, but over a small and important part of the world," Peter Thiel cries. "You are not a lottery ticket."[23] *That's just billionaire talk*, we say to ourselves. But deeper, if we listened in the silence, we'd hear a truer voice, admitting we've stopped the conversation before it starts. We won't listen to Thiel because we already bow at the altar of Chance.

Tocqueville saw it all coming, because he began where we, like Rorty, least want to—with faith. The key to fully receiving our crazy world is acknowledging our all-too-

---

*Peter Thiel with Blake Masters, *Zero to One: Notes on Startups, or How to Build the Future* (New York: Crown Business, 2014), 81. Nor is Thiel a fan of Gladwell's, either.

human habit of mistakenly drawing and erasing dividing lines. Try as we might, pantheism cannot unite what life amid equality insists we distinguish. Try as we might, er, *chancy-ism* cannot diversify what life amid equality makes uniform. Tired of talking ourselves in vicious circles, religion becomes a conversation *re*-starter.

And it doesn't happen by choice or by chance.

It happens, let's say, gratuitously.

Recall (from the previous chapter) that Tocqueville begins with religion to reveal how we process reality, because America's Puritan origins best reveal how the aristocratic past *persists*, incompletely but stubbornly, into the current age. Loosened from their ancient moorings, the spirit of religion and the spirit of freedom may be maddening, but they can also be tremendously fruitful. For while they conflict in the old world, they combine in the new. Now, we can see that Tocqueville's religion-first approach also actually operationalizes that insight, making us receptively *unafraid* to experience our *apparent crises* as something other than *solvable problems*. We love equality; we want unity; we fear uniformity. The promise of formal religion (and Christianity, as we'll see in particular, though not for the reasons you think) is not to *obliterate* these indefinitely imperfect realities, constitutive of life in the Great Transition. Nor is its promise to somehow defeat or destroy the role of chance and choice in our constitutionally crazy times. Instead, it is simply to reconcile us to those things—not by fleetingly blissing us out in some kind of all-and-nothing trance, but by *gifting* us with the grace to prevail, fully present, in the face of the trials that must necessarily arise in a time so far out of joint.

In the old world, Hamlet faked his madness to escape the burden of setting his world to rights. Here in the new, only by surrendering that burden can we truly escape our madness.

Sentence one: "I am a Christian."

Sentence two: "My Christianity is not a way of life."

Sentence three: "That's why I'm okay with the fact that I'll never get this chapter right."

EMPIRE STRIKES BACK

To sum up: Tocqueville has spilled the beans on not one but two secret longings that give rise in our time to spiritual worldviews—comprehensive visions commending particular, but cosmos-defining, ways of life. Increasingly ruled by money as the single standard of value or meaning; increasingly anxious about our apparent insignificance and interchangeability in what seems an indifferent universe; increasingly drawn toward competitively *hedging* our bets in the hopes of *edging* out people less ready to adapt in whatever way Chance would demand—all these democratic experiences solicit a prideful reaction that *conceals* a deeper, universal desire: to surrender our pride. Hence the allure of nihilism and, even more so, pantheism.

But these two secret longings fail to satisfy. The first parodies our craziness, domesticating it into the superficially harmless but deadening unity of empty kitsch. The second teases us with an escape from our craziness into blissful unity, only to fail us when the winners break through and the losers break down, dividing and distinguishing us in a way that feels unforgiving and arbitrary.

But there are two more secret longings.

Both speak to the fundamental reason that neither nihilism nor pantheism can save us: they're impossible masters to serve. We *want* them to master us—we want to *trust* in their definitive and comprehensive mastery of our universe and our lives, but when we really try, we discover we can't, because they lack the authority to be masters at all. Not only do they actually fail to *explain* it all; they fail to discipline us—in the original, religious sense of making us disciples. Both nihilism and pantheism are too vague, empty, and abstract to give us the gift of discipleship. They do not possess any *charisma*, in the original, religious sense of *kharis*, or grace.

There are plenty of nihilistic and pantheistic "gurus," of course, brimming with charisma in today's devilishly ambiguous and ambivalent sense of *talent*. Browse the featured reviews of Patricia Highsmith's *The Talented Mr. Ripley* to recall what experience has taught us to fear: "In this period of transition, our would-be charismatics are better understood as terrorists"—a point that seems absurdly outlandish when a social theorist makes it, but titillatingly clever when a novelist does.* Probably the best of the *Ripley* re-

---

*Philip Rieff, *Charisma: The Gift of Grace, and How It Has Been Taken Away From Us* (New York: Pantheon, 2000), 5. The novelist is Bret Easton Ellis; the novel is his follow-up to *American Psycho*, wherein a top model retires at the top of his game to ensnare others in a game of utterly lowering political violence. "How did he recruit people? . . . It was only models . . . and famous models. . . . He wasn't interested in anyone else. . . . He would use the fact that as a model all you do all day is stand around and do what other people tell you to do. . . . He preyed on that . . . and we listened . . . everyone wanted to be around us." Bret Easton Ellis, *Glamorama* (New York: Alfred A. Knopf, 1998), 352. "Holy terror is . . . fear of oneself, fear of the evil in oneself and in the world. . . . Without this

views comes courtesy of Mark Harris, writing with calm
amorality in *Entertainment Weekly*: "This young, charismatic
American protagonist is, it turns out, a murderer, a gentleman of calm amorality." But there's also the director Anthony Minghella, calling Ripley "one of the most interesting
characters in world literature," and *New York Times* reviewer
Michiko Kakutani, who says Highsmith "forces us to re-
evaluate the lines between reason and madness."* Tocqueville does this, too, of course—somehow, without making
a killer into a hero.

Tocqueville is no naif. He knows, more in the manner of
Shakespeare or Socrates than Minghella, just how "interesting" supposedly "charismatic" killers can be. That is to say,
he understands tyranny. "Up till now no one in the United
States has dared to profess the maxim that everything is allowed in the interests of society," he noted—"an impious
maxim apparently invented in an age of freedom in order
to legitimate every future tyrant." But in Europe, at the cre-
scendo of *Democracy*'s first volume, religion had "lost its
sway over men's souls," throwing "the natural limits of des-
potism and the bounds of license" into terrible question.
"Unburdened by the weight of public esteem, princes may
henceforth abandon themselves without fear to the intoxi-
cation of power." In the aftermath of Napoleon's fallen empire, the returning possibility that charismatic killers could
rule led Tocqueville to invoke "the terrible centuries of Roman tyranny, when mores had been corrupted, memories

---

necessary fear, charisma is not possible. To live without this high fear is
to be a terror oneself, a monster." Rieff, *Charisma*, 6.

*These and other nuggets of "praise" appear at the start of the 2008 edi-
tion published by W. W. Norton.

obliterated," and "customs destroyed"—"when men made sport of human nature and princes exhausted heaven's mercy before their subjects' patience."[24] As the twentieth century then revealed, "charismatics" could be terrorists or tyrants in equal measure.

Now we begin to glimpse the first of our last two secret longings. No falsely charismatic virtuoso of violence can bring the unity we crave. But what about, as Tocqueville says, a *single master*? In the closing pages of *Democracy*'s second volume, he whispers that, though the democratic age is "still half buried" amid the Great Transition, "in the ruins of the world falling into decay," the way of the gun and "vast confusion" aren't the only things to fear. There's vast order, under the peaceful yet forcible hand of a supreme leader. Some "already worship the master" they believe is "bound soon to appear," enlisting reason in the surrender of their pride and their taste for freedom."[25] Translation: just as pantheism seems to grant our secret wish to be united by promising to *unburden us* of our anxious individuality, the rule of a single master addresses our secret wish to be united by absolving us of our failure, amid the breakthroughs and breakdowns of competitive conformity, to unite ourselves.*

---

*The allure of the single master holds a special warning for artists, whose experience of being freely is so apt to turn excessively inward: "Once decay has reached its climax along with the infighting of all sorts of tyrants, the Caesar always appears, the final tyrant who puts an end to the weary struggle for sole rule—by putting weariness to work for himself. In his age the individual is usually ripest and culture therefore in its highest and most fruitful stage—but not for his sake or on account of him, although the men of the highest culture like to flatter their Caesar by pretending to be *his* creation. But in truth they merely need peace

Look into this longing, and what do we see? Another secret wish—for a single *heavenly* master. "The spirit of man, left to follow its bent," will "seek to *harmonize* earth with heaven."[26] And Christianity arose from decidedly imperial origins.*

> At the time when Christianity appeared on earth, Providence . . . had united a great part of mankind, like an immense flock, under the scepter of the Caesars. The men composing this multitude were of many different sorts, but they all had this in common, that they obeyed the same laws, and each of them was so small and weak compared to the greatness of the emperor that they all seemed equal in comparison to him. One must recognize that this new and singular condition of humanity disposed men to receive the general truths preached by Christianity, and this serves to explain the quick and easy way in which it then penetrated the human spirit.[27]

In an essential way, the ancient Romans were more like us today—*in their experience of interchangeable insignificance and their instinct for unity*—than we are like the denizens of ancient Athens or Jerusalem, Western civilization's acknowledged founders. Rather than seeing Christendom as rooted in Greek freedom or Hebraic law, Tocqueville wants us to

---

from outside because they have enough unrest and work inside themselves." Nietzsche, *Gay Science*, bk. 1, sec. 23.

*"The advance toward universal empires is always also an advance toward universal divinities." Friedrich Nietzsche, *Genealogy of Morals* (New York: Vintage, 1989), second essay, sec. 20.

wake up to the way our patterns of thinking and wishing still reach back to imperial Roman universality—to a comprehensive vision of the cosmos institutionalized and united by a single (shall we say *catholic*?) regime.*

That's why Tocqueville expected us Americans to eventually split off into two main groups: non-Christians on the one hand and Catholics on the other. "Our contemporaries are naturally little disposed to belief, but once they accept religion at all, there is a hidden instinct within them which unconsciously urges them toward Catholicism. Many of the doctrines and customs of the Roman Church astonish them, but they feel a secret admiration for its discipline, and its extraordinary unity attracts them." After all, it's just so maddening and wearying, for mushy quasi-Christians, to have "submitted to authority in some of their religious beliefs" while still seeking "to exempt some of their other beliefs from it"; as a result, intentionally but crazily, their minds "float at random between obedience and freedom."[28] We experience so much of that adrift, hassled, unreliable feeling in the material world that it seems extra crazy to choose it—and extra hard to maintain it—in the realm of the spirit. Catholicism, by contrast, offers a unity so ideal that even the most insignificant and interchangeable of us can get a trusty toehold on life and its meaning. Plus, it's easy to adopt without the pride and envy issues the denomination still dredges up in Europe. Here, Roman Christianity just isn't tainted by centuries of complicity

---

*"In his victory, Jesus represented the defeat of the Jews in their particularity, as Jews; this is very different from representing the defeated Jews," as Nietzsche would have it. Rieff, *Fellow Teachers*, 171.

in feudal control and absolutist oppression (if it is by more recent quiet atrocities). Here, Mark 12:17 is just common sense: just as we render unto Caesar that which is Caesar's, we give to God the things that are His. If our country does grow ever more uniform, and our taste in rulers grows ever more imperial, that doesn't necessarily upset the Catholic spirit, while for many Protestants, it's virtually a sign of the end times.

THE MYSTERY MACHINE

So Tocqueville ties it all up with a bow, right?

Not quite. There are, as always in the Great Transition, complications.

And it's with the complex possibilities of faith that Tocqueville will leave us.

Let's unwind the tangle backward—starting with Catholicism, where there's an all-important caveat to Tocqueville's prediction. In order to prevail among American Christianity's many denominations, Roman Christianity must "ultimately escape from the political animosities to which it has given rise"—that is, stay out of politics. But there's another condition. To triumph in our time, a religion must not only lean out of politics but lean into society. The greater equality of experience becomes, the harder it is to orient people where the hive mind does not already incline them to look; "religions, while remaining studiously aloof from the daily turmoil of worldly business, should not needlessly run counter to prevailing ideas or the permanent interests of the mass of the people."[29] Many Catholics and other Christians understand how hard it can be today to thread this needle. Even beyond the troublesome question of where "politicizing" lines should be drawn in the public sphere, the simple notion that *one* denomination is *right* and others are *wrong* is anathema to public opinion today. The hive mind inclines us all to seek out what *works*. And it turns out Tocqueville sought this out too. What varieties of faith, he asked, work to keep us all sane—in a world where we wish to seek out what works?

Here, we go further than many Tocqueville analysts might be willing to venture. At first, Tocqueville seems not so adventurous. Channeling the apostle Paul, for whom "diversities of gifts" are united by "the same Spirit,"[30] Tocqueville asserts that we drive ourselves crazy by refusing to grasp the superhuman majesty of God's gift of unity, revealed most fully—practically speaking—by Jesus.* We mortals *try* for unity, yet achieve only uniformity, because the "greatness" of unity resides in a kind of consummation that *does not result from* trying. Receptivity to reality reveals something reason does not. "To encourage endless variety of actions but to bring them about so that in a thousand different ways all tend toward the fulfillment of one great design—that is a God-given idea."[31] Our struggles for unity are impotent; God's gift of unity is fertile.

Exactly this, says Tocqueville, is why Christianity is at an advantage for us. Its entanglement with politics has con-

---

*"Jesus Christ had to come down to earth to make all members of the human race understand that they were naturally similar and equal" (Tocqueville, *Democracy*, 439). The equality of earthly empire *prepared* the ancient *spirit* for Christianity's reception, but could not *discern* equality's true measure through earthly *reason*. For each among all to occur as a gift, an ultimate gift was required. "In a casebook of charismatics, Jesus must come first, of course; without Jesus, the concept 'charisma' would not have come into being" (Rieff, *Fellow Teachers*, 213).

fused us on this score, but, in fact, the Gospels "deal only with the general relations between man and God and between man and man. Beyond that, they teach nothing and do not oblige people to believe anything."[32] Rather than dragging us into a way of life complete with enumerated rules about science, law, diet, and more, Christianity gives us the grace to move toward human unity without trying to force uniformity.

Today we make the mistake of being threatened by faith, which seems poised to close in around us, choking off communication, breaking through only aggressively and breaking down under pressure. On the contrary, says Tocqueville, Christianity has the capacity to open vast vistas—precisely the kind that it drives us so crazy to feel like we're losing as the Great Transition rolls on. That's because Christianity asks so relatively *little* of us. Love God fully. Love others as yourself. Beyond that, the Gospels follow us where we go. "In the democratic age, everything moves; a religion that does not place man in that flow of ever-changing events while at the same time giving him hope and encouragement will be at odds with the spirit of the age"—and not long for this world.*

Our age, in this sense, is a mystery machine—but not to lead us, Scooby-Doo style, from "solve" to "solve." The time is out of joint; the length and course of our journey are unclear; if our destination is foreordained, it is not given to us to know. Ruh-roh.

---

*Joshua Mitchell, *Tocqueville in Arabia* (Chicago: University of Chicago Press, 2013), 166. For me, this book first made explicit Tocqueville's pregnant, implicit question of what forms of Christianity are and aren't ways of life.

Americans that we are, we want a decent response at its quickest and easiest. So, under our mysterious circumstances, beyond Christianity's few supreme commandments, its seemingly ineffable accommodations of ever-changing human diversity raise a question we should welcome, not fear: how "minimal" a faith of that sort could help us?

Tocqueville's answer involves what he calls materialism's vicious circle—in our terms, a sort of democratized version of the vast apathy[33] and paralyzing sense of doom that was once recognized as a malady only afflicting celebrities. Giving up on religion exaggerates our love of physical gratification—even its most banal varieties like food and drink and simple pleasure. Materialism is a vicious circle because, in handing ourselves over to those fleeting gratifications, we quickly dispose ourselves and each other to "believe that nothing but matter exists"; but once we do that, we find ourselves swiftly drawn into "mad impetuosity"— crazy because we resent the material world for being too predictable and orderly on the one hand but too fleeting and chaotic on the other. Think of Macbeth's crisis of confidence:

> I 'gin to be aweary of the sun,
> And wish th' estate o' th' world were now undone.—
> Ring the alarum-bell!—Blow, wind! Come, wrack!
> At least we'll die with harness on our back.[34]

The dark secret of the world of mere matter is that it can't convince us *we* matter as much as we helplessly hope to. Forsaken in the material world, hollow even in victory, we are born to lose, haunted by the worry that we can't afford to pay attention to anything that isn't about us.* Because we so "often feel doubts" it seems "no one can resolve," we ping-pong between manic hopes of victory and depressing fears of defeat; "without the strong pressure of any directing force, nothing more than oscillation to and fro, without any progress, occurs."[35] Trapped in the merely material world, that ping-ponging sends us lurching for material excess one minute and collapsing into exhaustion the next. Though sometimes we halfheartedly long for a guru or a worldview to deliver a breakthrough that will leave all this madness behind, what we need, by Tocqueville's lights, is a minimal degree of faith in an *enduring* infinite and eternal. The chic minimalism and fashionable detachment feted today to disrupt conventional materialism isn't enough. That alone, Tocqueville would say, can't really escape the psychodrama—the melodrama—that penetrates far deeper than a floor-to-ceiling whitewash or an enlightened garage sale can reach.

And if Tocqueville is to be believed, all you need to escape the drama is hope. Hope in what, you ask? In the possibility that we can be how we are when we're being freely—forever. Because our imagination reaches further than our own lives and our own powers, the melodrama of materialism is just an especially desperate version of the drama of being human. "Alone among all created beings, man shows a natural disgust for existence and an immense longing to exist; he scorns life and fears annihilation." What-

---

*"It is very difficult to make the inhabitants of democracies listen when one is not talking about themselves. They do not hear what is said to them because they are always very preoccupied with what they are doing." Tocqueville, *Democracy*, 642.

ever our lot in life, it takes a self-induced stupor to blunt our longing for a joy more complete than mortal existence can provide. Despite our best efforts, our "taste for the infinite and love of what is immortal" betoken a soul whose "needs . . . must be satisfied. Whatever pains are taken to distract it from itself, it soon grows bored, restless, and anxious amid the pleasures of the senses."[36] No, "the longing for immortality equally tormenting every human heart" cries out for hope, and the hope of faith is the promise of the soul: the promise that we are not cursed to strive toward a freedom of being that our material bodies forever foreclose.

Today, if the fear of that curse is what works against us, what works for us is to simply disbelieve it. In fact, Tocqueville says, "even when it is not united to a conception of rewards and punishments," even when "one believes no more than that after death the divine principle embodied in man is absorbed in God or goes to animate some other creature," faith in the soul has perfectly "fine effects" upon us.[37]

Are we now in the land of heresy? Have we not left "orthodox" Christianity far behind? Perhaps. But Tocqueville's aim is to reveal just how forgiving of our crazy circumstances the Christian faith can be. Being human is hard enough as it is; in our time, our increasing experiences of interchangeability and insignificance send our oscillations between breakthroughs and breakdowns to what could be called a crisis point. Worse, seeing our struggle *as* a crisis just seems to worsen it, though deadening ourselves to the problem brings apathy, paralysis, and doom. Therefore, our instinct is to seek refuge: in doctrines that explain away our

anxiety, filling up the universe with comprehensive answers. But such strategies put us at war with our own moment, luring us toward a mournful remembrance of an
irrecoverable past or a delusional anticipation for an unat-
tainable future. Though the soul may endure forever, on
earth, the art of being free entails the art of enduring the
here and now, however out of joint. The crazed "but *why?!*"
of our rational minds may only be ameliorated, not annihi-
lated. Ours is not the land of heresy, but of mystery.

Our silver lining, our grace note, is this mystery's graceful irony: were it any other way, life would cease to be recognizably human. Not only would the art of being free ebb
away but indeed all art would too. "If he saw himself clearly,
his imagination would remain idle and would have nothing to add to the picture. But the nature of man is sufficiently
revealed for him to know something of himself and sufficiently veiled to leave much in impenetrable darkness, a
darkness in which he ever gropes, forever in vain, trying to
understand himself."[38] Yet to plumb these depths is no exercise in vanity. Tocqueville envisions our faith as our link
between the freedom of being artful and the art of being
free. "Human destiny, man himself, not tied to time or
place, but face to face with nature and with God, with his
passions, his doubts, his unexpected good fortune, and his
incomprehensible miseries, will for these peoples be the
chief and almost the sole subject of poetry." And not just
poetry. Writers in our time who reach for these themes
won't just seek "to record the actions of an individual, but
by exaggeration to illuminate certain dark corners of the
human heart." Finally, a kind of excess we can trust.

I wonder how this chapter would have turned out had I

been able to stride ahead as purposefully and confidently as I'd intended. I wonder *if* it would have turned out. Guided by Tocqueville, the purposeful, confident guy who hit a wall the minute he started still only managed to make it three sentences into his religion chapter.

I am a Christian. My Christianity is not a way of life. That's why I'm okay with the fact that I'll never get this chapter right.

Not at that rate, genius.

Then again, Mr. Formerly Purposefully Confident is no longer sure the world really needed his chapter on religion. Mr. Formerly Purposefully Confident now suspects he had just four lines to say anyway. He was convinced of this by that last extremely poetic bit of Tocqueville's about writing and art, reality and exaggeration. Truth be told, it was quite a relief.

Sentence four:

Did I mention I'm also writing a novel?

Which brings us to the subject of money.

Money

So, yes: I'm writing a novel. (Now that we're comfortable with Tocqueville's pattern of thinking, let's get more casual. Let's pick up the pace.) I've been at it now for most of my literate life. There's an unnerving thought. Then again, it'd be more unnerving simply to let it go, unconsummated, into the same slipstream of fruitless human endeavors that we struggle to deal with as we ping-pong from believing in nothing to believing in everything, and back. One reason it's taken so long: I didn't quite understand what I was doing until I beheld Tocqueville's vision of how being artful and being free calls for a certain kind of fiction.

But another reason is that the novel I'm writing hasn't been the kind you can knock out quickly for a big payday and a nice multi-sequel contract. A third reason is—yes—

it's taken me this long to figure out that I really *want* to turn the book into that kind of novel. The fourth reason (brace yourself): only now do I really believe I can do it.

This, Tocqueville tells me, is yet another instantiation of a supremely American pattern of thinking.

He invites us to imagine somebody "active, educated, free, comfortably off, and full of desire"—both "too poor to live in idleness" but "rich enough not to be in fear of immediate want," so "anxious to improve his lot."[1] Sounds familiar.

But that's where things get interesting. This person, you see, "has formed a taste for physical pleasures" of the quality that "thousands around him" are actively enjoying; "he himself has tasted some too, and he is very keen to acquire the means to enjoy them more. But life goes by, and time presses. What is he to do?" The answer, says Tocqueville, is all but a foregone conclusion. Rather than sticking to something safe and sedentary, tending a small garden, we middling sorts turn to commercial activity to embark "on some risky but lucrative profession."[2] We hazard our nervous compulsion to maximize our experience of satisfaction, as soon as we think we can.

Wait, sorry, you're laughing.

Oh, novel writing. How hazardous.

Well? Did J. K. Rowling think she had a sure thing? Is there anything more dispiriting today than trying to be artsy and failing? Ask Hitler: with the aristocratic age irrecoverably past, so much as presuming to still be in touch with the lofty culture of yore is sure, as Tocqueville hinted, to lead to sterile, fatuous art and some real peals of mockery—if anyone pays you attention at all.* Even more hazardous than wagering your time and life on art worth taking seriously is betting that you can do it in a way that's also "buzzworthy," or relevant to a wide audience of busy, picky, regular human beings.

And even when you do this, beyond your wildest hopes of success?

Guess what.

People hate you. Disdain you. Belittle you as much as they can.

Take Jonathan Franzen, whom everyone hates. (Or so you'd gather from cruising the internet.) Famed alpha nerd and literary white guy whose books, including *The Corrections* and *Freedom* and *Purity*, have hit the magic sweet spot between artistry and commerce, selling millions of copies while still garnering breathless reviews. But many revile him, notwithstanding how hard or how long he had to wait and work and wager. They're bothered, for instance, by the idea that he—a relatively well-advantaged person—should get the platform for moneymaking he now has. But if you think this is the root of the matter, Tocqueville would suggest you go deeper.

Don't worry: no deep dives into Franzen here. *Below* the farrago of identity conflict surrounding Jonathan Franzen,

---

*"Gods and heroes gone, they began by painting rivers and mountains," says Tocqueville, not thinking, as we do, of Hitler's decent landscapes. "Some have thought that this poetry embellishing the physical and inanimate things that cover the earth is the true poetry of democracy. But I think that is a mistake. . . . In the long run I am sure that democracy turns man's imagination away from externals to concentrate it on himself alone." Alexis de Tocqueville, *Democracy in America*, ed. J. P. Mayer, trans. George Lawrence (New York: Harper, 2006), 484.

below his work itself, is *our* great uncertainty or confusion over just what sort of practices it makes us happy to see huge amounts of money flow toward. That's what, with Tocqueville's aid, we need to explore. Should novelists be wealthy? Should they be stars? Why only novelists with *these* qualities and not *those*? Not just chance is at play, we worry (or insist), but a certain kind of slanted caprice: a set of baked-in biases that often favor some groups—what we might call the *pre-successful*—and disfavor others. But exactly which groups, or why, and how we can make sense of who's side we're on, has become a bewildering matter to analyze, not least in popular culture. Why should some musicians make it and others not? What level of success do all musicians deserve, if any? Our heads hurt. (Probably our souls too.)

We just want someone to give us the answer.

Yet we don't trust in the least that there is one.

So our inability to draw stable, durable lines in these realms causes us either to fall silent or to become impotent in the face of what seems to be the extremely confident and assertive line-drawing activity conducted by *money*. Success speaks for itself with the same kind of authority as public opinion. In fact, the market, which we sometimes think of as a disembodied entity, is actually just a way—like the "expertise" it rewards—of *clarifying* public opinion, our true master. How better to demarcate the bounds of public opinion—the voice of the people—than by "putting some skin in the game"? Money is the measure of our physical presence in the real world—even more reliable, we semi-secretly believe, than people's so-called convictions or their "conscience," political, religious, or otherwise.

Unfortunately, our passivity in the face of money doesn't supply the rest, repose, and reconciliation we seek. Instead, it makes us fear that money is asserting its rule over us, even though we tacitly grasp that this is happening because nothing else about us seems capable of drawing boundaries and assigning due measures on any other basis. We semisecretly understand this is an inherent problem when vertical authority in our society is reduced to broken, dangling chains, and the equal option to freely love anything takes hold.

Bottom line, as money itself would say?

Money is a special problem in transitional times like ours.

Be warned: Tocqueville is going to tell you some things you may not want to hear. It is not unlikely that the things he says will set off alarms—*ideological* alarms. When you grasp the claim, for instance, that we can never make ourselves feel okay about the amount of monetary inequality in society today—or the claim that only religion can ameliorate the craziness that comes up for us so characteristically in the realm of money—you may well suspect that Tocqueville is in fact an obsolete fop who doesn't truly care about the less fortunate. You may feel the temptation to angrily decide that all these *ideas* are a very clever, well-nigh masturbatory way of avoiding the simple truth: that the solution to the problem of money is to give it to whomever has little. Do not succumb.

Tocqueville is a richer thinker than you or I—and, no, not in the monetary sense. Because he goes deeper than we can, he is better at this than public opinion—better even than our experts. You may be surprised at what he yields. Tocqueville, for instance, concludes that it's a terrible idea to let the very wealthiest successful people hoard their riches in unbound fashion—not because they're terribly dangerous, but because their ability to bankroll a very glamorous knockoff version of "the aristocrat experience" makes the rest of us feel as if we are too interchangeably insignificant for life to be worth living.* With the craziness of life always just a few steps from breaking our spirit, even in conditions of great equality, the vision of all that equality producing a nonstop Rich Pride parade is more than we can bear.

This is just an example of Tocqueville's approach to our distemper around money and, as we'd say, "issues of money." And it may feel unfamiliar, uncomfortable. Dive in anyway. Not only is it "worth it," but, to be honest, you really don't have a choice. You can run from what Tocqueville is telling us, but you can't hide. You can try to bargain your way out of reckoning with the strange peace that his pattern of thinking reveals, but in the end, it won't work. You just have to, well . . . DEAL WITH IT.

---

*Equality, he says, "makes the passion for physical pleasures and an exclusive interest in immediate delights predominate in the human heart." This fusion of heart and mind infuses the ambition of even the most gifted and talented with the same bottom-line agenda the rest of us have—to "gratify trivial and coarse appetites more easily." The result is that our pride is grievously wounded by watching, amid the competition to which all must conform, those who are well-dealing, well-driven, and well-endowed to reach extraordinary results enjoy the material pleasures we all want to find satisfaction within. Tocqueville's answer is not the gospel of upward mobility. It is to put a cap on how much material enjoyment ambition can buy: setting down, "in advance, limits beyond which it would not be allowed to break"—while being "very careful not to hamper its free energy within the permitted limits." Tocqueville, *Democracy*, 631–32.

AMERICAN PSYCHODRAMA

Seeing as how the title of this book is *The Art of Being Free* and the motto of this book, in response to the constitutive craziness of everyday American life, is DEAL WITH IT, there are grounds for suspicion that another or truer name for this book could be *The Art of Dealing with It:* a most American-sounding title indeed, as no one can better attest than the author of *The Art of the Deal,* that human colossus astride our American crossroads of freedom, money, and crazy.

Of course, I'm talking about Donald Trump.

Emanating out of Trump's book and his mouth and his body and visage is a powerful signal we all receive that, today, our ideal is the motto *I Deal!* We all intuit, though we rarely care to be so explicit, that for us the art of *dealing* with life, in the sense of functional flourishing, can hardly be pulled apart from the art *of* the deal—in its crassly clever sense of manipulative machination designed to make people like you so that you can get the better of them. We know in our bones that life's constitutive crazy is quintessentially American, in the way money eggs us on and we egg it on right back, using it, no matter how much we grumble and moan, as the closest thing we have to a universal yardstick, a measure of all things.

Yet we also know that we can't bargain with money's role in our distemper. Rather than dealing with it that way, we have to deal with it in the sense introduced in this book: the one in which there isn't any opportunity to bargain with reality—only an opportunity to reconcile ourselves to it.

Most likely, *Democracy in America* has never occupied your thoughts in the same instant as *American Psycho*. Then again, if ever there were a novel hell-bent on using exaggeration to illuminate certain dark corners of the human heart, surely that would be it.* In fact, by no coincidence, even Patrick Bateman (when he isn't busy fantasizing about inhuman acts of slaughter) experiences a fleeting moment of clarity about the limits of the art of the deal as a way of life. Trump references and Trump sightings crop up continuously in the novel. Bateman explicitly uses Trump's book as an escape from reality, drawing prying detective Donald Kimball's attention to his desk copy of *The Art of the Deal* and describing his admitted hero's writing as "very good."[3] But Bateman recoils from his brother Sean's demand, when faced with bad news about a restaurant reservation, to "deal with it," rather than trying to best it through some kind of negotiation.† At a moment of weakness, plunged into the American nightmare of losing a status competition for a table at a nice restaurant, Patrick eventually labors—sadly, hilariously, and unsuccessfully—to try the approach. "This is reality," he concedes, "and as my loathsome brother Sean would say, I have to deal with it."[4] Where Patrick, a genuinely insane person, fails, we, merely trapped in a lifeworld suffused with craziness, can succeed. But to do so, we need

---

*Then again: "In democracies the springs of poetry are fine but few. They are soon exhausted. Finding no stuff for the ideal in what is real and true, poets, abandoning truth and reality, create monsters." Tocqueville, *Democracy*, 489.

†Bret Easton Ellis, *American Psycho* (New York: Vintage, 1991), 229. In *The Rules of Attraction*, "deal with it" is introduced as Sean Bateman's signature catchphrase—in the portentous sense that there is no bargaining to be done, rather than in the sense that there is.

to recognize how to reconcile ourselves to the way our craziness is fueled by the *monetariness* of life.*

Tocqueville is going to show us that, no matter how hard we try—and we try *hard*—we can't bargain our way to a deal with the thoroughly monetary quality of life's craziness. Instead, here we must *surrender* the art of the deal—to *receive* the art of being free.

We won't be free *from* the crazy monetariness of life, just as we can't be free from its fleetingness.

But we can be free *amid* it.

Let's start from the beginning. From our earliest years of socialization and education, we're trained to take life's monetariness for granted. We're groomed for monetization—not because we're ruled by greed but because we're obsessed with the single standard of mortal measure money affords above all. Peter Thiel describes our system of preparing young people to make money as one where, "in exchange for doing exactly what's asked of you (and for doing it just a bit better than your peers), you'll get an A."[5] It's Competitive Conformity 101. Habituation to one scale for all, with nobody off the charts, prepares us for the constitutively monetary character of our collective craziness, wherein we have no choice but to compete at competence in the art of the deal. So the psychodrama begins.

Then, habituated to monetary measurement, we're thrown into the paradox of egalitarian prestige that so de-

---

*We have the same kind of love-hate relationship with money as we do with moments. "The actual moment completely occupies and absorbs them," Tocqueville says of our most ambitious (*Democracy*, 631). We know all too anxiously how this captivity to the instant seems a curse as well as a blessing.

fines the Great Transition. Lived out over time, our art of the deal is the art of hedging to edge out, competing to conform yet also come out on top. The trick is to be better in quality, but not different in kind, from everyone else—an achievement that confers the sense of uniqueness in identity that, in the aristocratic age, came from a difference in kind, not in quality. *Money never sleeps; the relentless pursuit of perfection; engineering the impossible:* these mottos of dealing with the competitive conformity made ubiquitous by money's regnant role as our universal yardstick reveal that obsessing over *quality* is the characteristic practice in an age of *equality.** That's the theme of the psychodrama—our inescapable yearning to seem, feel, and maybe even *be* prestigious in a world where the universal yardstick of money makes more and more of us feel increasingly, interchangeably insignificant.

Our fully fledged proud *I!* or "ego" comes from well-*dealing*, in the artfully Trumpian sense, much more than the old-school kind of well-*being* that the "well-born" aristocrat knew in his blood, so very differently from you and I.† (Today, of course, our idea of well-being is different

---

*That's why we all (nervously) laugh when Patrick Bateman and his interchangeable friends, routinely mistaken for one another in public, ritually compare and contrast their business cards. See Ellis, *American Psycho*, 44–46.

†Especially amid the Great Transition, the residual romance of an aristocratic sense of manners and mannerisms helps the pre-Seinfeldian soul, still obsessed with the idea that life has to be about something, see money and love as inextricably mixed business pursuits. Binx, the qualities-challenged hero of Walker Percy's first novel, conceives his favorite schemes "in the interests of money and love," certain the two are inseparable. "Everything depends on a close cooperation between business and love," he insists. "The trick, the joy of it, is to prosper on all

in kind: to experience the same quality of satisfaction that everyone wants and works to spend on accessing and experiencing.) We know Donald Trump, for example, is no aristocrat, his wealth, status, celebrity, personality, and superficially peculiar genius notwithstanding.* He is the king of the deal, which is to say no king at all—a high-quality *representative* of an identity he *shares with us*, not a bred officer of separate rank, the kind of Nietzsche's antidemocratic fancy, to whom we bow precisely because we *don't* share a universal yardstick; we're unable to measure up to his, or even to measure ourselves with it. In an age of inequality, it is not quality—and, therefore, *qualities*†—that capture the imagination, possess the mind, and move the heart, but rather *kinds*. Rather than ordering ourselves horizontally, like a market or department store, where the highest-quality goods are at the center and the lowest at the margins, the (bygone) aristocratic age ranks us vertically, not by measuring how marginally better or worse versions of one another we are, but by the sharply

---

fronts, enlist money in the service of love and love in the service of money. As long as I am getting rich," he adds, I feel that all is well." To his consociation of well-being and well-dealing, Binx ascribes "my Presbyterian blood." Walker Percy, *The Moviegoer* (London: Methuen, 2004), 102.

*Whereas the more corrupt winners of democratic competitions characteristically emit "something coarse and vulgar which makes it contagious to the crowd," Tocqueville ventures, "even in the very depravity of great noblemen there is often a certain aristocratic refinement and an air of grandeur which prevents it from being communicated." Tocqueville, *Democracy*, 221.

†While the Seinfeldian soul is replete with qualities, rich in signature manners and mannerisms even or especially when bereft of meaning, a soul from an earlier era, more helplessly rooted in ruins surfeit with dangling chains, is much more likely to fear becoming a man without meaning than, as Robert Musil presented, a *Man Without Qualities*.

demarcated relations of superiority and inferiority that define the classes to which we belong. In that age, money is not relevant to "value" and "values." In our age, our grasp of value and values, in Trump's New York or anywhere else, is beyond comprehension absent our grasp—and grasping—of money.

Here is the secret to the failure of our fitful quest to put faith in money's measure of us all; here is the secret to the inequality that drives us crazy by arising from that egalitarian endeavor; here, too, is the secret to just DEALING with the strange truth that the art of being free from life's monetary craziness requires us to surrender the art of the deal, just when we want to put it to use the most.

THE DARK HALF

In the annals of *not* dealing with it, it feels inevitable, or only natural, that famed reporter Jane Mayer would go from writing about the darkness of war to the darkness of money.* The latter is an even broader canvas than the former, but it also pulls us in deeper. We reject the proposition that war is a necessary part of being human†; and though we accept the reality that money is, we fear all the

---

*See Jane Mayor, *The Dark Side: The Inside Story of How the War on Terror Turned into a War on American Ideals* (New York: Doubleday, 2008) and *Dark Money: The Hidden History of the Billionaires behind the Rise of the Radical Right* (New York: Doubleday, 2016).

† "True lovers hate war with all their heart, since it demonstrates too well that others have not found the secret of life that they know: But perhaps even they may sometimes admit that they learned the secret only when suspended over the abyss of death." J. Glenn Gray, *The Warriors: Reflections on Men in Battle* (Lincoln: University of Nebraska Press, 1998), 78.

more what that means. We are obsessed with the secret idea that money is a kind of black magic—something so powerful that it can do the impossible. Like all powers so tremendous that they can only be imagined as evil, of course, money's imagined power to do what we all think is impossible can only be refined and unleashed in secret. And we're increasingly convinced that the most important kind of secrecy—the one that controls all, the one to most be coveted—is the kind you can buy (or, at least, the wealthiest among us can buy).

And what, you're asking, is this impossible dark power that only the wealthiest can use their money to gain access to and ownership of?

—Mmm, no, not the power to kill anyone instantly anywhere in the world. We're worried about that (the military is hard at work on it), but we're more afraid of something even more impossible.

—Nope, not the power to completely manipulate what only looks like public opinion, turning apparently free thinking and speech into a rigged simulacrum. We're worried about that, too (which is why we're spending our precious funds and time on Mayer's latest book), but, still, that's all too possible, all too imaginable.

Go further into the dark. Deep in the furthest recesses of our soul, there's something we fear the richest could do that would literally rip a hole in the space-time continuum, imprisoning us not in a grand illusion but in an all too horribly real dimension: the past.

Yes, what we fear most of all is that money is so powerful that it can, by a horrible magic, *resurrect* the aristocratic age, returning the true and scary difference of human *kinds*, obliterating our diverse but united humankind with its equalized, nonthreatening multitude of superficial human qualities. We really do fear that, in sufficiently concentrated form, money is like a demonic magic, capable of empowering our wealthiest to do true evil and create true caste, true superiority and inferiority, right here in the only world we've got—this world where, like heroic vaccinators, we have managed almost completely to eradicate every last trace of the fearsome, abusive, "dark" aristocratic age.

Money for us has an evil power—a dark side, to use Dick Cheney's and George Lucas's millennia-old metaphor, or a dark half, to use Stephen King's. Like the suddenly struggling novelist Thad Beaumont, King's tortured hero in *The Dark Half*, we fear that we need money so badly in order to make life worth living that we will conjure back into reality the killed-off evil twin who haunts us in our most twisted dangling fantasies, suppressed but living nightmares lingering like broken chains above a slaughter-bench of history we so naively had only partly destroyed.*

But when our dark night of the soul is over, when we

---

*"I enjoyed him for a long time . . . and hell, the guy was making money," Beaumont says of George Stark, his dark alter ego. "Just knowing I could quit teaching if I wanted to and go on paying off the mortgage had a tremendously liberating effect on me"—*not* the liberating effect of upward, *vertical* mobility so crazily marketed as a cure for our sense of hemmed-in-ness, but of an enrichment that offers *horizontal* mobility in the two vectors, as Tocqueville shows, that our true longings pull us along. Regardless of class, Tocqueville suggests—for in America class still demarcates qualities, not kinds, of human being—we ping-pong between the desire for free-ranging *outward* movement (away, in Thad's case, from the pen of the school), *and,* simultaneously, for an *inward* enfoldment into sedate self-enclosure (pishing away placidly until reverse-mortgage time comes along). "I'm as vulnerable to the siren-song of money as anyone else," Beaumont sighs. As he should have known better than anyone, in

have whistled past the graveyard, the sunlight returns, the bustle of the market takes over; our good dreams and brightly lit ambitions reassert themselves and crowd the landscape, and we re-believe the light half of money betokens the whole.

We want money's light half to define our whole life.

We fear that the dark half will instead.

Is Tocqueville about to frighten us?

Our terror, he tells us, is an inherent consequence of the Great Transition. Our spooky psychodrama surrounding money is a natural problem when society segues toward democracy without having let go of the prior, old, "dark"-seeming regime. Our lingering and very ambivalent memories of that bygone regime cause us to feel extra uncertainty and angst over how money will now set the rule for all. Our incessant fear is as real now as it was given voice by Louis Brandeis, so pure in his distillation that he wound up as the epigram to Mayer's jeremiad:

> We must make our choice. We may have democracy,
> or we may have wealth concentrated in the hands of
> a few, but we can't have both.

Money rules; must then, inevitably, Fate usurp Chance—and the moneyed rule?

Here, in his answer, comes one of Tocqueville's biggest challenges. But, almost bizarrely, along with it comes one of his greatest reassurances.

---

our age, twin sirens are singing that tune. Stephen King, *The Dark Half* (New York: Signet, 1990), 29.

MIXED BUSINESS

To back into a readiness to receive Tocqueville's challenging wisdom, recall that, in our age, money and love are
inextricably linked pursuits, each lending the other its color
and character. "I'm mixing business with leather," as Beck
puts it in "Mixed Bizness," the second single from his
1999 album *Midnite Vultures*, commingling "homework"
with (as we'd say) a partner who "can really do me" and
"look right through me." It's a portrait followed up with a
Brandeis-quality distillation of the way competitive conformity applies even to our most beautiful and unique snowflakes: "Freaks flock together." Lest you think these are the
chance ravings of a musician under pressure to go through
a phase, consider that Socrates said the same about us several millennia ago.

We fear the rule of money will lay bare a death wish inside of equality—a hidden logic that will throw us back at
the feet of an aristocratic master class. What's more, we fear
that this evil procedure will first plunge us into something,
in a way, even more outrageous and galling: a bogus aristocracy. "Aristocracy of wealth," Tocqueville explains, "comes
in between" the "two extremes" of social and political life
expressed in aristocracy and democracy. Although aristocracy of wealth "is like aristocracy of birth in conferring great
privileges on a small number of citizens," it is also "like democracy in that these privileges can be acquired by all in
turn." Befitting our terror of its untenable, mid-mutation
form, and the purer, darker power it might unleash, Tocqueville calls it "an exception, a monstrosity, within the general social condition." Indeed, "if ever again permanent

inequality of conditions and aristocracy make their way into the world, it will have been by that door that they entered." But instead of an unnatural portal to the past, the emergence of economic inequality is an outwork of the Great Transition hurtling us into the future: "One cannot say whether it brings the reign of aristocratic institutions to an end or whether it is already ushering in the new era of democracy."[6] But like Tocqueville, we all recognize that what has been known since Socrates as "oligarchy" is not at all like aristocracy in *kind:* oligarchy (or "plutocracy") is not rule by a caste of honor-bound and honor-bred nobles, however besotted and debased they eventually wind up. Oligarchy is a jumble of people marked only by their wealth, which does not correspond to a unitary *identity* because the *interest* of each in his or her own wealth is not exceeded by any other love higher in kind.

To be sure, the wealthy do share a sense that the love of one's wealth comes first. And, Socrates says, the oligarchic city's divide between richer and poorer paves the way for the poorer to triumph with the love higher in kind that arises as a rebuke and attempted correction to the incomplete, narrowing love of one's wealth: the love of all things equally or interchangeably—"democratic" love.* But however

---

*See Plato, *Republic,* bk. 8. Socrates intimates that covetousness toward honor(s) causes its own replacement by a covetousness toward wealth. Disillusioned by the fickleness and pettiness of the competition for increasingly hollow or artificial honors, the sort of person to whom this generational transition passes "will force the rational and high-spirited principles to crouch lowly to right and left as slaves, and will allow the one to calculate and consider nothing but the ways of making more money from a little, and the other to admire and honor nothing but riches and rich men, and to take pride in nothing but the possession of

the culture wars rage, it's as true now as it was in ancient Athens that when wealth rules, it does not really demarcate a difference between richer and poorer in tastes, habits, or mores. This is what Tocqueville means by the superficially strange observation that there is "no solidarity among the rich."[7] We fear so much they are becoming a *kind* that we begin to believe it ourselves. But, in fact, everyone wants the same thing, they as well as we; some have it, others have it not. The oligarchs may work harder or better than those they rule, but not always. *As* a rule, they want what we want, and they value what we value: material comfort, physical pleasure, a participatory sense of meaning, and the experience of living large. Socrates can't introduce to Athens's best and brightest the concept of wisdom as the highest kind of love until old, comfortable, and wealthy Cephalus goes to bed, off to (not really) experience the sound sleep he says is the true blessing of riches.*

The difference between our time and Socrates's, of course, is that our even greater underlying equality (we don't turn battlefield losers into our slaves, for instance)

---

wealth and whatever contributes to that." Repeating the pattern of the generational corrective that itself misses the mark, the person disillusioned by the narrowness and banality of the love of wealth will become a "devotee of equality," hoping to be "stuffed with most excellent differences . . . , the fair and many-colored one whom many a man and woman would count fortunate in his life, as containing within himself the greatest number of patterns of constitutions and qualities."

*Yes, money in the *Republic* recalls money in *The Dark Half*—superficially alluring in the illusory *upward* orientation it seems to offer the soul, but *truly* alluring in its correspondence to the soul's two ruling *horizontal* desires: for the *outward* thrust into the crazy quilt of experiential motion (such as the marketplace from which Socrates must retreat in order to philosophize) *and* for the more secret *inward* thrust into self-enclosure, stasis, and, ultimately, the nothingness of deathlike sleep.

greatly increases the amount of churn among those at the top of our pyramid of wealth—increasing, in turn, the similarity, imitation, competition, and equality we experience with them. Those of us who imagine we have a big caste of permanently wealthy Americans are just much more wrong than we think. Even when generations manage to hold onto wealth, the gymnastics they must perform are risky and laborious, the failure rate is high, and the casualties can be enormous. (Exhibit A: the Hilton family.)* Yet the growing recognition of commonalities regardless of wealth, a product of the apparent rule of money itself, does not make us feel more together or more relaxed. It nags us and makes us feel more interchangeably insignificant if we're not earning (as opposed to saving) the big bucks. It makes us discount the legitimacy of wealth, because chance and caprice

---

* A recent IRS report confirms that even many of the most fortunate Americans are still subject to the wheel of fortune. "Of the group of 4,474 unique top earners from 1992–2013, there were 3,213 individual taxpayers who made it into the 'Fortunate 400' only one time during the 22-year period," as economics professor Mark Perry observed for the American Enterprise Institute. "Those 3,213 one-timers represent 71.8% of the total 4,474 taxpayers, and therefore only 1,261 taxpayers that make up the rest of that elite group (28.2% of the total, or about one in four) were able to make it into the Top 400 more than one year between 1992 and 2013." Because "3,213 earners made it into the Top 400 once (71.8%) and another 535 taxpayers (12.0%) made it into the top group twice between 1992 and 2013, that means that about 84% of the top earners made it into the 'Fortunate 400' only once or twice (3,748 out of 4,474), and only 16% (726 taxpayers out of 4,474) were able to make it into the top group in more than 2 years out of 22." All told, "only 129 taxpayers out of the 4,474 total taxpayers in the top earner group (2.88%) . . . were in the Top 400 in 10 or more years out of 22." See Mark J. Perry, "New IRS Data Show that 72% of US Taxpayers Who Make It into the 'Top 400' Are There for Only a Single Year," AEI, January 5, 2016, http://www.aei.org/publication/new-irs-data-show-that-72-of-us-taxpayers-who-make-it-into-the-top-400-are-there-for-only-a-single-year.

exercise such a fundamental pull on our imaginations and experience when we all compete to conform to the same standards in pursuit of the status that, we hope, brings peace. And since so many of the wealthy are just like us "but with money," as we might say, they're inclined to ape aristocratic manners in a way that is off-putting precisely because it's so phony.

But—and here's where Tocqueville now disrupts our pattern of thinking—there is one all-important way our wealthy really can act like aristocrats: by physically separating themselves off from the rest of us. Access, not ownership, provides today's wealthy with the closest thing left to a truly exclusive experience: the experience of persuasively feeling, *in a momentary way*, like a kind of person—the aristocrat—who no longer exists.* Let's carefully consider how this reality stacks up against the one Tocqueville describes in the America of his day:

> In the United States, the most opulent citizens are at pains not to get isolated from the people. On the contrary, they keep in constant contact, gladly listen and themselves talk any and every day. They know that the rich in democracies always need the poor and that good manners will draw them to them more than benefits conferred.[8]

---

*Here is a clue as to why so many rich people do a lot of drugs—often to the point of self-destruction. What they chase in the moment—a feeling of difference in *kind*—continually decays into just another feeling of ersatz difference, a difference only in quality. Once again, the morbidity of the American Dream hinges on how the quest for autonomy decays into the quest for money.

Yes, that's right—his description feels like the complete opposite of what we experience now: whether in Silicon Valley or the hills of Los Angeles or the high rises of New York City, the ultra-wealthy have taken physical segregation to new heights. This is the era of the VIP section within the VIP section, the wristband so exclusive that most people don't even know it exists, and the recognition that even though money buys access, if you don't spend it on access, you're on the outside looking in. Even though it's so hard to get to the top, even though it's so easy for those who get there to fall back down, and even though we actually love so greatly being spectators to that churn that we're willing to pay to watch for decades on end, the *bad manners* of the wealthy, in Tocqueville's sense, drive us to distraction. No matter, to us, that even the most heavily guarded trailer at Coachella or the slickest board room on Wall Street lacks stars or plutocrats with the degree of *radical* distance and difference from ordinary people—in kind, not quality—that the bygone aristocrats maintained. In a warped way, we almost feel *today* about the merely rich how people felt in *Tocqueville's* time about the aristocrats; in a key clue about how equal we've become, Tocqueville already noticed that the wealthy in Europe who clung the most to aristocratic pretensions were destined to drive themselves crazy. "The rich do not immediately appreciate this truth," he wrote of the French upper crust who had nothing of the well-mannered instinct for practical intermingling he saw among America's wealthy. "They generally stand out against it as long as a democratic revolution is in progress and do not admit it at once even after the revolution is accomplished." The problem was not, repeat not, that they weren't *nice* or caring overlords. It's that they misunderstood human nature—and what ordinary people, being human, hate about inequality *no matter how much* they experience upward mobility. Confused plutes "will gladly do good to the people, but they still want carefully to keep their distance from them. They think that that is enough, but they are wrong."

> They could ruin themselves in that fashion without warming their neighbors' hearts. What is wanted is not the sacrifice of their money but of their pride.[9]

Once again, the vertically oriented envy we sense reveals its root to be a more profound longing to find peace in our horizontal positioning. In fact, with the rise of more virtual, or networked, forms of performing proximity, it turns out we really don't mind billionaires most of the time if they constantly, authentically signal that they're very much like us, even if from afar. (Just ask Mark Zuckerberg.) Our real enmity is reserved for those who performatively pretend to be apart in a way they—and we—know they're not. And even some of those—onscreen celebrities we feel a skin-tight closeness to, for instance—routinely receive a reprieve.

We feel and act this way, in a word, because of one thing: love.

In our time, it is not for us to disentangle the busy-ness of money and love. They are of a piece, crazy as it seems, crazy as it is.

So long as we feel the love from the rich, Tocqueville reveals, we really don't envy them. And, in a telling sign of what makes us all the single human kind we are, we *can't* truthfully feel the love unless the rich are physically proximate *enough* to us that we can experience them in the same kind of direct, unmediated relationship as—ready?— *we want from God/the Source of the Universe/the All in our spiritual life.*

THE RED AND THE BLACK

This insight is one possible takeaway from the famous novel about thirsting for fame written by Nietzsche's favorite novelist, Stendhal. In *The Red and the Black*, set a decade and a half after the French Empire's fall, the ambitious and obscure Julian Sorel channels the glories of Napoleon Bonaparte to embark on a monomaniacal, imitative, and ultimately disastrous personal project. Napoleon was, bizarrely, thoroughly modern yet evocatively ancient; it was easy for Julian to see him as a democratic-age solution to the problem of the broken yet persistently dangling chains of the aristocratic allure. By emulating Napoleon, he hoped, he could plug directly, unmediated, into the mainline of greatness that unified and summed up the true qualities of being human.

Unfortunately, Julian couldn't quite recognize that his enterprise was doomed because he had become too crazy to know how to distinguish himself from Napoleon. He had lost the ability to draw the right lines—between himself and those he felt himself superior to, and between himself and those he should have kept a better-mannered distance from in his selfish and melodramatic quest for a peak experience of the All.

This should sound familiar. Recall Tocqueville's intimation in the realm of faith that the key to receiving our crazy world as it really is, undeceived, is receiving the folly of our all-too-human habit of mistakenly drawing and erasing dividing lines. Amid the Great Transition, we fruitlessly struggle—rancorous in public and resigned in private—to understand and articulate the location of personal, social, and conceptual boundaries. Reaching up vertically, amid life's dangling chains of residual rectitude, we find little to lift ourselves out of life's craziness; but a great horizontal line seems to offer a better deal.

Of course, I mean the bottom line.

First, we need to revisit, as Tocqueville says, that money really is more important in our times than before the Great Transition. After all, it almost magically confers three grand transitive properties, such valuable currency in the current of our transitional age: *mutability, commensurability,* and *passability.*

Consider how and why we love money in its mutability. Whereas well-being in the aristocratic sense shows forth as a "lofty disdain for physical comfort," an attribute of honor and separate kind passed through lineage by the wellborn, in our time it comes as the actualization of a "passion for physical pleasures"; not grandiose but petty, not debauched or haphazard but detailed and orderly,[10] "public sensuality has adopted a moderate and tranquil shape to which all are expected to conform. It is as hard for vices as for virtues to slip through the net of common standards."* Those common standards can only be expressed in terms of our great monetary interchange—as *values.* Whereas different human ranks and kinds want *radically* different things, our single

---

*Tocqueville, *Democracy,* 533; "No sovereign will or national prejudice . . . can fight for long against cheapness" (406).

human kind, enabled by money to inhabit an encompassing standard of valuation, wants *radially* different ones. Rather than living, separated, into measures of virtue and vice exclusive to our particular ranks and breeds—ones whose family trees, so to speak, trace to different *roots* than those unlike in kind from our own—together we pursue diverse diversions all thrusting outward from the single *centerpoint* of value that unites them—and so unites us—at their origin. But we do not just pursue diverse diversions because we are beautiful and unique snowflakes, each with his or her special custom preferences. We do it less because we wish than because we must, egged on by Chance, by our hedging and edging, and by the fleeting character of fortune shared by fashion and food, the two great diversions open, like money itself, to all tastes and all comers that accede to the value system of qualities instead of the virtue system of kinds. The further or longer we feel we radiate out from our single root, the more we long to reaffirm in experience the sense of unity that is our obsession. Money, which underwrites and overarches our "search for material blessings" through every change and convolution, perfectly fits the bill.[11]

With the mutability money confers comes commensurability. The more things change, the more things interchange. Money allows us to change like it does by allowing us to *ex*change—to "reconnect" (as we say) with our unity by participating in a kind of interchangeability that carries, however fleetingly, a sense of import. Our experiences of significant interchange are an inspiring bulwark against the dispiriting experience of our interchangeable insignificance. Without the commensurability of goods and services—in principle, *any and all* goods and services—access to that experience is imperiled or lost.

In fact, if we couldn't make goods and services that *aren't* commensurable somehow *seem* that way, we'd feel our love for money grow stale or wear thin. Our love for money is contingent on its conferral of passability. "When only the rich wore watches, they were almost all excellent. Now few are made that are more than mediocre, but we all have one," Tocqueville noticed so long ago. "Diamonds are already so well imitated that it is easy to be taken in. As soon as sham diamonds can be made so well that they cannot be distinguished from real stones," he surmised, anticipating today's current ambition for a higher authenticity than true or false gems can confer on a vow, "it is probable that both will be disregarded and become mere pebbles again."[12] So long as it lasts, passability is possibility.

Notice a familiar resonance in the triad of mutability, commensurability, and passability? All these transformational properties superficially promise to alleviate our craziness, selfishness, and melodrama. We're crazy, but we want to personally change; we're selfish, but we want to share in exchange; we're melodramatic, but we want to pass as truly confident. Yet in our worship of all things *trans-active*, we lay bare the absurdity of trying to find stability by measuring all against money. Our changeability complicates our lives. Our fear of being on a deal's losing end makes us grasping. Our shifting and shifty struggle to pass as more than we are deviously deepens our melodrama. The bottom line passes as a lifeline; but as soon as we cling on, it wriggles away.

SINGLE AND READY TO MINGLE

Because of this, we possess, and are possessed by, our bizarre obsession with inequality. Everywhere we look, we see it. Many of us would not tune in to the news were it not for the nagging suspicion that inequality was worsening. For many of us it is difficult to put meat on the bones of the abstract idea of things getting worse without thinking of increasing inequality. We are all so touchy—about the way money paradoxically breeds inequality as it entrenches a single standard of value that equalizes us through interchange—that even some of our most seemingly sober-minded observers suggest that Tocqueville's world, and his analysis, have simply been surpassed. Time has elapsed, he's been lapped, his promise of the ever-spreading equality of conditions is simply no longer accurate, if ever it was; it certainly isn't relevant, they say, except as a marker of how wrong it is to think democracy will successfully play out on its own. Most recently, Thomas Piketty's hit book *Capital in the 21st Century* claimed that, left to its own devices, democracy would not stop money from producing ever-greater inequality.*

The problem with this thesis is that it fails to comprehend the way money and love are inextricably mixed in our era. We can't sanely live without the rich mingling in

---

*I once shared a pointed exchange on this subject in *The Daily Beast* with Tocqueville translator Arthur Goldhammer, who refused to concede or consider Tocqueville's counsel that, although money matters more in the Great Transition than in the aristocratic age, pride and love matter even more than that. See James Poulos, "What's at Stake in the Tocqueville/Piketty Debate," *The Daily Beast*, April 27, 2014, http://www.thedailybeast.com/articles/2014/04/27/what-s-at-stake-in-the-tocqueville-piketty-debate.html.

our midst, and the rich can't sanely live without mingling in ours. Increasingly delinked and isolated from one another as we are, in our singledom, the desire to experience our deeper equality reaches a fever pitch. For all our Trumps, we lack, conspicuously, any lords or overlords radically different from us. Recurring once again to the all-important distinction between the past era of different human *kinds* and the present era of different human *qualities*, it's still true that our wealthy "never form a body with its own mores and way of enforcing the same; no opinions peculiar to their class restrain them, and public opinion urges them on."*

True, our big corporations are great engines of inequality. And as potentially immortal corporate persons, they can cheat at amassing and sustaining wealth in a way mere rich *people* cannot. Then again, we fully love corporations as much as rich people, if they show us love the same way our favorite rich people do. So our corporations have staffed up, in the blink of an eye, with Heads of Diversity and Inclusion, departments unintentionally designed to reveal just how much life can superficially grow superficially unequal and qualitatively variegated, while on a deeper level we grow ever less different in kind. Within a corporation that heaps its people with riches that shock the egalitarian conscience, co-workers ideally deal with things, like themselves and others (known colloquially as "stakeholders"), with ever-increasing equanimity—interchangeably, all-inclusively within the single rubric of value and values erected by money.

---

*Tocqueville, *Democracy*, 553. We constantly fear the rich have "gamed" or "rigged the system," as we say, because we know as well as they do that *we're all playing the same game.*

In sum? Money is more an engine of equality than inequality. But rather than bringing us peace, this fact further aggravates our crazed condition. Tocqueville's challenge is simple. We think we hate to feel inequality. But what we really hate to feel is hate. That's why we have a love-hate relationship with inequality itself. "In democracies, private citizens see men rising from their ranks and attaining wealth and power in a few years; that spectacle excites their astonishment and their envy; they wonder how he who was their equal yesterday has today won the right to command them. To attribute his rise to his talents or virtues is inconvenient, for it means admitting that they are less virtuous or capable than he," warns Tocqueville. The alternative? Blame, as we say, his value system:

> They therefore regard some of his vices as the main cause thereof, and often they are correct in this view. In this way there comes about an odious mingling of the conceptions of baseness and power, of unworthiness and success, and of profit and dishonor.[13]

We want to think that, rather than simply winning the so-called lottery of life, those who suddenly rise to fortune have *cheated* the system that constrains us all. We can't stand the idea that, in fact, money is a force that produces such sharp superficial inequalities because it holds us all to single standard, the closest we have come to a universal, unified mechanism for spreading and deepening equality.

Alas, says Tocqueville, we must deal—*not* in the sense of striking a bargain with it, but in the more profound and lasting sense of *reconciling* ourselves to it. For "as men become more alike and the principle of equality has quietly penetrated deep into the institutions and manners of the country, the rules of advancement become more inflexible, and advancement itself slower."[14] We long for unity through the *medium* of our equality—seeing ourselves *in the image of money*, not (for instance) the image of God; if only we could be as mutable, commensurable, and passable as that which constantly reinforces and reminds us of our interchangeable insignificance.

Alas, says Tocqueville, we "have abolished the troublesome privileges" of the past era's aristocratic kind only to "come up against the competition of all." Where once the many were held back by a vertical impediment to advancement—whether physical, material, or mental—now they are hemmed in by a horizontal impediment, all the more galling for its money-like quality of popping up everywhere, in every field of endeavor, with equal force.

> When all prerogatives of birth and fortune are abolished, when all professions are open to all and a man's own energies may bring him to the top of any of them, an ambitious man may think it easy to launch on a great career and feel that he is called to no common destiny. But that is a delusion which experience quickly corrects. The same equality which allows each man to entertain vast hopes makes each man by himself weak. His power is limited on every side, though his longings may wander where they will. . . . This constant strife between the desires inspired by equality and the means it supplies to satisfy them harasses and wearies the mind.[15]

The reason that gaining money does not diminish our hatred of monetary inequality, Tocqueville hints, is because pride, being of the heart, paradoxically does *not* arise out of our selfish interests, which belong to the calculating, manipulative mind. The rich err when their pride leads them to pretend as if they were different from the rest of us in kind, not in quality—living lives apart, like a separate race or caste distinguished by settled, natural rank and not by the artifice of competing qualities. Even if inequality could and should be diminished in the interests of the rich, the rest of us, or both, simply by handing over some wealth, Tocqueville surmises that the very universality of money's measure makes us see we belong so equally to a single human kind that bankrolling any pretense to deep "aristocratic" inequality will worsen the crazy, anxiety-inducing envy we already automatically feel toward one another as we compete to win.

This is why money is so constitutive to our craziness. We feel enslaved to its rule, yet we can't live without it. In fact, we *want* to be the most successful and prized of slaves to money. So we both fear and secretly encourage the degeneracy of democracy into oligarchy, risking the creation of a fake caste with enough concentrated wealth to unleash the real dark magic of a new aristocratic age.

"TAKE THE WHEEL" –JESUS

With any luck, I'll bet at this point you've got just one question.

Why?

Why did this happen?

We didn't just wake up one day locked into a love-hate relationship with money. Despite our manifold powers of obsession and forgetfulness, we know deep down that, no matter how profound our transitions, we must have transitioned *from* somewhere, out of something. And so, if you've begun thinking like Tocqueville at all, you'll sense what's coming. Back at our origins—the same ones that show how the aristocratic past stubbornly persists through to now in a state of maddening, alluring, entangling dereliction—we can discover why money makes us so crazy in the first place.

You'll recall that some of us, in our bid to unburden ourselves of the adaptive responsibility we face day in and day out, are fond of asking Jesus to take the wheel.

Tocqueville wants to suggest that money puts us in that frame of mind (Jesus, the Universe, the shrink, a mountain of drugs, whatever) because at our origins, our forebearers understood Jesus to have told *them* to take the wheel.

Yes: America's religious origins put us in a frame of mind—and a practical situation—that bumped money to the top of our list of earthly, material priorities. Not only did religion define the way we felt a need for money, by anchoring us to eternal, fixed rules only in a small circle of life, leaving the whole field of commerce wide open to dramatic competition and change, but it also created our sense of the possibilities that money could unlock for us. That combination of anxiety and ambition made for a productive economic life, but, as we know all too well, it's also a recipe for rash thoughts, feelings, actions, and even dangerous inaction. Money wound up playing an unsettled, conflicted, and sometimes unbearable role in our everyday lives. It reminded us uncomfortably of our spiritual origins *and* gave us an excuse to try to lose ourselves in temporary distractions that promise an escape from the very kind of reckoning that will ameliorate our madness. (That's why those distractions, which give us hope that *entertainment* can *divert* us, are the focus of the next chapter.)

From here, we can almost see the moment where the Great Transition kicked into high gear. President Calvin Coolidge, known as "Silent Cal," was the last Puritan president. Americans never elected another simple, disciplined, and quiet Yankee, and it's hard to see how they would again. That kind of character has all but died out. Coolidge's austere persona, however, accommodated a view of money that hasn't aged a day. In a famous speech, he affirmed that "the chief business of the American people is business."

> They are profoundly concerned with producing, buying, selling, investing and prospering in the world. I am strongly of the opinion that the great majority of people will always find these the moving impulses of our life.[16]

Tocqueville, of course, saw it coming. "I once met an American sailor," he recounts, "and asked him why his country's ships are made so that they will not last long. He answered offhand that the art of navigation was making such quick progress that even the best of boats would be almost useless if it lasted more than a few years."[17] Although artisanal goods are making a modest comeback among some of the hipper niche cultures in America, most of us are well aware of the role of so-called planned obsolescence in our economy. And though we may grumble, we pretty much accept it. In fact, our acceptance is growing as the generations pass, just as Tocqueville predicted. Bob Lefsetz, the influential music industry insider, has observed that older Americans will repair their cracked cell phones and keep their devices for years and years, while younger Americans will use their cell phones even if they're cracked, knowing that they'll just trade them in for the latest and greatest model in a matter of months.

How could this tolerance, or even hunger, for endless change, disposability, and updates arise—and remain undiminished—even as we find ourselves ever more at sea in the swarm of commercialism, advertisements, and the general scramble for what feels like ever scarcer resources and opportunities?

Tocqueville points us back to our—and America's—origins. For the Puritans, religion was a realm of unquestioned authority, but one that receded from the world. Although they initially sought to hardwire biblical law into their municipal codes, as Tocqueville points out, they quickly accepted an idea already present in Christian theology: that religion ruled morals and mores but not politics and laws.[18] So if, as Tocqueville theorized, "in the moral world everything is classified, foreseen, and decided in advance," in politics "everything is in turmoil, contested, uncertain. In the one case obedience is passive, though voluntary; in the other there is independence, contempt of experience, and jealousy of all authority."[19] If "everything in the moral field is certain and fixed," everything in "the world of politics seems given over to argument and experiment."

If you suspect that, because our political life is influenced by our religious attitudes and the frames of mind that persist, like dangling chains, even after the fervor of particular belief has waned, it will influence another aspect of our lives in turn, you're thinking like Tocqueville. You might even also find yourself thinking that political life looks like a sideshow from this vantage point. Here's something we still haven't dealt with: how the practices and sentiments opened by our religious attitudes flowed—and still flow—into our economic life. "Democracy," says Tocqueville, "does not provide people with the most skillful of governments, but it does what the most skillful government often cannot do: it spreads throughout the body social a restless activity, superabundant force, and energy never found elsewhere."[20] Our economic life adopts the character of our social life! *We* invested money with the power it has.

This is a big deal, and for two reasons. One, if we lose the interest or ability to step outside our comfort zone and collaborate on handling our shared affairs, our economic productivity will suffer. Even more important, it illustrates Tocqueville's understanding that *economic life has no independent internal logic of its own.* (Yep—that's a hell of a thing to say to a people who almost instinctively trust that economics is what happens when each person freely acts on their own independent internal logic.) Rather than the typical free-market story about our natural, ingrained propensity to freely exchange goods for money, Tocqueville paints a much more challenging picture. Without a more foundational understanding of what it means to be human, neither capitalism nor free exchange nor any kind of commerce can answer the big questions. And if we strain to convince ourselves that it can, we'll be painfully, bewilderingly let down time and time again.

The sad paradox is that even though money can't tell us who we are, in an age of equality, we're stuck having to care a lot about it. We don't want to love money. We can't really love it the way we want to love, for instance, other people. But we can certainly have a *love-hate* relationship with money. And we do.

That's why, looking far into our future, Tocqueville expressed his own fear: our "anxious and eager" love of wealth, amid an ever-churning and unstable economy, would lead us to "become so engrossed in a cowardly love of immediate pleasures" that we would give up on the future.[21] Rather than striving for our own advancement or that of our descendants, we would "tamely" go where fate seemed to push us instead of making the "sudden energetic effort necessary to set things right." Tocqueville wasn't just speaking of our personal fates, but of the fate of America as a nation. If we all gradually abandon our anxious striving, we could wear ourselves out "in trivial, lonely, futile activity," and despite the "constant agitation," stagnate completely.

Are there signs that this twilight is already upon us? On the one hand, it strikes us as reasonable to give up in the face of seemingly insurmountable odds—odds so unfavorable that sometimes we don't even calculate them. Americans "see a multitude of little intermediate obstacles, all of which have to be negotiated slowly"—and simply anticipating that effort exhausts their "ambition and discourages it. They therefore discard such distant and doubtful hopes, preferring to seek delights less lofty but easier to reach. No law limits their horizon," as Tocqueville puts it, "but they do so for themselves." Who hasn't guiltily felt that attitude creep in? Even the extraordinarily ambitious, talented, lucky, and fortunate few are just as likely to succumb eventually. Among the wealthy, remember, "very vulgar tastes often go with their enjoyment of extraordinary prosperity, and it would seem that their only object in rising to supreme power was to gratify trivial and coarse appetites more easily."[22] Our wealthy are, characteristically, just as isolated and alone as the rest of us, feeling just as singled-out for a crazy love deficit. Their extreme monetary prosperity often doesn't grant them even middling relief of a spiritual, social, or psychological kind. That "lonely at the top" feeling is real—as real as our feelings of being lonely at the bottom or lonely in the middle.

That's because the wealthy ultimately lack the power to open a portal to the aristocratic age and make of themselves a higher human caste or kind. The evil future of our shared nightmares takes more than money. Not only does it require a devotion, increasingly alien to us all, to building multicentury projects out of human beings and families but it also requires an immense forgetfulness of the reality of our equality as a single human kind. Partial devotion and partial forgetfulness—of the sort that can be seen among some of our futurists and those ultimate trans-worshippers, the transhumanists pushing for radical life extension, artificial intelligence, and augmented reality—won't lead to a new aristocracy. So long as our civilization is not shattered by apocalyptic war, scary tech-driven change will lead at most to a grotesquely exaggerated version of our transitional times, where a super-rich bio-elite finds itself secretly unwilling, and therefore unable, to disentangle its destiny from our own.*

THE GOSPEL OF WELL-DEALING

Think back to Socrates again. In our unwillingness to reconcile ourselves to an out-of-joint world, in which democratic and oligarchic urges swirl together indefinitely and irresolvably, we strangely echo Socrates in one important respect. Like him, we frame the problem of money without reference to religion—specifically, Christianity, the religion that takes equality to the highest level (if Tocqueville and Nietzsche, to mention a few, are to be believed). To be sure, Socrates does discuss the relationship between the love of money and the love of equality from the standpoint of "divine" reason—that is, the sort of reason that can at best interrupt our inherently flawed and mistaken mortal reason. For Socrates, divine reason alone orients us successfully toward an understanding of the art of dying, while mortal reason alone leads us to die poorly by tricking us into thinking it can help us master the world.† Just so, in our common disenchanted view of money, we try to enlist reason in the service of our longing for a greater unity than money can truly provide. We hope either to perfect money's drawing

---

*It is always sketchy to predict the far future, but it is always prudent, even in times like ours, to bet on the persistence of mythos. *Mad Max: Fury Road* (2015) is the latest and greatest proof of how hard our collective imagination comes down on the anti-aristocratic side—even in the most delinked and vulnerable of possible futures.

† "Other people are likely not to be aware that those who pursue philosophy aright study nothing but dying and being dead." Plato, *Phaedo*, Vol. 1, trans. H. N. Fowler (New York: Macmillan, 1913), 223.

of boundaries or correct it, typically by mastering the re-allocation of money this way or that. We don't really buy into Socrates's wager that the person oriented toward pursuing life's appetites can discover the spirited part of the soul, and that the person who has discovered spirited-ness, which pridefully wants more than the appetites can afford, can be oriented toward the unpredictable gift of divine reason.* But many of us really do like the idea, however implausible it sometimes seems, that we can perfect the world by using reason to order money in the perfect way. We reject the Socratic vision of accessing transcendent goals through initially materialistic means because his, which leads toward salvation by philosophy for the few, isn't democratic enough. Money, we half-consciously decide, will be our philosophy. After all, in a way unlike all other things, it's for everyone. But this vision of ours, no matter how expertly executed, fails to ameliorate our profound confusion and fearful uncertainty over what measure is due to ourselves or others—just as Socrates predicted.

This Tocqueville knew. That's why he says it's only natural that we turn to religion for answers, specifically about money. But this, too, instantly gives rise to a fresh wave of difficulties. Pious believers complain that the faith is being profaned and lowered. Skeptical secularists complain that religion is being turned into an even bigger and more lucrative con than it already was. But if we begin by assuming that religion can ameliorate the craziness that causes money to come up for us so consistently as a source of angst

---

*See the so-called Chariot Allegory in Plato, *Phaedrus*, *The Dialogues of Plato*, Vol. 1, trans. Benjamin Jowett (New York: Random House, 1937), 250–51.

and anger, as Tocqueville shows us to do, we end up taking a much different path.

The gospel of the deal is often not particularly good news—for the would-be preachers or the congregation. Discord at home, loveless personal lives, difficulties with children, substance abuse, and the simple realization that nice things can't make you happy all conspire against the well-being of our economic elite. Instead of apostles of a prosperity gospel, these people often become the kinds of cautionary tales you hear from actual preachers. That's why it's easy to mock and dispute the prosperity gospel. That's why it's a doctrine ripe for abuse.

Nevertheless, embedded in Tocqueville's logic is a version of the prosperity gospel—well-dealing rightly understood, to borrow a turn of phrase from his description of true self-interest*—that doesn't get the same media coverage as the preachers in the suits with the Jumbotrons and the megachurches. In short, it goes a bit like this:

First, have faith in God and in the reality of your own soul. Being human is about inhabiting a created consciousness built to last forever, if you treat it right.

Second, recognize that everyone on earth has the same equipment as you in this regard. That identical equipment is the most important thing about you and everyone else.

Third, surmise that your equipment has features and capabilities that extend well beyond passively suffering spiritual and psychological angst. You're always able to make choices and create possibilities, even in tough situations.

---

*On "self-interest rightly understood," see Tocqueville, *Democracy*, vol. 2, sec. 2, chap. 8–9.

Fourth, you're surrounded by other people in the same situations—and together, you can stir up possibilities that nobody could have anticipated in advance, even smart people who have run the numbers.

Fifth, it's okay to admit that money's important because the equality that defines us and our time makes so much of life's goods easy to buy and sell. We're all so similar that we readily agree to use money as a stand-in for just about anything.

Sixth, if you accept the preceding five points, you'll gain access to a powerful peace, confidence, and stability in at least one part of your life. And we know from experience that life becomes a lot easier for us to face when we've got even one special realm we can count on for rest, calm, care, and consolation. The best part is, you can share this realm with others—friends, colleagues, strangers, to be sure, but especially intimates, including family.

Seventh, and finally, when you go out into the world, you can get really adventurous and improvisatory. You can set big goals and try for unreasonable successes. You might not win in every instance, or even most, but if you keep the reality of your fellow humans' special equipment in the forefront of your mind, you'll be able to pursue your fortune justly, fairly, and honestly. Best of all, when you come upon even a modest fortune by these means—some money in the bank, some property to your name, and resources large enough to share as you please—you'll recognize that the prosperity gospel isn't about becoming a zillionaire.

This, when it comes to money, is how you surrender the art of the deal in favor of the art of being free.

Obviously, this worldview no more guarantees material

prosperity than writing a novel. Nor does it police this or that line-drawing exercise. What matters most is that the rise and rise of the most ambitious and talented not send us over the edge—or drive us too deeply into the sterile labyrinth of its endless machinations. Tocqueville's advice for dealing well with our moneyed world is to assume a spiritual disposition that can strongly ameliorate our feelings of resentment, exhaustion, bitterness, depression—the ravening craziness that dogs us throughout our day. And it's all consonant with the possibilities that Tocqueville says still persist in our time, even with its paradoxical constraints on opportunity.

The end?

Not yet.

Like all scary novels, there's a twist.

Tocqueville suggests that Coolidge missed just one thing. We're not only obsessed with money. We're obsessed with *what money gets us*—especially when it gets us a reprieve, however momentary, from our obsession with money. Because our frenetic embrace of the art of the deal reveals a more secret hope that it will grant us well-being, a transitory, transitional realm of life exists between our financial frenzies and our inertia of "just being": the realm of play, with its myriad entertainments, diversions, and distractions. Of course, the pursuit—as well as the *experience*—of ostensible amusement and relaxation is rarely without its own crazy-making properties. In the next chapter, we'll take that ride. Get ready to have some fun with fun.

Play

I love *Zoolander*. In Los Angeles, in transit, rolling through the city's long and lateral surface streets, it seems so right, as Oscar Wilde famously said, that we're all in the gutter but some of us ogle the stars. Here, the human stars frolic frozen overhead. Advertisements try to distract or engross us with faces we recognize, to talk us into taking a chance on whichever diversion or entertainment they're selling. For the person who feels like he or she is in danger of being no one from nowhere, the stars can offer poignant particularity in the sea of indifference. But even if you've lived in Los Angeles long enough to be that person from that place, the stars can actually console you. Not long ago, while I was staving off this anxiety or the other, the trademark inquisitive pout of Ben Stiller's Derek Zoolander swam into my field of vision, with Owen Wilson's chill bro Hansel and Will Ferrell's fashion villain Mugatu striking adjacent poses I hadn't seen astride the city since the week of September 11, 2001. (The first *Zoolander* hit theaters on September 28.) "Shots of the Twin Towers," the A.V. Club noted, "were digitally excised." (Bad timing for a movie about a vapid model brainwashed to assassinate the prime minister of Singapore.)

But I loved it, that final film of the late 1990s era, and the sudden resurrection of its world, however fleeting—*Zoolander 2* was released in February 2016—sent through me a wave of warm if slightly tenebrous reassurance. Even here, even now, more than a decade later, it was still okay to accept the illusion that the culture hadn't become what it is today.

Well, almost okay. The wave was more than a little tenebrous. As is often the case with playing along, it seemed to yieldingly bleed into the realm of the ominous. This is a film wherein Donald Trump intones that "without Derek Zoolander, male modeling wouldn't be what it is today." This is a film that so closely parodied Bret Easton Ellis's late-1990s models-and-terrorism nightmare, *Glamorama*, that it may or may not have led, as Trump might have steered it, to an out-of-court settlement.

And now is the time that I have to admit—if you've read my other writing, this will not be a shocker—that I really do think a switch of some sort flipped in the late 1990s; that coming of age in that time (and in London, specifically, at the exact moment *Glamorama*'s sex-and-death-soaked models carried out cosmopolitan bombings and killings on a scale that ISIS would have envied) made one an eyewitness to something of real importance in the playing out of the Great Transition. This was a time when the celebrity bubble got so big, and its members so numerous and ubiquitous, that fame absolutely dominated and enchanted the culture—yet reality TV effectively did not yet exist, and the internet effectively didn't yet exist, and smartphones were a dream, and terrorist groups largely belonged, for most people, to an opaque and extraneous fantasyland. The late 1990s were the culmination of an era when playful illusions were still controlled by an elite big enough to rule the zeitgeist but not yet defined by a few ultra-stars who totally dwarfed the rest (like Kanye and the Kardashians and Taylor Swift). The way those stars now have to command the second-to-second pace of the online ecosystem, looming over everything while also paradoxically carpeting the culture's sedimentary ocean floor, just didn't apply at millennium's end. (Trump couldn't have run for president then. So he didn't.)

And everything was very indoorsy. Stardom was a siloed warehouse party heavily influenced by Europe—the vogue for New Balance sneakers hadn't yet hopped to New York—and the playful illusions, confining motion in strobing, shadowy spaces, functioned as a hall of mirrors within which monsters and demons could work their way in and out of the crowd. There was no Coachella.* Pot was illegal. There were no rich kids of Instagram, much less a *Rich Kids of Instagram* (2015), aired suitably enough on BBC Channel 4.

So in a way, bringing us back to the stubborn throughlines that also define the Great Transition, the late 1990s was not just a high-gloss freeze frame, about to be vaporized, in a blast of democratization, by the internet. It was also a

---

*The first Coachella festival took place in October 1999. It didn't return until 2001.

weirdly "aristocratic" hiccup, when celebrity and artistry became stable and well-funded enough to produce all these far-seeing touchstone commentaries on the world about to come: *Glamorama, Fight Club, The Matrix, Midnite Vultures, Celebrity Skin,* and *Mechanical Animals,* to name just a few enduring artifacts. The internet soon democratized life in just the way Tocqueville foresaw, locking the many into a pattern of competitive conformity that only the most bizarrely talented and ambitious could break through—though even they, no matter how high their privacy gardens grew, could never break away from the commonality of taste, habit, desire, and mores they shared with the people. But the culture, to us today strangely indifferent to technology, democratized the good and bad dreams of the best end-of-cycle fame artists. Their works are not replicable because, in some uncanny measure, we live them every day.

Perhaps that's why our play—and our illusions—lurch so wildly between the physically isolated space of the technological network and the organically immersive, outward-facing space of the natural world. You could see that coming in *Zoolander* too. "So I'm rappelling down Mount Vesuvius when I suddenly slip," says Hansel, teeing up a story any globe-trekking gym rat/tech bro could rattle off today, "and I start to fall. Just falling—*ahh, ahh* . . . I'll never forget the terror. When suddenly I realize: 'Holy shit, Hansel, haven't you been smoking Peyote for six straight days, and couldn't some of this maybe be in your head?' "

Zoolander: "And?"

"And it was. I was totally fine. I've never even been to Mount Vesuvius."

Even in the joke of it, these yearnings, these socially

desirable goalposts of meaning, have quietly loomed over time into a commanding view. One very successful woman in digital media once reminisced to me about growing up in Hawaii, eating psychedelic mushrooms, and descending into a massive cave with the kind of friend posse that now serves as a touchstone and ideal for the kids on the festival circuit. Whatever miraculous view awaited at bottom morphed, unfortunately, into a hellhole of serpents. Convinced that massive descending vine tendrils were actually snakes—you decide how well this works as a metaphor for Tocqueville's dangling chains—our heroine scrambled up and out of the cave in a fugue of horror, only to discover at the earth's surface that she had shredded her arms and legs on a ladder of outcroppings. You live, you learn, as Alanis Morissette says.

In that sense, *Zoolander*'s ridiculously exploratory and posse-driven world is as familiar and American, despite the obvious changes, as the America of Tocqueville's time, when Tocqueville's acquaintance* Ralph Waldo Emerson mobilized his squad to avail themselves of nature's hall of mirrors as spiritualistically as the lovably entitled outdoorsy hipsters of today:

> The mysteries and scenery of the cave had the same dignity that belongs to all natural objects, and which shames the fine things to which we foppishly compare them. I remarked, especially, the mimetic habit, with which Nature, on new instruments, hums her

---

*Emerson met Tocqueville in Paris during France's abortive 1848 revolution.

old tunes, making night to mimic day, and chemistry to ape vegetation. But then I took notice, and still chiefly remember, that the best thing which the cave had to offer was an illusion. On arriving at what is called the "Star-Chamber," our lamps were taken from us by the guide, and extinguished or put aside, and, on looking upwards, I saw or seemed to see the night heaven thick with stars glimmering more or less brightly over our heads, and even what seemed a comet flashed among them. All the party were touched with astonishment and pleasure. Our musical friends sung with much feeling a pretty song, "The stars are in the quiet sky," &c., and I sat down on the rocky floor to enjoy the serene picture. Some crystal specks in the black ceiling high overhead, reflecting the light of a half-hid lamp, yielded this magnificent effect.[1]

Concluded Emerson: "Our conversation with Nature is not just what it seems." The ad agency that cribbed Whitman for the Levi's *Go Forth* campaign would swoon. Tocqueville, naturally, saw it coming. "In America the majority has enclosed thought within a formidable fence," he already realized; the "state of perpetual self-adoration" in which public opinion keeps "the majority" is a gilded cage from which we endlessly flee into America's readiest refuge[2]—the still remarkably "empty cradle" of our national wilderness.*

---

*Alexis de Tocqueville, *Democracy in America*, ed. J. P. Mayer, trans. George Lawrence (New York: Harper, 2006), 30. The Native Americans, Tocqueville knew, echo through our souls long after their presence is all but effaced from the land and living memory. "The ruin of these peoples

Yet once we're there, we find it all too hard to stay inert. In Europe, a continent filled with people and history and guilt and memories, "simple tastes, quiet mores, family feeling, and love of one's birthplace" are considered "great guarantees of tranquility and happiness," notes Tocqueville. "But in America nothing seems more prejudicial to society than virtues of that sort."[3] Here, our Puritan origins hold our spirits to a fixed point that allows, within the limits circumscribed by its anchor, our bodies' free range in nature's sphere.

---

began as soon as the Europeans landed on their shores; it has continued ever since and is coming to completion in our own day. Providence, when it placed them amid the riches of the New World, seems to have granted them a short lease only; they were there, in some sense, *only waiting*" (30; emphasis in original). We Americans remain staunchly but incompletely haunted and charmed by a dangling promise embodied for us by the peoples we subjected to a genocide unparalleled in history—a redemptive, revitalizing unification of play and peace, illusion and revelation. At the same time, the current thrust of our retreat into nature often seems to trend toward celebration in the harshest of environments. Desert festival culture, with Burning Man at the top, taps into a long Christian and post-Christian tradition (from Luther on) of seeing the wilderness as the site where the human will may be made pure. "If peoples with a democratic social state could not remain free when they live in the wilderness, one would have to despair of the future of the human race," Tocqueville quipped, "for men are progressing rapidly toward democracy and the wildernesses are filling up" (312). But his theological tradition was once wherein "Christianity speaks to reason, not to the will; it teaches forbearance, not inner perspicuity." Joshua Mitchell, *The Fragility of Freedom* (Chicago: University of Chicago Press, 1995), 190. One pattern for curbing the craziness in our culture could be formed if our desert festival circuit opens itself to pursuing purification without forgetting the crucial relationship between forgiveness and freedom. Here, Tocqueville whispers, plunging face to face into preparatory details will be more important to acquiring such a habit of mind than individually hovering over the wilderness in collective celebration of the blazing ideal of the Whole.

But how fixed a spirit and anchored a heart was, say, Emerson's? How close did he come to a brush with the cave's darker, more hostile illusions? After Zoolander gives him snide condolences for failing to book Mugatu's *Derelicte* campaign, Hansel repays him in kind, insisting he didn't blow it because he's so cosmopolitan he'd "never even heard of it. Me and my friends have been too busy bathing off the coast of St. Barts with spider monkeys for the past two weeks, tripping on acid." Of course, you're supposed to laugh when the dueling models make faux-deadly sport of each other with the ultimate walk-off. "Who you trying to get crazy with?" Hansel glowers. "Don't you know I'm loco?" But in real life, making sport of your fellow human beings tips us quickly into the violent side of crazy. At what point in our "free time" do our rangers without anchors become rebels without a cause—or, Zoolander-style, conformists without a clue?

ALL THAT GLITTERS

Oh so much of our free time is me time. The straightest path to learning why we play this way is to consider how we don't.

To wit: the old way of leisure is gone. "In aristocratic ages the chief function of science is to give pleasure to the mind, but in democratic ages to the body." Not so now. While "the Americans always display a clear, free, original, and creative turn of mind," Tocqueville says, "hardly anyone in the United States devotes himself to the essentially theoretical and abstract side of human knowledge"—the distinctive practice of leisured minds in aristocratic civilization. Back then, meditation meant something much different than it does in the cross-legged sunrise wellness workshops of Malibu's Point Dume. It meant what Marcus Aurelius did in his *Meditations: taking*, in the literal Latin sense, the *measure* of ultimate things. Now, "nothing is less conducive to meditation" in the old manner "than the setup of democratic society. There, in contrast to aristocratic societies, one finds no numerous class that remains at pleasure because all is well with it, nor that other class which does not stir because it despairs of any improvement." (If you feel particularly cynical about the idleness of today's best and least well off, this may ring a bit hollow. Then again, your standards reflect just how far we've come from the aristocratic castes of old, when complete freedom and utter servitude were inherited in an unbroken chain for centuries upon centuries.) "Everyone is on the move" now; in "the midst of this universal tumult, this incessant conflict of jarring interest, this endless chase for wealth, where is one to find the calm for the profound researches of the intellect?"[4] Tocqueville would see in today's fussy fixation on mindfulness and mind-body health an ironic attempt to fight fire with fire, using our fitful, restless spirits to cope with what ails them.

The replacement of leisured meditation with this kind of "me time" is perfectly captured by 2 Chainz, the rapper whose sophomore album, *Me Time* (2013), "gives people a sense of going away sometimes—without really going on vacation," as he once told MTV News.[5] "I feel like when people listen to me, they feel like they're goin' somewhere, taking time off; they're relaxing, lettin' their hair down. Every time somebody wants to have some 'me time' or whatever, this is the type of vibe, this is the type of project. I'm putting together different sounds to make people be

like, 'This is about me. Me and my people, this is our time.' "
Settle in for a minute, however, and the restlessness within
rises swiftly to the surface. "It's all about showing growth
and maturation. It's supposed to be better than the last time.
I'm coming with a new album, a new way of life," he told
New York City radio station Power 105.1. "I wanted to
show progression on this album. I wanted to show prosperity."[6] What could be more American than creating a
fake vacation—and a whole ethos of relaxation—that in
fact celebrates your own productivity?

As contemporary as 2 Chainz seems, his ethos and ours
reaches back in an unbroken chain to the supposedly old-
fashioned *Mad Men* era, to the even quainter Gilded Age,
back yet again to the mid-nineteenth-century moment of
Democracy in America, and, finally, all the way (as Tocqueville
said it reached) to the Puritans.* David Riesman, the famed

---

*As Robert Bellah and his coauthors observe in their own Tocquevillean
inquiry into "individualism and commitment in American life," Philip
Rieff suggests that the therapeutic view of the human condition is "more
native to American culture than the Puritan sources of that culture
would indicate." Rieff, *Triumph of the Therapeutic*, 58, quoted in Bellah
et. al, *Habits of the Heart: Individualism and Commitment in American Life*
(Berkeley, CA: University of California Press, 2008), 311n22. Recurring
to America's origins, Tocqueville insists, reveals that the fixed point of
human reconciliation to God, made accessible through the experience of
Jesus, allowed Americans to develop a radically free range of experiential motion outside the deep but limited orbit of faith—and the "habits of
the heart" essential to maintaining the balance in freedom. "Both the
Old and the New Testaments speak of the heart as involving intellect,
will, and intention as well as feeling," Team Bellah recalls. "The notion
of 'habits of the heart' perhaps goes back ultimately to the law written in
the heart (Rom. 2:15; cf. Jer. 31:33 and Deut. 6:6)." Bellah et. al., *Habits*, 312
n28. Whether biblical or not—"both Confucianism and Buddhism have a
notion of the heart that is somewhat compatible"—it is the loss of the
point fixed in the heart, Tocqueville leads us to believe, and not the

sociologist behind *The Lonely Crowd* (1950), traced "the middle-class leisure pattern" to "the sobersides of the Puritan revolution," so "urban, uplifting, strenuous." This is the land of professional play. "In democratic times, enjoyments are more lively than in times of aristocracy, and more especially, immeasurably greater numbers taste them."[7] Extreme sports, professional sports, professional extreme sports—here is why we have them. In an age of equality, the home is the closest we can get to a safe place of quiet, restorative repose. We also know it can be isolating. And we know that we can't spend all or even most of our time relaxing at home. We are sent out into the world again and again, to compete with an ever-growing number of people who seem so much like us that our social and economic position never feels certain. At the same time, we know that even when we do establish a modicum of predictability with regard to our competitive advantage, our habit of mind and our awareness of our mortality send us questing after physical and material gratification on top of it—which may dazzle or sate us for a moment but which never lasts. Our "hopes and desires are much more often disap-

---

presence of some rival origin point, that makes "Americans experience more doubt about who they 'really' are and more difficulty in finding an authentic self. Thus over time guilt declines but anxiety increases" (ibid., 319n21)—perfect preconditions for a practical triumph of the therapeutic. In this book, I want you to consider that the quest for the "authentic self" is even more apt for us than for an aristocratic-age royal like Hamlet to spiral into selfish, ugly, and destructive melodrama. "In our day everything threatens to become so much alike that the particular features of each individual may soon be entirely lost in the common physiognomy" (Tocqueville, *Democracy*, 701). The art of being free requires you to hold fast to what Rieff calls your "irreducible I"—the *particular* constitutive heart you've been given, always and already there.

pointed" in our age than the aristocratic age, "minds are more anxious and on edge, and trouble is felt more keenly." There is always something better out there, and we want it—even if we know, deep down, that we're very unlikely to reach the level of the most talented and ambitious among us.

The physicality and extreme experience of sports serve as an outlet for these frustrations. Daredevil pursuits on skis, skates, boards, and bungee cords give us the momentary sense of pushing ourselves to the limit, although we can safely return home or "retire" from practicing them professionally. Meanwhile, the latest studies confirm our hopes that strenuous workout sessions help fight bad moods and depression. Team sports give us "something bigger than ourselves" to focus on while demanding far less from us than aristocratic institutions like the dynastic family, the tribe, the guild, the priesthood, or the military. The most powerful and ambiguous consequence of that democratic approach to participation and representation is the multibillion-dollar pro sports industry. Here, all our forms of play seem to fuse into a single, awe-inspiring whole. Ultra-wealthy businessmen who don't want to piddle around with politics can spend real money buying franchises (or maintaining megayachts, winning sailing competitions, or fielding Formula One racing teams). Those lower on the socioeconomic ladder, who seem least connected to the world of high talent and ambition, become one of the main pools for extraordinary athletic talent and ambition. Anxious middle-class Americans can use sports events as a regular ritual way to drink and eat their way into a respectable, but ultimately infrequent enough, stupor. In a democratic age, Tocqueville helps us understand, sports are like medicine. They give us access to a diluted form of the intense experiences that dissipated with the aristocratic age, but in a way that works harmoniously with our democratic sensibilities and democratic society.

In our crazy way, however, we tend to make semiprofessional sports out of everything. In the pages of Henry James's late-nineteenth-century novel *The Bostonians*, Riesman noted, a so-called gentleman of leisure was to be found mooning around Provincetown, Cape Cod's ultimate resort destination. In the mid-twentieth century, Riesman surmised, "it may be that a few fossils of the species are preserved"; but

> my impression is that people who go to such places for the summer appear to lead strenuously artsy and craftsy lives: even if they lie on the beach, they are getting a competitively handsome tan, but most of the time they appear to be playing energetic tennis, taking exhausting walks, . . . and in the evening attending lectures, the experimental theatre, and colloquia in private houses.[8]

Here are the "bourgeois bohemians" *New York Times* columnist David Brooks announced at the end of the late 1990s*; here, too, today's bohos, tech bros, disaster tourists, and social-good nomads jet-setting and backpacking their way

---

*See David Brooks, *Bobos in Paradise: The New Upper Class and How They Got There* (New York: Simon & Schuster, 2000).

from festival circuit to conflict zone and back.* "While they may be less systematically engaged than many students," Riesman allowed—this was before today's amenity-happy campus culture was even a dream—"they are gainfully improving themselves in body and mind; and, perhaps unlike many students, they are subject to the additional strain of

---

*We all "try to affiliate ourselves with the ordeal lifestyle," Brooks sighs. "It's like going into a nightclub where everybody is constantly shoving their endurance cleavage in your face" (*Bobos*, 211). But all that work quietly imposes diminishing returns. Rising generations who act as if they're on to something exclusive and new are moving too fast, in air too thin, to inhale any mold spores from the mustier truth. Languishing during a break from writing this book at Sunset Junction, the epicenter of L.A.'s terminally hip Silverlake neighborhood, I realized everyone was still patterning a style and substance Beck had established in a fold-out poster insert from 1999. Their sense of novelty ensures nothing in hipsterdom is new under the sun. "*Bobos in Paradise* is frustratingly relevant," Brooks confessed in a 2011 introduction. "I have waited for a new and different culture to replace the culture of Whole Foods, Restoration Hardware, and locally grown, thick-textured breads [I read 'beards'!] that I wrote about in that book. Alas, this new replacement culture has not yet come." David Brooks, *The Paradise Suite* (New York: Simon & Schuster, 2011), 1–2. That is because it, like hipster culture, is not really distinctive of the upper class. It has been democratizing steadily since the moment it first grew apparent, and it grew apparent because it was already so familiar to all—giving particular voice and form to the same abstract and basic longings we all share to have it all in our pursuit of well-being. To be sure, we are struck by the separation, acutely documented by Charles Murray in *Coming Apart*, between those who have and haven't been fully democratized into the not-so-new standard culture. But still, Tocqueville counsels, this inequality is best understood as what happens when actively maintained vertical barriers to advancement crumble along with the aristocratic age—and the passively sustained horizontal barriers arising in our age ensnare most of us in a competitive conformity that only the most ambitious and talented can surpass. Some high performers may be relatively more sheltered from our constitutive craziness, but some are even more exposed than the rest of us.

having to feel and to claim that they are having a good time, being victims of that new form of Puritanism which Martha Wolfenstein and Nathan Leites in their book *Movies* have termed 'fun-morality.' "[9] Our human illusion of play relies on artifice and machinations—a sharp contrast to nature's playfully organic illusions. For nature offers an equality of experience that even democratic life cannot. "In the confusion of classes each man wants to appear as something he is not and is prepared to take much trouble to produce this effect."

> Such feelings are not born of democracy, for they are all too natural to the heart of man, but it is democracy which applies them to material products. The hypocrisy of virtue is of every age, but the hypocrisy of luxury is peculiar to democratic centuries. To satisfy these new cravings of human vanity the arts have recourse to every kind of imposture.[10]

Think again of Tocqueville's prophetic remarks on fake diamonds, or Marilyn Manson's Shakespeare-aping quip (in "Posthuman" from *Mechanical Animals*) that "all that glitters is cold." Our play often throws off such a fevered chill for the same reason our work does. "Appearance counts for more than reality"; while "Renaissance painters generally looked for mighty subjects over their heads and far away in time so that imagination could have ample play," our artists "copy trivial objects from every angle, though nature provides only too many originals." Our fixation on quickly and constantly changing perspective, of a piece with our mania for the feeling of breakthroughs, entrenches our systematically crazy pattern of viewing everyday life in one selfish and melodramatic key. "American society appears animated because men and things are constantly changing; it is monotonous because all these changes are alike."[11] All too often, in our me-time theatrics, we can run but not hide from a frantic fear that we've lost contact with any reference point fixed enough to anchor true repose, the kind of passive rest that graces us with the possibility of peaceful play. Like Gertrude after Claudius murders Hamlet's father the king, just at the moment we want to relax, we find ourselves all too busy—and deep in denial about it.

Unlike Gertrude, of course, we're not royalty. Whatever our income level, whatever our net worth, we're all confronted with the same question after we take a break from the hustle: now what? In play, we only summon forth more questions. Seeking fixed points and anchors, we turn first to ourselves, then to one another—first deepening the isolation we say drives us crazy, then aggravating a performative publicity that also likens us to Hamlet. Our experience of play is haunted by the death of fun, a parody of our own death. How can fleeting experience ever ease our own incessant sense that time is always running short, that we are always falling behind?

The question feels like a cruel trick.

But, industrious Americans that we are, we've improvised a few ideas.

A few options emerge from our practical experience. We could possibly succeed by trying to escape the categories of work and play, finding some transcendent place to hover. Or we could try fusing work and play together in a unified, all-purposeful whole. Perhaps we could thrust deeply into the most engrossing experience of play—or the opposite, launching into forms of play that distract us most from work life.

These all seem plausible, all worth gaming out.

But maybe, just maybe, there's a way we can oscillate between inwardness and outwardness, in play no less than work, without losing our way or losing our minds.

TOYS OF DESPERATION

Despite the occasional outburst of enthusiasm for a "work hard, play hard" mentality, we are mostly more ambivalent about our more ambiguous reality. For anyone with a smartphone or a virtual office, it's obvious that one of the hallmarks of modern life is struggling to stave off attention-deficit experiences on the one hand without actually "unplugging" on the other. It sounds nice to levitate above the dilemmas of working and playing with too much or too little commitment. But Tocqueville saw how the logic of equality makes us characteristically too agitated to wallow in our leisure, yet too easily dismayed to lose ourselves in our labors. Our inability to repose at either pole makes it too hard to transcend both. Rather than rising above the distinction between work and play, we're more apt to slip between the cracks, slinking away from working *or* playing full out.

There's something creepy about this behavior. It's as if we're trying to shirk two calls of duty at once. Think of Hamlet. Confronted with the ghost of his murdered father, he faced two temptations. The first was to disbelieve the ghost. The second was to believe. But for half-faithful Hamlet, both options led to the same destination—a dangerously noncommittal pursuit of whatever fate might await. Horatio, sensing the problem, tried to ward him away from the abyss. "Think of it," he gasped. "The very place puts toys of desperation, without more motive, into every brain that looks so many fathoms to the sea and hears it roar beneath."[12] We're free to wonder whether Horatio was referring to a literal plunge into the depths, a figurative one, or both. Driven crazy by the anxieties of work and play alike, we know with all too great a certainty how it feels to peer into the deep crevasse between them. On the one hand, the vertigo we feel inspires us to fill up the gap the same way we fill up the world—busily, excessively, with a fixation on the surface of things. On the other, we're inspired in the frightening way that standing on a real cliff-side sometimes tugs at us with ten thousand hands, crazy little voices saying *jump!* Both these kinds of desperation toy with us, and we with them. Whether by trying to fill ourselves up with some alternative to labor and leisure, or trying to empty ourselves out by somehow fleeing the whole problem of an alternative, our entertainments and our diversions alike are poised to put us back in mind of the troubles we're trying to escape.

Yet we pursue them anyway. After all, what's so bad about food and fashion, sports and hobbies, and all the rest?

The answer has to do with who's doing the playing: us.

Let's revisit the logic of equality, beginning with the things that tend to happen inevitably just because of how the similarity of our American experience gives us such similar senses of life. Note: there's nothing in that logic that claims increased equality fosters increased togetherness: "When social conditions are equal every man tends to live apart, centered in himself and forgetful of the public." While "the duties of each to all are much clearer" than in aristocratic times, "devoted service to any individual" is "much rarer. The bonds of humanity are wider but more relaxed."[13] Rather than feeling bad or guilty, Tocqueville simply wants us to recognize this for what it is. Delinked from a legacy of family bloodlines, aristocratic pride, feudal allegiance, or centuries-old homesteads, our imagination and our experience confirm that everyone is equally human.* That idea draws us outward, but our relative disconnection from our neighbors and even extended family members prevents us from favoring them with our attention and care. We might even be uncomfortable with the idea of "privileging" those relatively comfortable people we know, while strangers in distant, troubled lands eke out a hard, meager existence. If we can be of real help to such people without using up much of our time, we will often gladly do it. That's why donation-driven charity is so popular, and Americans sometimes seem more inclined to worry about the worst off in foreign lands than the badly off in their own country. On

---

*But! Our need to *justify* our imagination (or faith) *through* experience, our most trustworthy guide today regardless of natural and human illusion, makes us demand *direct, unmediated* experience—in this case, of the equality of all. Sometimes, illusion demands of us that we learn the art of being taught: even in ancient times, when authority was mediated through noble and priestly classes, "Jesus Christ had to come down to earth to make all members of the human race understand that they were naturally similar and equal" (Tocqueville, *Democracy*, 439). Now, not even Jesus can escape our desperate desire for direct experience—in this case, as millions of Americans will testify, of his equal *personal* love and salvation for all. Despite the avowedly high stakes, there is something of a game at work even here: we "distractedly launch out into the world of spirits for fear of being held too tightly bound by the body's fetters" (535).

the other hand, there's so much in life that makes us feel (as we say) like "just one person" can't "make a difference," even if we try to salve our anxieties by "being a part of something bigger than ourselves."* Unless that something is the biggest possible, with the most money and power, we tend to doubt its effectiveness. We tend to doubt the point of trying.

Increasingly, we even tend to feel disgust or embarrassment around ordinary people who do try to pick away in a small manner at society's biggest problems. We're hypersensitive to how unglamorous and inconsequential it feels to participate in local government, local news, and other small-time pursuits that bump up against big-time challenges. That kind of disenchanted thinking, Tocqueville tells us, is the result of what he called individualism—the way we live in democratic times. Individualism isn't *necessarily* egotistical or selfish in a greedy sense. But it is much different from the kind of thinking and being that prevails when we're deeply inspired by loyalty to family, tribe, country, or party. "Individualism," he explains, "is a calm and considered feeling which disposes each citizen to isolate himself from the mass of his fellows and withdraw into the circle of family and friends; with this little society formed to his taste, he gladly leaves the greater society to look after itself."[14] In an era of special friends-and-family networks on our cell-phone plans, this shouldn't be a controversial idea.

---

*There's also a last vestige of guilt here in our low-guilt world of high anxiety. "Ridiculous yachts and private planes and big limousines won't make people enjoy life more, and it sends out terrible messages to the people who work for them," said Virgin CEO Richard Branson at the 2013 Ultimate Success Summit. "It would be so much better if that money was spent in Africa—and it's about getting a balance."

It is, though, because we hear it as an attack on our morals. We fear that someone describing us this way is about to criticize us for being a bad person. That's not what Tocqueville is after. He does, however, offer an important caution. Since individualism "is of democratic origin and threatens to grow as conditions get more equal" if it is left unabated and nothing is set up to work against its influence, it "finally merges in egoism" after all.[15] Tocqueville feared that we'd get so good at the art of being egoistic that we'd close up comfortably in our own personal nutshells, the way Hamlet fantasized: "O God, I could be bounded in a nutshell and count myself a king of infinite space, were it not that I have bad dreams."[16] Recall that, in the *Republic*, Socrates can't begin his erotic pursuit of wisdom about the human condition until Cephalus—convinced that the great value of wealth is to let you sleep soundly, assured that you don't owe "sacrifices to a god or money to a human being"— trots off to bed.[17] Not only do we dread becoming too crazy but we're also in terror of becoming too sane—so well-adjusted to cookie-cutter fates as harmless, domesticated pets that we become nightmarishly depersonalized. At our point in the Great Transition, turning into humble little creatures of habit strikes us as so crazy it just might happen. It's as if Tocqueville had told us we might be in danger of turning into cartoon teddy bears. Such cheerful, ingrown beings would not be recognizably *us*—there would be something insanely, unnaturally wrong with them. Like Tocqueville, we know that "animals only know how to satisfy their primary and coarsest needs, whereas we can infinitely vary and continually increase our delights," and, like Tocqueville, we fear that the Great Transition might pull us inescapably toward a less than fully human future—a Potemkin global village.[18] For all our passionate advances and retreats into play, our confidence in playdom often slips away for no more complicated reason than we really do still know who and how we are: not cartoon teddy bears at all, but *humans*, creatures whose lives are caught up in the highest of stakes—and who act like it.

HAVING IT ALL

That stubborn awareness means life is always going to get complicated. Afraid of being, by turns, too individual or not individual enough—not to mention constantly concerned that we're either spending too much or not enough money on fun—we're driven away from the small-ball of hobbies and potted interests by a grand vision of fusing work and play. So many of our most successful *workers/players* do this. Why shouldn't we? Don't we live in a world where, as Tocqueville knew we believe, we can emulate and replicate success if only we adapt and adopt its patterns quickly and heroically enough? "I don't think of work as work and play as play," said Richard Branson, at the 2013 Ultimate Success Summit. "It's all living." With "much curiosity and little leisure," our "contrary instincts" lead us "straight to looking for generalizations," ways to "paint vast canvases very cheaply" and express a unity of ideas "without trouble."[19] We're primed to fuse work and play.

Nevertheless, the all-purpose sense of undifferentiated living we long for strikes us deep down as throwing off illusions, the kind you see when playing with fire. The fantasy of play is actually *subsumed* to the reality of work,

Tocqueville intimates, because our *like* of liberty is sub-sumed to our *love* of equality.* Of all the features of life in the democratic age, the one we might love and hate the most is how much we have to start seemingly fresh every day. Already, we are harassed by a sense that our possibilities are always narrowing, our time is running out, our competitors are outpacing us, and fate is threatening to displace faith in our lives. And those feelings are intensified by the nagging sense that we can't rest on our laurels any day of the week. Our torments around playdom plague us because we love equality so much that we can't rest or relax amid its incomplete aspects. We have to *do* something about them. Like all our biggest of challenges, equality's incompleteness throws our interchangeable insignificance into the least flattering relief.

We realize the problem is so all-encompassing that if we paltry creatures try to solve it, our reason will give way, as Tocqueville puts it, before our will.[20] But in a more selfish sense, we also know we must work just to keep our guilty feelings toward play at bay. Not only can play be *permissive* of inequality, after all, but some forms of play seem positively *productive* of it—making us fall behind as others steal a march. (When we're active on social media but *not* promoting ourselves, it all too often appears that we're just consuming others' self-promotions, losing ground with the internet's attention-conferring algorithms.) If we don't

---

*When it comes to equality, we would almost "rather die than lose it" (Tocqueville, *Democracy*, 57). Americans "have a natural *taste* for liberty; left to themselves, they will seek it, cherish it, and be sad if it is taken from them. But their *passion* for equality is ardent, insatiable, eternal, and invincible" (506).

throw ourselves back into the world anew each day, some-how refilled with the energy and the hope necessary to en-dure the daily grind, we'll cease to advance, and slip into ruin. To succeed at working for the "physical pleasures" we always want, we "need to be free"; but we know that we'll fall behind our equals in their enjoyment if we put play first, because that temptation "turns against itself and uncon-sciously drives away the very thing it wants."[21] If work isn't preeminent, we know and fear, our play will be hollow, bitter, in vain.

So we anxiously hope that by combining work with play in an *equal* way, we can reconcile the anxieties arising from each—or, perhaps more accurately, cancel them out, render-ing their attendant anxieties as unnecessary as sacrifices to two rival deities. We ascribe great privilege and prosperity to people we think we see pulling this off. We sigh when we watch intellectuals catch themselves and one another "midschmooze," as Brooks observed, enviously certain they "are enjoying an activity that deliciously combines work and play, which is a characteristic reconciliation of the Bobo class." What if we saw them straining less deliciously, and just as the rest of us do, to cancel out competing bets? The pattern of herding into superficially sociable groups, mask-ing our anxious sense of individual insignificance, reap-pears in a less stage-managed light all over—especially on college campuses, where calculated insouciance can mark the difference between social life and social death. Perhaps "it's not surprising" bourgeois bohemians "should make play more like work," Brooks ventures. "Bobos are recon-cilers, after all, so maybe it is inevitable they would strive to blur their duties with their pleasures, making the former more enjoyable and the latter more tame."[22] Alas, taking pleasure in the illusion of reconciliation leads to what novelists ranging from Milan Kundera to Ian McEwan have diagnosed as "moral kitsch": sentimentalism that involves taking a figurative step back from ourselves, the better to feel poignant about the fleeting cuteness specific to small aesthetic pleasures. Indeed, that quietly melodramatic kind of pleasure opens onto dismayingly infinite inward depths we neither can fathom nor anchor ourselves within.[23] "We get here," as Riesman says,

> into very deep waters indeed, where the boundaries between work and play become shadowy—waters where we are looking for a quality we can only vaguely describe: it is various and rhythmical; it breaks through social forms and as constantly recreates them; it manifests itself in tension, yet not too much of it; it is at once meaningful, in the sense of giving us intrinsic satisfaction, and meaningless, in the sense of having no pressing utilitarian purpose. It is some such model as this, I suggest, which haunts us . . . elaborated in our culture, and yet which transcends most, and perhaps all, given cultures.[24]

Or, as Hansel puts it, "I wasn't like every other kid, you know, who dreams about being an astronaut. I was always more interested in what bark was made out of on a tree. Richard Gere's a real hero of mine. Sting. Sting would be another person who's a hero. The music he's created over the years, I don't really listen to it, but the fact that he's making it, I respect that. I care desperately about what I do. Do I know what product I'm selling? No. Do I know what I'm doing today? No. But I'm here, and I'm gonna give it my best shot." In a world with no boundary between meaningful and meaningless activity, no wonder *Glamorama*'s working-hard-or-hardly-working models found it so easy and inevitable to take orders from an international terrorist who used to be one of their own.* Riesman's and Brooks' high-middlebrow transcendence collapses, with all-too-familiar earnestness, into *Zoolander*'s. No surprise, is it, that Derek and Hansel's nemesis in *Zoolander 2* is Benedict Cumberbatch's gender-transcending supermodel All? Whose signature catchphrase is *All is all?*

Despite our best efforts to fuse work and play into the same undifferentiated All as everything else, we may find that the more we push, the less control we exert over their reappearance. It turns out we're too desperate to profitably play with them. Think of all the club songs exhorting you to work, from Britney Spears's "Work Bitch" to Daft Punk's "Harder Faster Stronger"—the backbone of Kanye West's "Stronger": *work it harder, make it better, do it faster, makes us stronger, more than ever, hour after hour, work is never over.*† Think of all the hardworking songs exhorting you to

---

*"He gave his last interview to *Esquire* during the winter of 1989, which was where he said, not at all defensively, 'I know exactly what I'm going to do and where I'm going' . . ." Bret Easton Ellis, *Glamorama* (London: Picador, 1998), 267.

†See Spears's *Britney Jean* (2013), Daft Punk's *Discovery* (2001), and West's *Graduation* (2007). It's true that the "Stronger" ethos can manifest in a much more richly personal and relational way than the dance floor can always offer. In a certain kind of mechanic's workshop, for instance, "the dialectic is between people, but also between iterations—you break

party, an aim taken to the level of a spiritual discipline by self-styled King of the Party Andrew W. K.[25] Think—but not too much, because that's next chapter—of sex.

Sometimes negotiating this force field of exhortations is fun. Sometimes it's not.* As Rieff suspected, these days, the old historical conflict "between instinct and institution may be secondary to that between the values of competition and cooperation," a binary that sends us ping-ponging along a line that intersects with the work-to-play axis. Within those Cartesian coordinates, we can compete or cooperate at work or at play. Fusing the matter together *should*, theoretically, create a blissfully smooth terrain offering infinite glide paths. But in real life, it's a crazy quilt—especially for the beleaguered, disenchanted, lonely, or lost—a treacherous web of convoluted meanings. The Pu-

---

things, and learn something new by taking them apart and talking it through. Here work and leisure both take their bearings from something basically human: rational activity, in association with others . . . directed toward something that appears as good within the horizon of a certain way of life." Matthew B. Crawford, *Shop Class as Soulcraft* (New York: Penguin, 2009), 186. The Tocquevillean attitude adopted in this book, however, suggests that this dialectic depends upon something very similar to a way of life. For most of us, recall, refuge in ways of life will never feel as real as we want it to because ways of life occur to us so accurately as too comprehensive yet paradoxically incomplete. Though many of them, to be sure, can coexist, they are not oriented fully toward the precondition for practicing the art of being free in our constitutively crazy society—an anchored heart from which to roam within wide but compassed bounds.

*Team Bellah cites a San Franciscan, quoted in Steven Tipton's *Getting Saved from the Sixties*, "who complained that all through school he had been expected to 'decide what is right and wrong and why I was alive and what I was living for. . . . That's the worst thing to do to a man—make him decide everything for himself, because he can't.' " See Bellah et. al., *Habits*, 325n17.

ritan "Protestant ethic lingers, but it is very doubtful that it in any way dominates the expression of Western energies," Rieff frowned. "The man of ambition is still with us, as in all times, but now he needs a more subtle initiative, a deeper capacity to manipulate the democracy of emotions, if he is to maintain his separate identity and significantly augment it with success. Pick up almost any post-Freudian book on our emotional condition and you will find this theme."[26] Rieff set forth a different theme in its place: the charismatic renunciation of much that passes today as fun, through a relationship of integrity with sacred authority.

Tocqueville is not so strict. For him, America showed how binaries that bedeviled Europe's violent democratization "naturally and constantly balance and correct each other."[27] Abstract ideas and particular experience; activity and passivity; outwardness and inwardness; the tacit and the explicit; settled faith and unsettled fortune—all these manifestations of the oscillating quality of democratic life find, in America, a workable and hopeful means of amelioration. Rather than curing our crazy by curbing our will, our anchored hearts ease our restless scheming minds, making them gentler, more circumspect, readier to forgive. Where once was disgusted impatience, here we find the time to forbear the mess, the tumult, and the imperfection of our fleeting but filled-up world. Could work and play be yet another ticking time binary *defused* by the art of being free?

BACK TO THE FUTURE

To be sure, Tocqueville proposes that free being, well understood, secures fruitful labor and fruitful play by reconciling *us to the future* more than by reconciling work to play. Again, our point of origin logically reveals why *we*, and not *what we do*, can and must be reconciled. Rather than marking a dramatic, unexpected break from aristocratic leisure, democratic play emerges gradually amid the Great Transition.

Already on the small homestead of mid-nineteenth-century America, Tocqueville saw its first stirrings. He saw that the American "soul cleaves to" our "petty aims" of making "life ever easier and more comfortable," orienting our lives around "keeping irritations away" and "satisfying one's slightest needs without trouble and almost without expense."[28] We "dwell on" these goals "every day and in great detail"—so much so that they sometimes "shut out the rest of the world" and "come between the soul and God." That's why Joel Osteen, for instance, spends valuable sermon time telling his megachurch faithful to put down the cell phone when they walk through the front door after work.

Just as important as our desire for an exceptionally large quantity of comforts is our longing for comforts of an exceptionally simple quality. That makes us very unlike the old aristocrats, who used their leisure time in pursuit of insanely exaggerated and bizarre enjoyments. Equality's vice is not that it leads people "astray with forbidden delights" but that it "absorbs them in the quest of those permitted completely. By such a means a kind of decent materialism may come to be established on earth, which will not corrupt souls but soften and imperceptibly loosen the springs of action."[29] Yes, although Tocqueville could not imagine the lonely couch potato or internet junkie snacking his or her way through the night, he already knew why they would seek the kind of play that they do.

And in fine oscillating form, we lurch from our private, secret play for simple pleasures into a public party indulging "a multitude of artificial and arbitrary classifications"—brands, trends, fashions, fads, affinity groups, personality types, astrological signs, and all other kinds of identity markers—"to protect each man from the danger of being swept along in spite of himself with the crowd" into the always-encroaching oblivion of felt obscurity.[30]

In this ping-ponging, Tocqueville sees that equality "kindles" people's "desires and limits their powers." The sensation of every day being a new day morphs into a feeling of time accelerating beyond our control. We feel most vividly "the imperfectly satisfied desire to have it"—whatever it is in the moment—"and the continual fear of losing it again." We want to slow down the clock, but we fear someone else will turn it back on us. "The actual moment completely occupies and absorbs" us all. So "anxious and eager," will we not "become so engrossed in a cowardly love of immediate pleasures" that we will give in to a prejudice against the future? Such is the fear that grows from the Puritan kernel at our heart, which still makes so many Americans apt to beg Jesus to take the wheel. Recall the way people "see a multitude of little intermediate obstacles, all of which have to be negotiated slowly"; simply gaming out that effort exhausts their "ambition and discourages it. They therefore discard such distant and doubtful hopes, preferring to seek delights less lofty but easier to reach. No law limits their horizon, but they do so for themselves."[31] What is lost in the frenzy of work and play, cooperative, competitive, or carried out in isolation, is a view of both time's horizon and our own—something we can see only by lifting our gaze upward and outward. Play, at its worst, is a temptation to the kind of excess that saps our frazzled energies: a surfeit of short-term planning, arrayed around securing our most immediate interest in our most pedestrian pleasures.

Play at its *best*, however, arises from a recognition that ameliorating our craziness is much more a matter of giving up on fruitless frenzy *in work or play* than of doubling down on the will to power *in either*. Amid all the "perpetual fluctuations of fate" in our age, "the present looms large and hides the future, so that men do not want to think beyond tomorrow"; yet "it is only by resisting a thousand daily petty urges that the fundamental anxious longing for happiness can be satisfied."[32] This is our true so-called self-interest, well understood. This is being free.

> There are as many pillows of illusion [writes Emerson] as flakes in a snow-storm. We wake from one dream into another dream. The toys, to be sure, are various, and are graduated in refinement to the quality of the dupe. The intellectual man requires a fine bait; the sots are easily amused. But everybody is drugged with his own frenzy, and the pageant marches at all hours, with music and banner and badge.[33]

Once we realize that snatching at the chance of sudden material gratification is the opposite of fun, we can form the long-term plans that give us such freer play than the frenzied moment. In so doing, crucially, we begin to forgive ourselves, and one another, for being the mere humans we are.

Sex

———

"I'm selfish, impatient and a little insecure. I make mistakes, I am out of control and at times hard to handle. But if you can't handle me at my worst, then you sure as hell don't deserve me at my best." This mantra, allegedly first uttered by Marilyn Monroe and so expressive of our sense of the foundations of sexual romance, has swept the internet with an intensity reminiscent of an STD. You probably still can't survive a session on Tinder without having it pounded into your head—and heart. If you're of the most appealing age to advertisers, chances are good you've had sex with at least one person who'd tell a pollster The Mantra describes them pretty well. For more than a few women, it has become a hallmark of self-regard. But although few will admit it, it's equally applicable to guys, who are equally at sea in the awkward, crazy, needy, and passive-aggressive individualism that defines our sexual—and social—situation.

In today's awkward, paranoid world, where "How are you?" might always be a pickup line, The Mantra preemptively strikes at unwanted acts of autonomy. What it really says, by this point in this book, is all too familiar.

I am crazily; I am selfishly; I am melodramatically.

DEAL WITH IT.

Of course, the most revealing thing of all about this revealing quote is that it wasn't actually uttered by Marilyn Monroe, everyone's favorite doomed romantic. It's apocryphal—yet another phony attribution that emerged anonymously from the depths of the internet, our collective half-consciousness. Somewhere deep in our souls we want it to be true that Marilyn Monroe said exactly the thing that construes our powerful performance of shared powerlessness as a unique personal entitlement. (Turns out, the way it speaks to us is yet another dispiriting reminder of how interchangeably insignificant we really are.*) Marilyn is one of our few national authority figures in sexual culture—naughty enough for Lady Gaga to reference in the song "Government Hooker" but nice enough for the Madame Tussaud's Wax Museum. Part Norma Jean, part Marilyn Manson, she's up there with Lincoln and Einstein

---

* "Truthfully when I first saw this quote, I loved it so hard. It's like one of those things you rely on when you feel particularly undateable, right after crying into a tub of cookie dough and watching that *Sex and the City* episode where Carrie finds out Big's engaged. It's an ode to a complicated woman. On a base level, I get that. But again, there's absolutely nothing out there that attributes this to Marilyn Monroe, and having seen it mass produced so many times, I'm entirely disenchanted." Mary Grace Garis, "Marilyn Monroe's Best Quote Wasn't by Marilyn Monroe," *Elle*, June 1, 2014, http://www.elle.com/culture/celebrities/a15424/marilyn-monroe-misquotations/.

in the apocryphal quotes department—but alone among giants in representing our sense that inescapable craziness only *seems* to expand our possibilities for sex, romance, and intimate partnership. The reality sends us zinging away from melodramatic performance, toward the no-drama Seinfeld-and-chill refuge that's also a popular touchstone in dating app world.

How could Tocqueville possibly shed light on our sexual predicament today? Simple. It's fueled by the same social logic that shapes all our mores, habits, feelings, and beliefs in the present age. And it shows how what seems to be an ego problem is actually something much different—and more solvable.

FUCK IT

In our ordinary language, there are few more popular and useful ideas than that something is fucked. If we like to imagine that civilizations still connected to the ancient world of honor have many different words for the same thing, like Eskimos with snow, we ourselves communicate our contemporary democratic selves by using the same word for many different situations—perhaps *any* different one. In good egalitarian style, anyone and anything is, potentially, fucked.

There's a logic to the remarkable adaptability of this particular piece of slang. It reflects our strange intuition that there's some connection between futility, or fruitlessness, and the pursuit of purely sexual gratification. At the same time, however, we pour endless amounts of energy and money into the pursuit of sexual relationships, no matter how much drama and dismay surrounds them. We're weirdly comfortable with squandering our time and life force on banal entertainments, but the pursuit of sex returns us to anxieties and ambitions often far more intense than those surrounding money. No surprise, considering how desperately we toy with one another. But despite all the complications brought about by the confusion and irregularity of shifting gender norms, the vast majority of us still refuse to just say fuck it. We all know how much of an emotionally debilitating time suck sex can be. So why do we keep doubling down?

Tocqueville has some unexpected answers.

To get them across, he first helps us see how sex orients us toward something essential about our human personality. Sex crystallizes why it's so easy for us to act crazy, and why we're driven, in spite of it all, to seek in sexual relationships a sane shelter from the frantic, unstable world around us. We're conflicted: we want a refuge *and* a playground. We want to gratify our egos by experiencing the rush of power that sex supplies, but we also want to hide, if only for a moment, from the striving desire that defines our interactions everywhere else in the world. That's why Tocqueville doesn't just focus on sex as a pleasurable haven. He also recognizes its role as a den of madness, offering the kind of experience Oscar Wilde described as "feasting with panthers."

Let's dig into *that* metaphor for a minute.

Socrates, for whom only the lover of wisdom really experienced pleasure unmixed with pain, claimed that the democratic soul half-intentionally papered over its secret longing for tyranny with a superficially feminine and juvenile appreciation of the kind of meaningless diversity and interchangeability of, say, fashion. (Intentionally or not, this grave judgment echoes throughout both *Zoolander* and *Glamorama*.) Oriented away from the love of wisdom, and the anchored preparedness of heart that would sustain the possibility of receiving it, Socrates sees the democratic soul "feasting on crumbs" of diluted and transient pleasure.[1] Because the pleasures sought by those unawakened to the love of wisdom are all fated to come into being and pass away, much faster than any mortal would hope, they are, for Socrates, inherently sadomasochistic, always mixed with pain. But for us, the paradox of S&M in a not-just-sexual sense can't consume our lives the way it did for the most uninhibited aristocrats. They didn't confront the paradox of feasting on crumbs in the same way we must.* And so, while someone trying to sustain an aristocratic moral framework sees feasting with panthers as an all-out assault on sacred and social order,[2] Tocqueville is, again, more forbearing. "Not that equality of conditions could ever make man chaste," he wryly suggests,

> but it gives the irregularity of his morals a less dangerous character. As no man any longer has leisure or opportunity to attack the virtue of those who wish to defend themselves, there are at the same time a great number of courtesans and a great many hon-

---

*When aristocrats "turn exclusively to sensual pleasures they usually force into that one direction all the energy accumulated by long experience of power," demanding "sumptuous depravity and startling corruption." While the grander the aristocracy was, the harder it will fall into depravity, "love of physical pleasures never leads democratic peoples to such excesses." See Alexis de Tocqueville, *Democracy in America*, ed. J. P. Mayer, trans. George Lawrence (New York: Harper, 2006), 533.

est women. Such a state of affairs leads to deplorable individual wretchedness, but it does not prevent the body social from being strong and alert; it does not break up families and does not weaken national morality.[3]

Whereas much of what Tocqueville says cuts against the instinctive grain of the progressive mind, now it's conservatives' turn to object. Surely the sexual revolution and the culture war have debunked Tocqueville's gentle view of the perils of licentiousness? In fact, Tocqueville would whisper—to those with ears to hear—that the explosion of sexual appetites in our democratic age betokened a collapse in *pride* more than a collapse in *virtue*.* As a matter of sheer

---

*Alasdair MacIntyre, following Rieff's lead, described our age as playing out *After Virtue* (Notre Dame, IN: University of Notre Dame Press, 1981). Tocqueville admits the difficulty in maintaining morals of any type in the absence of pride; the second volume of *Democracy in America* could almost be called *After Pride*. But his corrective to our cultural reactionaries stems from the idea that no moral awakening can occur without a reorientation toward the pride that arises only from reckoning with the irreducible I that is found in the anchoring of one's heart. Many conservatives blame what they see as a revolutionary new culture of *egoism* for our selfish and melodramatic craziness. But that "passionate and exaggerated love of self" is "a vice as old as the world," and not our special, constitutive problem; "individualism," defining our new era, "is based on misguided judgment rather than depraved feeling. It is due more to inadequate understanding than to perversity of heart" (Tocqueville, *Democracy*, 506). The complicated and intense sexual "feels" burdening our heart today are less the product of an *impurity of the will* than an *illusion of the mind*. We are pushed into *what looks* like proud sexual egoism by *what's really* a miscalculation that we lack a rational basis for pride in ourselves. As we'll see in the next chapter, the way to constructively cope with this lie that our rational minds create under the pressure of everyday life is found through experiencing relationships of face-to-face forbearance.

logic, our thirst for well-being and physical comfort combines with our disenchanted view of our and others' insignificance to hurl us into sex as the last bastion of ultimate meaning accessible immediately—without mediation— through direct personal experience. Sex is just *one way* that we throw ourselves with such "strange melancholy" into our sense of *both* superficial "abundance" *and* of deeper "disgust with life" that characteristically grip us in such deceptively "calm and easy circumstances."[4] Crazily trapped in our ping-ponging between the frenzy of others and the isolation of inward brooding, when it comes to sex, we alternate unstably between desiring the dirty, dangerous den of panthers and desiring the all-too-clean and safe teddy-bear household that we glimpsed in the last chapter (and are about to see in more detail). Even when we find ourselves living closer to panthers than teddys, we oscillate between enchantment and revulsion in sex no less than in other realms of life, struggling just as much, and for the same reasons, to find a stable mooring. But it's especially through sex that we're brought face to face with one another, and with ourselves, stripped bare—in the delicious sense of immediacy, intimacy, and honesty, yes, but also in the nauseating sense of interchangeability, disposability, and banality.* Sure enough, the recipe for craziness repeated throughout everyday life is brought to a climax sexually.

And if our sex lives are crazy, Tocqueville counsels, our social lives will be as well—to a degree that can turn the whole character of our society upside down.

---

*Have a look at Marcel Duchamp's *The Bride Stripped Bare by Her Bachelors, Even.*

Whereas most moralists emphasize the transgressive sources of de-moralization, the logic of the Great Transition tells us that the overt behavior of the more sexually active is less determinative of our developing future than the covert behavior of the more sexually passive. The art of being free requires spirit, morale, a measure of pride: all things diminished more by the sexless life of the teddy-bear household than by libidinous excess. This should send a shiver of recognition through anyone who has experienced the frightening moment in a relationship when both sexual partners realize they have, as we say, let themselves go. It's much, much easier to say fuck it and give up on erotic life than it is to say fuck it to everyday life and disappear fully into the erotic.

Unlike many contemporary critics of our sexual culture, Tocqueville has no illusions about the supposedly virtuous home life that promises to calm and control our sexual passions. We know the ideal: Husband and wife are older but hardly seem to be aging. They've got "great" kids, "great" bodies, "great" amenities, and "great" taste in furnishings and food. They might have a great drawer of erotic aids too. But they play it as healthy as they do safe. Rather than focusing only on the crazy extent of our outwardness in sexual matters, Tocqueville asks us to attend to the secrets contained in our all-too-docile sexual inwardness. The perfect nuclear family home is far too easily romanticized. Tocqueville grasped how well a family could function as a little world unto itself—all too well. He marveled at the way a pioneer husband, wife, and kids could survive in tranquility out in the literal middle of nowhere. He considered silence, repose, and fertility to be naturally intertwined, restorative qualities of life and associated them far more with the female sex than the male. Gazing into the future, however, he also saw a perversely self-sterilized way of life wherein men and women alike retreated so far into their own petty cares that the nuclear family became a lazy, indulgent, isolated, and soulless way to play house.*

So when it comes to sex, even if we say fuck it, we're screwed from two directions. If sex isn't driven enough by what we, unlike Tocqueville, are too used to calling "family values," it will become a site of competition so pleasurable and painful that it will first turn us into maniacs and then turn us loose on society at large. But if we're using sex as a means of pursuing the perfect home, the perfect kids, and the perfect lifestyle, it will disappear into the "moral kitsch" of Bobos and teddy bears. Few of us are complete strangers to that kind of masturbatory tear-jerking, which now shows up at the emotional core of movie after movie and advertisement after advertisement. Today, even once-dangerously scandalous forms of sexual entertainment are morally kitsched up. For women, we have everything from bad *Sex and the City* sequels to all-too-tame sex toy parties. For

---

*As is well known, these perils are not confined to two-person heterosexual households. No matter which performance of pride we indulge in, our preference and identities are subsumed in the experience of sex losing its grace or charisma with frightening swiftness. Or perhaps we somehow inherited our disenchanted hearts: "When I was young, I dreamt of a passionate obligation to a roommate," as Father John Misty faux-ironically sings in his teddy-bear household nightmare "Bored in the U.S.A.," the lead single and opening track off of—yes—*I Love You, Honeybear* (2015).

men, we sell prescription drugs that promise spontaneous sex after magic moments such as a last glass of wine, a
candlelight dinner, or (apparently) a dip in some his-and-
hers bathtubs. We are just a few innovations away from
Saturday Night Live's classic "Love Toilet" sketch, which
pitched the conjoined commodes "designed for two people
who love spending time together." When moral kitsch hi-
jacks sex, sex becomes just another tastefully flavorless fea-
ture of the tame and toothless narcissism we pump up with
sentimentality to shore up our self-esteem.

The current cavalcade of popular articles fretting over
these issues confirms that sex will remain a public obsession, not just a private one, even if the boundaries between
public and private continue to erode or blur through endless, faulty drawing and redrawing. Therapists will cash
in. Experts will blur the line between news, science, medicine, and hype. Real and phony charismatics will promise
to sort out sex lives that don't work for us. Yet the burden
for productive yet restorative sexual relationships will continue to fall on us, as individuals and couples. If we just say
fuck it, trying to hide from that challenge in the panther's
den or the teddy-bear suite, our human predicament will
only worsen.

Note: were we true egomaniacs, we'd be much better at
stubbornly indulging in either panther or teddy-bear life.
Our problem is subtly different, as we're about to see. Much
as the death of fun we considered in the last chapter gives
us an anxiety-inducing foretaste of our own death, a sane
view of sex issues a related kind of wake-up call about our
mortality. And as we'll discover as this book nears its end,
the better we are at dealing with craziness around *la petite*

mort, the better we'll be at dealing with the craziest of all life's aspects: the big death.*

CIRCLE JERKS

To get to that eventual link between sex and death, we have to think back to play. Obviously sex can be playful beyond the usual measure of entertainment, and in play, Tocqueville sees us make choices that reveal huge insights about the human condition. Recall that when it comes to money, we tend to shuttle between two ways of life; at home, we hunker down, and outside, we forge ahead. Play promises us a way to break out of that back-and-forth. But Tocqueville sees something else happen time and again. In our effort to stop cycling between an insanity that pulls us inward and one that pushes us outward, we just end up changing the *site* of our oscillations from work to play. To chill out about money, we wind up oscillating between two suspiciously similar patterns of life: playing with ourselves and playing with other people.

Stop me if you've heard these analogies before.

Actually, don't—Tocqueville's going to extend them. Recall further that sometimes we can find fleeting moments of rest and relaxation, within the home or without, but too often those moments segue us helplessly back into the chaos we struggle to keep at bay in our workaday lives. When we're alone, Netflix and smartphone binges give us a chance

---

*"The future can't be real, I barely know how long a moment is," Misty goes on, "unless we're naked getting high on the mattress, while the global market crashes."

at play that's safe from the craziness of other (real-life) people. And when we venture out into the world, team sports and infotainment and the other competitive fields of professional play entertain and divert us in ways that typically make us feel much less lonely. But ultimately, isolated and social entertainments have something important in common: "The constant recurrence of the same passion is monotonous; so, too, are the details of the methods used to satisfy it."[5] If you're not already, imagine Tocqueville is saying that about sex. What goes for play goes for sex as well, because the overarching obsessions baked into our reality are the same in both realms. Chasing us down to the ends of our sex organs, our quest for unity is apt to lead, by merely mortal means, only to uniformity.

Sadly, we're half-aware of the mistake we're making. If you've glanced at a grocery store magazine rack lately, you already know that one of our biggest sex-related fears is the fear of uniformity. Nothing is a bigger turn-off than the use of monotonous methods in an effort to satisfy—or merely sharpen—a dulled passion. And little is more terrifying—in our historically easy times—than being absolutely stuck as a person whose sex life is definitively limited by that kind of failure. Adding to the fear factor, we recognize that our sex lives are always in danger of ceasing to entertain or even divert us, thanks to the craziness of everyday life. Our fevered existence is consumed by ubiquitous competition, constant commerce, and low-grade pleasure-seeking on a massive scale. All of this creates a steady drumbeat of uninspiring, routine activity. Our longings for that special something more—which is often what sex promises—go increasingly unfulfilled. "Society is tranquil, but the reason for that is not that it knows its strength and good fortune, but rather that it thinks itself weak and feeble," Tocqueville reports; "men have desires, regrets, sorrows, and joys which produce no visible or durable result, like old men's passions ending in impotence."[6]

Surprised that a nineteenth-century French aristocrat reaches for an analogy straight out of a Viagra commercial? Don't be. Tocqueville isn't as obvious about it as the silver fox in the TV ad who pours a gushing, gurgling bottle of water into the busted radiator on his classic car. But he knows sex distills our crazy condition of frantically joining competitive projects that screw with us because of how much they make us conform. At every site of everyday life, our rational minds tell us to press ahead, even though we feel so deeply that it's crazy to do so. And because our lives are ruled by oscillations between inwardness and outwardness, we can't even seek refuge in the sensation of saying fuck it and fatalistically pursuing one single-minded course. We chase our tails and we run in circles—even when we're alone, and even when our sex partners are virtual or imagined.

You could even say we jerk in circles.

Yes, one of the crudest and most effective terms we use to describe a self-indulgent waste of time is the so-called circle jerk, where a group of people, usually metaphorically speaking, get together to do little more than watch each other pleasure themselves. This practice may seem far removed from the genteel aristocracy that hung on in Tocqueville's France, but, as we'll see, although *Democracy* stays PG-13, Tocqueville is well acquainted with the idle perversion and debauched abandon of the European aristocrats.

Even more important, he understood that, in a time like ours, the democratic citizen's taste for sexual pleasure wouldn't at all mirror that of the decadent nobility. The madness we Americans would plunge into, he imagined, just wouldn't measure up to the gilded barbarism of a Marquis de Sade. We have too many ordinary cares on our mind. We have no taste for following abstract ideas to absurd and all-consuming lengths. Perhaps above all, we lack the free time and the big budgets necessary to, say, descend utterly into the shadowy world implied by Stanley Kubrick's *Eyes Wide Shut* (1999).* In that film, even the highly educated, upper-middle-class couple played by Tom Cruise and Nicole Kidman are interlopers at best in that terrifying realm—and unwelcome invaders at worst. That's as apt a metaphor as any for Tocqueville's view of our sexual future. Rather than being initiated into secret circles of untold transgression, we'd more likely wind up in a metaphorical circle jerk—fruitlessly, reflexively seeking sexual pleasure as a way to evade isolation.

Indeed, Tocqueville would be scandalized, but not confused, by today's massive masturbation industry. Rather than criticizing internet pornography from the standpoint

---

*A few years ago here in Los Angeles a secret and very shadowy private sex club, Sanctum, was formed. What started with a cryptic and vaguely Illuminati-esque logo, wheat-pasted on locations like the Beverly Hills Ralphs, has continued with a string of favorable eyewitness write-ups in major publications, a consumer-facing name change ("Snctm"), and other going-legit moves like a daytime pool party. As founder Damon Lawner now maintains, "the Snctm experience is not about sex. It's about the openness, acceptance and freedom we give ourselves and each other here that is transformational." (See his "Founder Manifesto No. 2," April 26, 2016, https://www.snctm.com/2016/04/26/founder-manifesto-no2 /.) Money talks.

of a moral scold, however, he'd reiterate his great theme: "The human idea of unity is almost always sterile, but that of God is immensely fruitful. Men think they prove their greatness by simplifying the means. God's object is simple but His means infinitely various."[7] That is, equality captures our imaginations as the one path to unity without which we're meaningless and alone, but equality also breeds a sense of personal insignificance that aggravates our passions even as we find it harder than ever to secure more than a fleeting release. In the Great Transition the watchword of our sexual lives is one we're (too) familiar with from Facebook: "It's complicated." During the transitional period in which we live, we can collectively remember our society's great feats and sudden renown amid the collapse of aristocratic impediments to achievement, but as we look around, we realize that secret impediments have arisen in their place—the competition of all against all, which today, as we well know, reaches its fever pitch when sex is involved. Sex with yourself, and someone else's image, offers a sterile relief.

GRIN AND BEAR IT

But it's only fleeting. In fact, even sex with a flesh-and-blood person doesn't last that long. Our selfish and melodramatic replacement for pride in an anchored heart enviously mutters to our hovering, haunted hearts that our status as desired creatures is in doubt, in peril, in need of the kind of affirmation that only comes, as is characteristic, from direct, unmediated experience. We begin to sense how barren and futile passion can be, as more of us are becoming interchangeably equal. Whether we're having a lot of sex or a little, whether we're living the dream or just watching *The Bachelor*, we can quickly become disillusioned and jaded when it comes to the relentless routine of racking up sexual conquests. But instead of plunging into bottomless misery or endless cheer, we oscillate between the poles of despair and enthusiasm. As many an internet think piece can attest, online dating is the latest outlet for such a manic-depressive experience, where the good news and the bad news are virtually identical: an endless cycle of new prospects is just a click or a swipe away—just as easily passed over as you are.

And so the temptation to retreat into the teddy-bear household returns, bolstered by the logic of equality. As it becomes stronger and more ubiquitous, the frenetic pace of our oscillations could gradually wear us out, and eventually the circle jerks, real and virtual, could cease. Think of Japan's brisk sales in body pillows with human features, or life-sized doll girlfriends, or aids like the virtual-companion smartphone game called *Love Plus*. That app, as Rachel Lowry noted for *Time*, grew popular among "thirty-somethings who have accepted living alone instead of looking for love. They share a common yearning for connection and found it on a touch screen. Many see it as just a game and can easily distinguish between the computerized and reality, while others are perpetually stuck in a love loop, desperately waiting for the next update of the game."[8] Somewhere between a soft bigotry of low expectations for the Japanese people and a chorus of whistling past the erotic graveyard, some of our smarter and deeper observers and creators of culture have warned that we Americans are disposed toward living out an even more disenchanted and unimaginative version of this egalitarian dystopia than Japan's. In Charlie Kaufman's painstakingly executed puppet film *Anomalisa* (2015), Michael, a traveling motivational speaker specializing in corporate sales, is afflicted with something like the so-called Fregoli delusion—"a rare psychiatric disorder," Zadie Smith explains,

> in which a person believes that many different people are in fact a single person. But a narrowly neurological interpretation of *Anomalisa* (i.e., the trouble with Michael is he has a brain lesion) can't account, I don't think, for the profound identification the viewer feels with Michael's experience, or the strong part desire plays in the scheme of his suffering. Weariness pervades everything he says and does, the simplest human interactions elicit sighs and groans, and yet this weariness of the world includes his own part within it; or, to put it another way, whatever is driving all the phenomena of the world surges up through Michael, too, taking the form, in him, of a kind of blind striving, a relentless desire for something, which, the moment it is achieved, is already exhausted.[9]

Watching this film very late, in a mostly empty highbrow theater in Hollywood, I was unnerved by the way the crippling awkwardness and alienation we so readily consume as news about Japanese people—about *the safely other*— oozed from every pore of *Anomalisa*, a film so aggressively American that it's set in Cincinnati circa 2005. It struck me

198 · The Art of Being Free

that Kaufman was hitting the audience over the head with this when he had his protagonist half-accidentally pick up a clockwork Japanese sex doll as a gift to bring back to his son. At film's end,

> Michael returns home to find his wife Donna throwing him a surprise party. The surprise is he knows nobody and they're all the same person. His son grabs his present, the Japanese sex toy. It starts singing. A liquid oozes from it. Donna asks Michael if it's semen. But Michael does not find that an important line of inquiry. Instead he turns to his wife: "Who are you Donna? Who are you really?" . . . Our final vision of Michael is of a man stuck in the middle of a party of nobodies—all with the same face—who is choosing to focus on a singing doll leaking semen.

For Smith, the lens to view all this through is the German philosopher—and Nietzsche nemesis—Arthur Schopenhauer, who saw in ejaculate (her words) "a clear manifestation of the will, seeking only its own replication and continuance, without regard for what we, as individuals, may 'want.' "

Now, to be sure, Schopenhauer's gaze and Tocqueville's overlapped: the second edition of the former's magnum opus, *The World as Will and Representation*, arrived four years after the second volume of *Democracy*. But it's telling that Schopenhauer—like Hamlet, a rich and moody lapsed Protestant schooled in Germany and bitter about how easily his mother got over the death of his father—wrote a willfully disenchanted book called *The Art of Being Right*, not a playfully earnest one called *The Art of Being Free*. Recall (from our glimpse, last chapter, of the secret longings at play on the desert festival circuit) Tocqueville's awareness that the only sane response to the constitutive craziness of American life is to *cope with it*, teaching the scheming mind *forbearance*, not to try *curing it* by *purifying* the force of will.* While Schopenhauer's would-be solution to the problem of the tyranny of the will was to retreat into extreme teddy-bear bachelorhood, Tocqueville (like Nietzsche!) sees that as a nihilistic cop-out.† There's no doubt that we're apt to be tempted. But the abstract logic of equality faces a very concrete hurdle in the form of us real-life people. For us, the reality of an irreducible I persists even when our artificial illusion of a constructed self collapses. Even when we feel at our most interchangeably insignificant, we're

---

* "Christianity is not a dialectic that unconceals the true ground of the will's purity amid the wilderness of Judea—as it was from Luther to Nietzsche. Rather, following Pascal, Christianity is a training in self-interest rightly understood." Joshua Mitchell, *The Fragility of Freedom* (Chicago: University of Chicago Press, 1995), 190.

† "Schopenhauer, though a pessimist, *really*—played the flute. Every day, after dinner," Nietzsche groaned; "a pessimist, one who denies God and the world but *comes to a stop* before morality—who affirms morality and plays the flute—the *laude neminem* ['cultured man'] morality—what? is that really—a pessimist?" Friedrich Nietzsche, *Beyond Good and Evil* (New York: Vintage, 1989), sec. 186. Los Angeles is full of "cultured" pessimists endlessly redrawing blurry lines between pleasure and pain. Of a representative lust interest who "says, like literally, music is the air she breathes," Misty sings on *Honeybear*'s "The Night Josh Tillman Came to Our Apartment:" "Someone's been told too many times they're beyond their years, by every half-wit of distinction she keeps around. And now every insufferable convo features her patiently explaining the cosmos— of which she's in the middle." Schopenhauer's Germany had enough dangling aristocratic chains to support a teddy-bear morality of wholesome self-care. More and more of our America doesn't, Misty attests: "I obliged later on when you begged me to choke ya."

still stuck being an I. That's what keeps us oscillating inward and outward again—even when the rational mind and the seemingly inevitable dystopia it detects promise we'll wake up one morning turned into teddy bears.

Without doubt, sex is one realm of life where it's all too clear that "general apathy" is the "fruit of individualism."[10] But that also makes sex the canary in the coal mine of the logic of equality. And we're still way too early in the Great Transition to make it die of autoerotic asphyxiation.

AMERICAN BEASTS

Knowing us, then, maybe we'll freak out in the other direction and end up way more sexually extreme than Tocqueville could ever have imagined. Among the most consuming challenges of our time is to square our hunger for individuality with our fear of the isolation and anonymity that individuality so often brings. We badly want to accomplish that trick through sexual romantic relationships. And many of us still try to do so through marriage—which, after all, can wind up housing its own kind of fantasies about sexual utopia.*

As we know well, however, those fantasies are on the rocks. Many of us are beginning to think that serial failure sits at the intersection of sex and freedom. America's sexual culture is defined by marriage anxiety and its attendant mores and consequences. But the most important quality of

---

*For a teddy-bear household nightmare even more harrowing than Misty's, see Mark Z. Danielewski's *House of Leaves* (New York: Pantheon Books, 2000).

those consequences, from a Tocquevillean standpoint, can't be tabulated on anyone's ethical scorecard. Instead, it appears in the fabric of everyday life. Wherever we turn, we encounter the unhappiness and dysfunction that emanate from America's failed relationships, including—but not limited to—dissolved marital unions.

Strangely enough, the best place to start feeling out Tocqueville's approach to sexual extremes—and active, not passive, sexual failure—is in his analysis of America's bankruptcy laws. To his eyes, the way America deals with bankruptcy struck a resonant and telling contrast with the way debtors are handled in Europe. Tocqueville marveled that we show an "altogether singular indulgence" toward businesspeople who go bankrupt. Having made "a sort of virtue" out of "rash speculation," he reasoned, we Americans can hardly "stigmatize" those whose recklessness in commercial matters leads them to ruin.[11] Here's where it gets interesting. Keep in mind that for Tocqueville, something more fundamental than "the market" is at work in this economy of forgiveness. Equality creates a frenzy that pushes so many of us over the edge that we develop mores and institutions that favor a safety net. But the safety net doesn't *prevent* us from going broke. It allows it! The ability to go bankrupt is the ability to be free from fate, even when you bring massive debt obligations crashing down around you. And the feeling of fatedness, of the closure of our horizons, hits those delinked, lonely, and anxious individuals with an ultimate feeling of illness and madness. Bankruptcy laws, simply put, help keep us from going crazy.

Look around for similar frameworks outside of bankruptcy law, however, and you'll notice something remarkable. Despite an explosion of judicial activity surrounding family law, we pretty much lack a cultural apparatus for dealing with what one might call familial bankruptcy. To be sure, the courts—and the lawyers—are working overtime to arbitrate and litigate family disputes, but the outcomes of family law cases almost always involve tying members of broken families to one another, especially financially, long after the family structure that linked their fates has been destroyed. We Americans, who long for a lifetime supply of fresh starts, are routinely deprived of a fresh start in the most painful and intimate realm of personal troubles.

At the same time, of course, a real fresh start in the wake of a failed family arrangement requires more than a court, or even a culture, can afford. After all, completely severing links with (former) family members, especially children, can be a gut-wrenching and guilt-laden experience. This fact looms over everything. Compounding the anxiety, people know it in advance. We're afraid to embrace the most humiliating and diminishing aspects of equality, which include giving up on the idea that any of us has a strong claim to long-term—much less lifelong—intimacy. When things go wrong in the realm of sex, family, and romance, one current in our culture tells us to seek a complete break from the past, but another warns us to fear the isolation, insignificance, and irrelevance that may befall us if we go back, at this late date, to square one.

> They are vaguely conscious [Tocqueville says] of the possibility of a sudden and unexpected change in their condition. They are afraid of themselves, dread-

ing that, their taste having changed, they will come to regret not being able to drop what once had formed the object of their lust. And they are right to feel this fear, for in ages of democracy all things are unstable, but the most unstable of all is the human heart.*

This is why, on the one hand, Americans are continually stripping away the stigma from divorce, remarriage, cohabitation, out-of-wedlock birth, and so on—but on the other hand, the burdensome "drama" and "baggage" and "issues" dragged around by those who've been superficially forgiven their failures continue to accumulate. You don't have to strain to see a moral problem here, but, again, Tocqueville wants us to understand that the *constitutive* instability of our hearts is paramount in corroding our shared ability to produce (and reproduce) sanity.

As these dramas play out within the confines of the household, the panther rears its head. We only need a film like dad-angst touchstone *American Beauty* (1999) to remind us that our families today—like Hamlet's—offer too few internal supports and safety nets when the constitutive craziness of life imposes a greater burden than its softened mores, hovering hearts, and harried minds can withstand. Like Hamlet's, our crazily rational mechanisms for alternately manufacturing and surviving family drama turn sex into a dangerously therapeutic playground.†

---

*Tocqueville, *Democracy*, 582. This insight arises from Tocqueville's look at Americans' feelings about property!

†Just as the democratic age is way more theatrical than the aristocratic age, the theater is the most democratic literary art. "The pit often lays down the law for the boxes," as Tocqueville puts it; people like us "want

Tocqueville might say we're democratically updating Schopenhauer's Old World teddy-bear ethos of wholesomely nihilistic self-care. Goethe famously anticipated that ethos by fearing that one day "the world will have turned into one huge hospital where everyone is everybody else's humane nurse."[12] For plenty of analysts, that hospital turned out to be the state or society.[13] For Tocqueville, the truth is deeper: the hospital is actually in the heart, and our Hamletesque half-lunacy is taking over the asylum. *The instability of our hearts*, baked into our crazy age, is responsible for our sexual instability. What looks like ego-driven melodrama is actually a reaction to our lack of anchored hearts to anchor real pride.

Even as the aristocratic age began to crumble, the pride problem was apparent. Social disunity in aristocratic France was rooted in the sexual disunity that corrupt and disintegrating aristocracies made possible. "In Europe almost all the disorders of society are born around the domestic hearth and not far from the nuptial bed," says Tocqueville. "It is there that men come to feel scorn for natural ties and legitimate pleasures and develop a taste for disorder, restlessness of spirit, and instability of desires."[14] All of society is directly affected by the personal relations between the sexes: if "tumultuous passions" disturb the household, it even becomes

---

the talk to be about themselves and to see the present world mirrored. . . . On the stage they like to see the same medley of conditions, feelings, and opinions that occur in life. The drama becomes more striking, more vulgar, and more true"—in real life, too (Tocqueville, *Democracy*, 491). Our constitutive craziness *compels* us to desperately toy with each other—and ourselves.

"hard to submit to the authority of the state's legislators." Sexual disunity breeds social disunity; boundaries drawn and redrawn on the battlefields of the heart bleed over (as Robin Thicke can now attest) into the most public of blurred lines.

But for us, the idle delirium or maniacal excess of the decadent aristocrats is not at play or at work. Neither is the sexual drama that arises from courtly scheming, arranged marriages, rival bloodlines, and all the rest. *Our* individualism doesn't fuel egoism—it saps it, isolating people so much that they "withdraw into the little circle of family and friends," formed by each "to his taste." Their idiosyncratic preferences are subsumed to a "habit of thinking of themselves in isolation" until they are "shut up in the solitude" of their own hearts.[15] Selfishness and melodrama that initially *seem* like mere self-indulgent ego-tripping arise from something deeper and more secret: the logic of isolation and insignificance. Our imprisonment in our hovering hearts' halls of mirrors does not lead us straight to becoming little European teddy bears like Arthur Schopenhauer. We American beauties are apt, instead, to become American beasts.

Transitional and transactive as we are, the kind of beasts we're most likely to become are chimeras—part passive and domesticated, part predatory and wild. Call us Wilde heirs *teddy panthers*. While Goethe's vision, in its aristocratic innocence, is one of "professional kindness" elevated to an art, today's "hospital personnel" of the heart do not "care so professionally," as Rieff warns. "Consider each humane nurse, rather, as the crippled pet of some other. Then it is that 'the world stands like a dog, pleading to be played with,' each plea representing the equality and inclusiveness of relations and experiences."[16] Here you can catch a glimpse of the dark spot where sexual extremism and sexual failure meet in a race to the bottom. That pleading-dog quotation is from Nabokov,[17] an Old World expert in just how many excuses Americans can make for their strategic instabilities of the heart. To be fair to us, *Lolita*'s villainous Humbert and Quilty are artfully exaggerated sexual failures. But in our own beastly ways, we, too, are busy insinuating the habits of the isolated heart into the fabric of sex and family intimacy. That's because no matter how tempted we are to find a stable point of exhaustion in the imprisonment of the closed-up heart, our stronger lusts and longings still make us feel like our hovering hearts are cages that offer no rest and no repose.

Unfortunately for us, our misguided effort to escape the restless cage is akin to bungee jumping without remembering to tie the cord to something.

Instead of tethering our hearts before launching off into freedom, we opt to play beastly sexualized games with our shifting selves—grasping, manipulating, thrusting, and luring one another into relationships that are destined to be lost in the wilderness, because we hide and deny our fixed point within.

THE ART OF BEING I

Recall that one powerful name for that fixed point and anchored heart is the irreducible I—that is, the particular, mortal, flesh-and-blood being who we are, regardless of which self we pretend to be or try on.* Traditionally, the family was the first and in some ways ultimate place to discover and inhabit the irreducible I. Where now, in the contemporary American family, can we experience that inescapable identity? How, to put it bluntly, can we learn to be an I?

Sex complicates these questions considerably. Today, all too characteristically we learn to be a selfish *me*—something we can posture, pose, and manipulate to pursue always-fleeting satisfactions—rather than a selfless *I*—someone who has stopped trying to find *meaning* in illusory, fleeting selves and has focused on how to freely be the particular human being he or she permanently is.

The aristocratic age had its issues, but that wasn't one of them. In America, born and raised in the democratic age, the problem of *locating* the I in the family is baked in—a core source of our constitutive craziness. "In America, the family, if one takes the word in its roman and aristocratic sense, no longer exists." Aristocratic families are like any

---

* Philip Rieff, *Crisis of the Officer Class: Illustrations of the Aesthetics of Authority*, Vol. 2 of *Sacred Order / Social Order* (Charlottesville: University of Virginia Press, 2007), 7. For such a reactionary, Rieff recognized the irreducible I in the Romantic tradition that Americans love so well, no less than in the biblical one distilled in Galatians 2:20. And guess who he compares it against? "Marilyn (as all us good old boys of therapy must call her), when asked about her belief, said: 'I believe in everything, just a little.' Marilyn was the noblest therapeutic of them all. She was never entirely beguiled by those sophistries of sin that are testaments to therapy in L.A. Yet poor Marilyn was beguiled enough." Spend enough time in L.A. or its East Coast cognates, and a tear of recognition will come to your eye too: "Marilyn Monroe is the Oscar Wilde of our time. Both were sexual comedians; and, in their schooled denials of the faith instinct, ultimately unfunny. Two sad cases." Lest we forget: "faith is the only permanent state of mankind" (Tocqueville, *Democracy*, 297).

other aristocratic institution—hierarchical, meaning that "authority never addresses the whole of the governed directly."* In a family context, that means "the father is not only the political head of the family but also the instrument of tradition, the interpreter of custom, and the arbiter of mores. He is heard with deference, he is addressed always with respect, and the affection felt for him is ever mingled with fear." To locate the I in the aristocratic family, children need only look at the father, who is the model of the I the sons will become. (Yes, this is all very male-centered. Stay tuned.) In the democratic family, that's not possible. But the aristocratic I is not free in any sense we would recognize today. The only way for people in aristocratic life to be an I is for them to fill their particular lives with specific and unchanging roles inherited in an unbroken line over the course of countless generations. For the sons to honor and obey the fathers in keeping with the character of the aristocratic I, they had to subjugate their romantic preferences to the fathers' criteria for young women selected to carry on the family line. (Or they had to simply not form romantic preferences at all.) When the aristocratic authority of the father disappears, however, that very particular kind of filial sexual anxiety goes with it. The democratic son "has known in advance exactly when he will be his own master, and wins his liberty without haste or effort, as a possession which is his due and which no one seeks to snatch from him."[18] The fathers turn inward and enjoy their children, enabling once-fully inward mothers to rotate their

---

*Tocqueville, *Democracy*, 586. "In aristocracies society . . . only controls the sons through the father."

own gaze outward; and the sons, eyes on the horizon, seek what advantage they may among young women—who have also been loosed in a new way on society at large. It's on this new and more complex sexual landscape that we Americans now have to locate the I.

For Tocqueville, it was an unnerving but impressive environment. Though he well understood the democratic family as a logical extension of the end of aristocracy, he was astonished by the way sexual roles had already progressed and adapted. "I have often been surprised and almost frightened," he said, "to see the singular skill and happy audacity with which young American women contrive to steer their thoughts and language through the traps of sprightly conversation."[19] Translation: guys on the make want to put power moves on girls, reeling them in with macho talk and bravado; girls nimbly disarm them, then survey their achievements.

At first blush, that may seem to us like a pretty unoriginal observation—almost a stereotype of male-female relations—but the subtext tells us far more about sexual craziness in a democratic age. Amy Nicholson, the noted Tom Cruise expert, identifies the exact same dynamic at work in one of the pivotal scenes in *Magnolia* (1999). Cruise, playing self-help alpha-male sex guru Frank "T. J." Mackey, sets out to sexually dominate a TV reporter, Gwenovier, who's interviewing him. "He wants to charm her and her camera; she wants to coo and smile until he drops his guard. Their dynamic is the distillation of every stereotype in the battle of the sexes," Nicholson writes: "men using blunt chemistry to exert their power and women pretending to be impressed until they're ready to wrest control."[20]

But that's where things get real. Mackey goes utterly crazy in an effort to crack Gwenovier's controlled, coy demeanor, stripping down to bulging skivvies, busting out an impressive handstand, yelling at random about "Terrorists! Babes! Beauties!" Gwenovier "talks to him like a naughty little child," Nicholson recounts, "and he cheerfully responds. 'Yes, ma'am!' he chirps, buttoning his shirt as though he expects her to be proud of his fingers for moving so fast. Mackey mistakes her interest for flirting—which, in fairness, is probably part of her plan. Uncharmed, she subtly asserts her control by telling him that he missed a button."

In the film, Mackey's sexual madness and arrested maturity can be traced to his abandonment at a young age by his father (a trait shared by the real-life Cruise). Tocqueville leads us to believe that the collapse of the aristocratic family opens up the possibility of a similar pattern. Just as the collapse of aristocracy creates a sudden freedom that sours as competition erects invisible barriers to quick success, the end of the patriarchal family throws sons into a fresh predicament. Not only must they fend for themselves in sexual competition; they find it harder than ever to seal the deal once they've dispatched their male competitors. On top of it all, they can never ascend to the heights of authority and confidence embodied by the fathers, whose age of dominance has faded into the past.

No wonder they're crazy.

But the secret roots of that craziness flip the stereotypical male-female script. Start with the obvious: we "realize there must be a great deal of individual freedom" in a world where everyone is so equal; "youth will be impatient, tastes ill-restrained, customs fleeting, public opinion often un-settled or feeble, parental authority weak, and a husband's power contested." *For that reason*, we expose the teenage American girl to "the vices and dangers of society," so she "judges them without illusion and faces them without fear, . . . full of confidence in her own powers," a feeling "shared by all around her." Put simply: we train our girls in the art of being sexual—to avoid the worst extremes and the worst failures. *But we don't do this for the teenage Ameri-can boy.* "In America there is, in truth, no adolescence. At the close of boyhood he is a man and begins to trace out his own path."[21] This is why young women are still the effec-tive arbiters of morals in our society, so strongly organized around the preferences of women and children. And this is why some Americans wrongly think the burden falls on women to somehow *tame* Mackey-men. Rather, it's that the burden falls most heavily on individual women to locate their irreducible I well enough to quickly and effectively screen crazy guys out of their romantic lives. That's what happens sociologically when the psychological agenda of young men suddenly shifts—away from impressing their coldly imperious fathers and toward competing for young women against lots of interchangeably insignificant relative equals and a few superstar specimens. So far, so conven-tional.

Now: here's where we break loose completely from any link to stereotypes. As young men and women become steadily more similar, yet never identical, the burden of screening out crazies increasingly falls on *both* sexes in a way that's as ill-restrained, unsettled, feeble, weak, and con-tested as American life *must* be. Increasingly, *both* boys and girls need to seek sexual refuge in an irreducible I they can't recognize and pattern after because they aren't raised to do so. Increasingly, *both* sexes cross a sudden threshold where one minute they're precious children who must be sheltered from harm, and the next minute they're sex objects who must be played with and profited from.

All this spins out from the end of fathers as the authoritative, commanding link between children below them and hierarchical society above. As the father's identity changes, everyone else's in the family's does too. Children trying to anchor their hearts, in a way that gives them an I to be proud of, are thrown back on their own resources.

Amid the chaos, we struggle to see how the family can keep us *all* not only sane but *free*. But we don't have to fear learning from the family women Tocqueville saw supply sanity and freedom to Americans beset by the tumult of life in and outside the household. Our love of equality is not imperiled by the lessons they have to teach about how to anchor our hearts for the endless bungee jumps that await outside our front doors.

> When the American returns from the turmoil of politics to the bosom of the family, he immediately finds a perfect picture of order and peace. There all his pleasures are simple and natural and his joys innocent and quiet, and as the regularity of life brings him happiness, he easily forms the habit of regulating his opinions as well as his tastes. Whereas the European tries to escape his sorrows at home by troubling society, the American derives from his home that love of order which he carries over into [public].[22]

To be sure, this idyll excludes such nineteenth-century horrors as male drunkenness, physical abuse, and other corrupt habits persisting in the Great Transition. It also summons to our minds the mid-twentieth-century caricature of the Alpha Dad kicking back with slippers and pipe as the rest of the family revolves around him. But consider how the pattern Tocqueville identifies changes its tone when bearing in mind how similar the sexes are growing. American women "are often manly in their intelligence and in their energy" yet "usually preserve great delicacy of personal appearance"—much, today, like American men!* Today, we can *all* become more like sitcom dads . . . *and* moms . . . *and* kids. Yes, that's what makes it even harder to get clear on what specific irreducible I we are. But the increasing similarity of men and women turns out *not* to be a problem for finding the I in democratic sexual life. The crossing and recrossing of "traditional" gender roles is not what ails us— so long as that activity isn't adopted as another way to pursue our typically flawed longings in typically fruitless fashion. Our obsession with unity, for instance, can lead us to frantically embrace mere uniformity between the sexes— making us more interchangeable but failing to bring us into closer accord. Remember, that obsession is fueled by our disgust with the divided world of the aristocratic age that lingers like dangling chains. In that age, "birth and fortune often make a man and a woman such different creatures that they would never be able to unite with one

---

*Tocqueville, *Democracy*, 601. Of course, at the same time, it also increasingly *seems* like both men and women are getting less attentive to their looks. But whatever our class or fitness level, we're all actually increasingly focused on appearances, necessarily including our own.

another. Their passions draw them together, but social conditions and the thoughts that spring from them prevent them from uniting in a permanent and open way. The necessary result of that is a great number of ephemeral and clandestine connections"—the powdered-wig equivalent of hookups, booty calls, and date rapes. In a dark irony, "although a European may often make himself a woman's slave, one feels that he never sincerely thinks her his equal."[23] We, by contrast, offer one another a lot less debasement and a lot more respect. The lingering inequalities of respect that do lurk today shouldn't obscure the reality that a shared experience of human equality defines sexual relations from a very early age. But Tocqueville would object to the relentless push for equal *lifestyles* among men and women—*not* because he believes women were created by God or by Nature to remain beside the hearth but because of the false hope and hollow disappointment that will invade the haven of the home whenever people try to anchor their hearts in any allegedly all-encompassing way of life.*

For us, comprehensive doctrines fail us amid reality's crazy complexity. The exhaustive exhausts us. The regular, by contrast, sanely shores us up, giving us the breathers we need to reasonably recognize ourselves as the specific individuals we are. Trying to make selfhood into the latest and greatest of comprehensive doctrines screws us twice over.

---

*Hopefully this book does not arouse the same kind of bipartisan but hostile ideological bewilderment as Christopher Lasch's fairly Tocquevillean critique of what has happened to intimacy, *Haven in a Heartless World: The Family Besieged* (New York: Basic Books, 1977).

KICKSTART MY HEART

Today, Tocqueville would suspect that *any* individual man or woman would quickly be overwhelmed by the tasks of work, play, and romance—all of which require us to conform to uniform standards of competition with relative equals, and all of which we take on feeling ever more isolated and alone. "The disturbed and constantly harassed life which equality makes men lead, not only diverts their attention from lovemaking by depriving them of leisure for its pursuit, but also turns them away by a more secret but more certain path."[24] Short on leisure and long on wounded isolation, we anxiously seek the same kind of shortcuts in romantic and erotic life that we do in every other sphere of work and play. That's why there's such a robust market for short, direct, repetitive guides to hot sex and relationship quick fixes—easy-to-master programs that will presumably work for anyone and everyone. Those are the same kinds of guides we seek no matter what we're trying to accomplish. Sex is no exception; or, rather, it's exceptional in a different way. Everyone wants it, but so many of us have such a hard time fitting it into the kind of life we all crave: the "type of deep, regular, and peaceful affection which makes life happy and secure." The drama and suffering that infuse our get-sex-quick schemes unleash so many of the "violent and capricious emotions which disturb life"— and even "cut it short"—that we're left feeling more helpless and isolated than ever.[25]

This is how we're brought once again to confront the basic fact that no one can have it all, no matter how much or how often the boundaries of roles and duties are negotiated, fought over, and redrawn. This limitation—just where we'd expect to triumph over barriers—drives us crazy. We can't resign ourselves to it, but we can't seem to use progress (not even technological progress) to get past it.* Although the better-off among us would probably scoff at this idea, since they believe they can buy their way out of most problems, for many Americans, including those facing hard landings into adulthood today, Tocqueville's suspicion is a prophetic one.†

So what can we do in the family to help ensure sex doesn't destroy our access to our I? Very few of us today are willing to say we'd be better off as a rule if women focus on

---

* "Is this the part where I get all I ever wanted? Who said that?" Father John Misty asks in *Honeybear's* "Bored in the U.S.A." "Can I get my money back?"

† There is a lot—a *lot*—of denial going around about how stable the hearts and fortunes of upwardly mobile assortative maters might be. The idea that the elites are pulling away, proving that inequality matters far more than equality, may flatter our fears about the dark magic of money, but it doesn't hold up to the kind of scrutiny an inquiry into American sex provides. In a noted *New York Times* article, Claire Cain Miller and Quoctrung Bui spotlit "Alena Taylor, 28, a management consultant [who] earns 40 percent more than her husband, Matt, 31, a nonprofit executive." Mr. Taylor's assessment of the situation? "It has felt like a nonissue." But what about Mrs. Taylor? "Because my earnings potential is much higher than his, over time we'll have to figure that out," she told the *Times*. "They said they knew that conflict could arise over their division of labor when they have children, including because she travels more and he has greater flexibility." Speaking from experience: this is not the kind of conflict that some economist could resolve. The division of labor is merely the tip of the iceberg, beneath which vast and shadowy secret divisions within the heart collide. But rather than pressing on this most pressing of points—especially assuming even the smallest reverberation of competitive churn that defines the American economy at all working levels—the authors scooted past it to reaffirm their theme. Claire Cain Miller and Quoctrung Bui, "Equality in Marriages Grows, and So Does Class Divide," *New York Times*, February 27, 2016.

mastering the "domestic economy." In part, that's because of our changing views on religion (and this goes beyond our changing views on Christianity). Although we often connect the culture of "homemaking" to the narrow, inherited views on gender long associated with devout Christianity, Tocqueville would make a broader, subtler, and more potent point. Certainly, he concedes, the age of transition is so forceful and dynamic that "religion is often powerless to restrain men in the midst of" the "innumerable temptations which fortune offers" amid competition among relative equals. "It cannot moderate their eagerness to enrich themselves, which everything contributes to," but—and here's the kicker—"it reigns supreme in the souls of women, and it is women who shape mores."[26] Now, don't worry, I said religion is *almost* the only stable point to anchor the heart. But we do need to deal with Tocqueville's claim that women find the I in the practice of crafting morality at home through religion.

Many of us would almost reflexively deny that this is true any longer, but few of us have calmed down enough to slowly reflect on what consequences and opportunities would flow if it *were* true—but is no longer. Consider the logic carefully: if women more or less suddenly cease to be the guardians of mores, because they've progressively abandoned any religious belief capable of supplying everyone with access to a sane, peaceful, and fruitful personal life, then society really will require a powerful revolution to replace what's missing.

And sure enough: since World War II we've tried out a number of revolutionary changes that might do the trick. We moved the work of most men far outside the home. We sent women to work, often at a similar commuting distance.

We used science and art to create a culture where not only was sex increasingly delinked from reproduction but sexual opportunity was increasingly delinked from emotional intimacy. We haven't just changed our sexual mores; we've used those changes to fundamentally alter the way we think about economics, education, entertainment, and culture. They've even affected the way we think about religion. As a result, we've seen remarkable gains in personal autonomy, and we've even significantly reduced some once-familiar ways of acting out craziness—like domestic abuse—that can flourish in the shadows of traditional mores.

It's important to recognize that these things have happened because we've been trying, so hard and for so long, to *replace and improve on* the authoritarian patriarchy and the moralistic matriarchy we inherited in crumbling form from the aristocratic age. So it's even more important to concede that, despite our half-crazy dedication to these sweeping and rationalistic projects, we're *still* deeply dissatisfied, disillusioned, and dismayed, and we're beginning to grasp that yet another barrier has arisen precisely where we expected a triumph. Despite all the progress—despite a rather grim sense that we have no choice but to pursue apparent progress at almost any cost—we still don't feel sane, peaceful, and fruitful. We feel dogged by the same grinding madness and dizzying oscillations that Tocqueville first described almost two hundred years ago. We might have beaten the cult of domesticity, but no cult of progress will strike at the heart of what's really driving us over the edge.

Here's where a more inclusive and radical restatement of finding the I comes in. One reason for our frustration is our crazy misunderstanding of what being free is. Americans don't wish to submit unless they feel it's absolutely necessary to their survival. We run ourselves into the ground, and only then crawl into rehab. We style ourselves as autonomous masters of our own choices, but cry out constantly to our elites for more credit, benefits, subsidies, tax breaks, health care, and complete security from enemies, criminals, and disturbed freaks. We often feel the same way about religion. Often only a complete meltdown (a lengthy prison sentence, a near-death experience, an utter collapse in our fortunes) drives us into the arms of an ancient religious creed. As Mötley Crüe reminds us in "Kickstart My Heart," we crave that all-consuming, life-changing, breakthrough "conversion experience."* But even that desire papers over a deeper, secret truth we are loathe to admit! *Only when we are pushed by exhaustion to the point of collapse do we let ourselves become available to the insight into who we really are that true passivity brings.* Characteristically, too skeptical and too anxious about the nature of this reckoning, we half-choose to just go crazier instead. We resist what Tocqueville teaches at every point: if we're to be free in our world, we must *submit in our heart* to that reckoning—because only with an anchored heart can we *be* an I where the practice of freely being can *happen*.

---

*"The second single off of the band's fifth album *Dr. Feelgood*," notes NC-Fan1231 at Genius.com, "Mötley Crüe's bassist Nikki Sixx wrote this song after an accidental heroin overdose in 1987. He was declared clinically dead before being revived by two adrenaline shots to the heart. . . . To that end, Sixx uses this song to describe his new methods of attaining the intense experiences he craves as he is trying to remain sober after the OD." In a crucial twist important to our next chapter, "the EMT who administered both shots was a Mötley Crüe fan and after the first shot did not work and Sixx was essentially dead, the EMT decided on a second one which ultimately revived him and saved his life."

This is why, from a Tocquevillean standpoint, sanity and shelter are far more important for men and women than upward mobility, social prestige, or any of the other measuring sticks that often control our behavior in public life. Without sane shelter, we're too badly exposed in our sexual environment to experiencing life as a selfish me, not a selfless I. It's true that *one way* to help ensure that we don't all go crazy is for wives and mothers to focus with singular discipline on anchoring hearts by ordering domestic space sustainably. By Tocqueville's lights, however, that option is best seen as an approach that arose because it squared with the realities of life at the time. Our anthropology isn't infinitely plastic, so we shouldn't expect our sexual mores to be either. But any replacement for moral maternalism that preserves the art of being free must arise from the real-life experience of our own time.*

At last we can look at what that replacement could actually be. Somehow, we need the same combination of creativity, confidence, sanity, and collective action that once showed up by routine in the faithful, morally matriarchal home. Amid the prisons hidden within our shifting halls of mirrors, we cry out for people, in and out of our families, capable of leading—and *loving*—us out of the labyrinth.

---

*Confronted with a socioeconomic situation that had become extraordinarily unfavorable and even hostile to women, moral maternalists of the early 1900s pursued through policy what Julia Lathrop called an effort "to create a family that can do things for itself." See Ross Douthat and Reihan Salam, *Grand New Party* (New York: Doubleday, 2008), 25. One of this book's animating ideas is that political questions of this kind can only be properly asked and answered once we have reopened our hearts to the art of being free.

Death

There once was a rich man—ridiculously rich, ridiculously good-looking—who turned his back on the black magic of money. Instead of ushering the dark ages back in, monstrously transforming their falsified premise of caste inequality into something unnaturally true, he spent his wealth in secret, in silence, on the unrequited defense of all. Blacking out his identity, he became master of his pride, pursuing justice in a state of renunciation so complete that he earned, in some cosmic sense, the moral right to his inherited wealth. Or perhaps that right had to be earned and re-earned each day, until his inevitable, final defeat. Either way, instead of a folk villain, the man is a folk hero, beloved by millions, his legend greater than the philanthropist-barons of yore and the tech titans of today.

His name?

Bruce Wayne.

THE SUM OF ALL FEARS

Bruce creates Batman because he fears death, and so fears its symbols, the most. But why, as Socrates once asked, fear death at all? Why fear the dark and the night, the pit and the bat? Death, says Socrates, merely ends our current powers in a way that leads to, well, we can't know what.

This ancient wisdom feeds neatly into the fearless aristocratic ethos. Having satisfied the "universal, natural, and instinctive human taste for comfort . . . without trouble or anxiety," aristocrats can "show a haughty contempt for the physical comforts they are actually enjoying and show singular powers of endurance when ultimately deprived of them." The peons of an aristocratic age follow suit: "Where an aristocracy dominates society, the people finally get used to their poverty just as the rich do to their opulence. The latter are not preoccupied with physical comfort, enjoying it without trouble; the former do not think about it at all because they despair of getting it and because they do not know enough about it to want it." But in America, our imaginations will continuously "snatch in anticipation good things that fate obstinately refused" us so far. In the dark ages, ironically, people "seem serene and often have a jovial disposition," while people today seem "serious and almost sad even in their pleasures."

> Americans cleave to the things of this world as if assured that they will never die, and yet are in such a rush to snatch any that come within their reach, as if expecting to stop living before they have relished them.

The Great Transition transitions us away from being at peace about death. A person today is practically at war with it.

> Remembrance of the shortness of life continually goads him on. Apart from the goods he has, he thinks of a thousand others which death will prevent him from tasting if he does not hurry. This thought fills him with distress, fear, and regret and keeps his mind continually in agitation, so that he is always changing his plans and his abode.[1]

In an aristocratic age, the great inequalities of caste that persisted for century after century reinforced the reality that human beings are just part of the natural world's great hierarchy. Death occurred to people as natural because they viewed the nature of people as both human and animal. Our human hearts and minds strive far beyond the animals'; yet, like the animals, we are born to die. This is not an agonizing, insulting paradox. "The short space of sixty years can never shut in the whole of man's imagination; the incomplete joys of this world will never satisfy his heart."[2] But in an aristocratic age, people bear that fact as one of many of life's natural sufferings, eventually to end. Death may not always be welcomed, but it is not seen as an adversary.

For us, by contrast, death is an unwelcome and inescapable reminder that our natural, animal bodies are forever pulling us away from our human wants and wishes. It pushes us toward the unhappy realization that our habits of living are constitutively at odds with our nature—and that since we can't seek full satisfaction in the solace of

natural life, we have little choice but to grapple with supernatural questions that themselves hinder our fugitive, fleeting enjoyment of the world. Contemplating our mortality
also leads us to contemplate time, and contemplating
time leads us to contemplate the fleeting character of all
things—ourselves included. We don't just die; we die too
soon. *Untimely* death threatens our pride as much as our
petty enjoyments. "Like our years upon the earth, the powers of society are all more or less transitory; they follow
one another quickly, like the various cares of life," today's
greatness and meanness alike becoming yesterday's equally
forgotten memories.[3] These realizations erode what's left of
the pride we had inherited from the aristocratic age—pride
not in any one person in particular, but in the greatness of
which humanity is capable.

Since the earliest years of Christianity, mortal pride in
earthly greatness has not been viewed as a virtue. Of course,
Christianity is not alone among creeds in counseling that
the path to salvation or enlightenment is to be found in the
sacrifice of our pride—not just in ourselves but in humanity itself. But Tocqueville has a subtler view. Our new age
presents new problems. Though "religious nations have often accomplished such lasting achievements" because "in
thinking of the other world, they had found out the great
secret of success in this"—namely, "a general habit of behav-
ing with the future in view"—in our time, our disconnection from experiences, memories, and exemplars of greatness
exacerbates our tendency to think of the future, so to speak,
as just one more false myth passed down by a naive and
outmoded age. "No power on earth can prevent increasing
inequality from turning men's minds to look for the useful

or disposing each citizen to get wrapped up in himself." Though some of us still look ahead to "rewards in the next world," our habits of mind, in the prison of the moment, "have grown accustomed not to think about what will happen after their life"; it is all too easy for us to "fall back into a complete and brutish indifference about the future," seeing ourselves as just as meaninglessly transient as everything around us. Our fear of our own death drives us to seek refuge in the death of the future: once people "despair of living forever, they are inclined to act as if they could not live for more than a day."

> For as their ultimate object is enjoyment, the means
> to it must be prompt and easy. . . . Hence the prevail-
> ing temper is at the same time ardent and soft, vio-
> lent and enervated. Men are often less afraid of death
> than of enduring effort toward one goal.[4]

Far worse than death, of course, is a life spent being cheated by death. With past greatness fading and our prospects for present greatness with future persistence already gone, we don't see death as a partner, whose union with life is grandly consummated. We see it as ingloriously humbling—as humiliating. Trapped in our human hearts and minds between the natural and the supernatural, craziness rushes in. The change we cannot control; the way of life that purports to explain it all but actually encloses us in isolation; the talented and ambitious rivals who pay to act like members of a caste they know doesn't really exist; the toil of play, in its all-too-engrossing entertainments and all-too-distracting diversions; the sexual Scylla and Charybdis of feasts with panthers and kitsch with teddy bears: all of the fears revealed in this book betoken our encompassing fear of death, which itself points back, with a bony finger, to each of them in turn.

To confront this madness, we need love, to be sure.

But we also could use a hero.

THE DARK KNIGHT

In some sense, you can love a hero. But our relationships with our heroes are characteristically about both more and less than love. What is behind our desire to draw near to Batman, a monster of a kind, albeit a strangely compelling one? Why do we pay, generation after generation, to watch him, in guise after guise, in action? What is the payoff? And what does it tell us about the place of death in our crazy lives?

Maybe mere entertainment is the answer. But before we jump to that comfortable, dreary conclusion, let's take a minute and go back a couple thousand years. Aristotle would have pegged Bruce immediately as the kind of fantastically superhuman-yet-subhuman figure who alone combines extreme self-sufficiency with an extraordinary inability to partake in common life. But Aristotle would also see, in our ritual relation to Bruce's performance, our human thirst for simple catharsis—for experiencing what he alone can do "onstage" in order to arouse ourselves in some expressive way.*

---

*"Tragedy, then, is an imitation of an action . . . through pity and fear effecting the proper purgation of these emotions." Aristotle, *Poetics*,

Now let's skip to last century. Riesman, more attuned to our democratic yearning to unite work and play as much as youth and adulthood, would see the Bruce show as a particularly rich example of the cherished "tasks which allow us to practice our skills on the universe"—in this case, the art of being self-expressive—"when not too much is at stake."

> Some of us, who lose this ability in our waking lives, retain it (as Erich Fromm points out in *The Forgotten Language*) in our dreams, which can be astonishingly witty, brilliant, and artistic—an indication, perhaps, of the child still buried within us, not so much in Freud's sense of the vicious child but rather of the child natively gifted with the capacity for imaginative play.[5]

Turn around to dip back several decades, and Freud himself excavates not just the secret child within us but also the secret hunger animating our use of theater for more than work or play. If children at play "repeat everything that has made a great impression on them in real life" so as to "make themselves master of the situation," we adults elevate our game, by transforming play into playacting, pursuing self-mastery as performers and spectators.[6] Although Freud's

---

trans. Richard Janko (Indianapolis, IN: Hackett, 1987), 1449b24–28. Like Socrates, Augustine associates the hunger for catharsis with the soft sadomasochism of the person whose lack of an anchored heart prevents him or her from locating their irreducible I. This person "wants to suffer the pain given by being a spectator of these sufferings, and the pain itself in his pleasure. What is this but amazing folly?" (Augustine, *Confessions*, bk. 3, 35–36).

shift away from "expression to self-mastery as the function of play—and, by extrapolation, of art—suggests a new(er) interpretation of catharsis" than Aristotle's, Freud recognized that our real opportunity for dramatic self-mastery lay in analysis, not mere catharsis. As much as we love the rush of cathartic experience, that love is painfully undermined at every turn by our nagging knowledge of just how *fleeting* it is. Even or especially at its most potent, catharsis is "caught within the dialectic of transience which characterizes the aesthetic process, as opposed to the intellectual one," Freud reminds us, which offers "an expression rather more *clear* than powerful."[7] Translation: the heart's catharsis doesn't bring us anywhere near as *lasting* an experience of self-mastery as the mind's analysis. It brings us face to face with the ugly truth we least want to experience because it already always haunts us—the truth of *our* transience, and the transience of all we materially achieve and enjoy. Catharsis drives us deeper into melodrama. It makes us more worshipful of life "in the moment" while reminding us of the moment's ultimate emptiness and futility.*

We, the aristocratic Freud seemed to sense, are acutely susceptible to cathartically induced craziness precisely

---

*Former heroin users will talk about the addictive quality of dropping out from time's inexorable march. Lest we think we non–heroin users are that different, the logic animating people's retreats into "softer" drugs shows we're all on the same spectrum, no matter how obscure or famous. "I was burnt out," Macklemore told Kris Ex for the cover story of the August/September 2015 issue of *Complex*, recalling how his success gave him an opportunity to revisit the habitual longing "to escape" that arose so long before his fame. "Straight up, driving all around here, like I was 15 years ago. Same shit. I felt so dumb. I felt like I'm just wasting time. What am I escaping here?"

because catharsis heightens the constitutive craziness of everyday life. "When everyone is constantly striving to change his position" and "an immense field of competition is open to all," the "perpetual fluctuations of fate" zap away our experience of time as something that opens gracefully onto inviting horizons; "the present looms large and hides the future, so that men do not want to think beyond tomorrow."[8] What equality reveals to us about humanity is *immediately* inspiring and empowering, amid our great transition, but *swiftly* daunting and dispiriting. The joys of catharsis available in Aristotle's time are quickly foreclosed to us—as, it seems, is so much else.

So we turn as quickly to analysis. Unable to use playacting as a way to experience mastery by heart, we use it as a way to experience mastery by mind. And in so doing, we cheat Freud at his old aristocratic game. We, he reasoned, could use our analytic intellect to ameliorate the sickness of soul brought on by our shared experience of everything, ourselves included, becoming imprisoned in transience. Psychotherapy could train us in strategies for being more than just safely present—being modest but purposive pathfinders, our horizons stably extended beyond the melodrama of the constantly dying moment. If "the hero, in Freud's view, is always a rebel," with "the enjoyment of art" always amounting to "vicarious, or safe, rebellion," the therapist was supposed to be an antihero of a very enthusiasm-curbing sort, using analysis to reconcile us to life and society by teaching us to master the selves they spawned within us and the selves we spawned within them.[9] But Freud, who realized how frightened we often are of real-life rebellion, didn't seem to grasp, as Tocqueville did, that the form of pride the analytic attitude offers is still too aristocratic to temper our fear that we *can't* rebel against the tyranny of transience. As Tocqueville knew, there's always something *more powerful* than our minds at work—something that makes us keep trying to reason our way out of the moment's labyrinthine prison *despite* our rational realization that it's an absurd, debilitating exercise in futility. The powerful use of the mind's feverish schemes is to keep us always on the move, unable to confront *and pass through*, in stillness, what we fear most. "However hard one may try to prove that virtue is useful, it will always be difficult to make a man live well if he will not face death."[10] In our hands, psychotherapy and psychoanalysis are all too apt to just offer us ways of being experts at manipulating our selves—a terribly tempting coping mechanism for those of us convinced that our imprisonment in the labyrinthine moment means the best we can become is master Minotaurs.*

BEASTS AND BURDENS

Life amid the Great Transition primes us perfectly to give in to lives as illusory and fantastic man-beasts, individuals with grotesquely outsized selves, incapable of living sanely

---

*This is the tragedy of Hamlet, the dark prince who does not know whether he is a knight or a knave. "I have heard," he says, "that guilty creatures sitting at a play have by the very cunning of the scene been struck so to the soul that presently they have proclaim'd their malefactions" (act 10, scene 10). Hamlet's analytic determination that playacting can make faith-deficient Claudius cathartically vanquish himself, so faith-deficient Hamlet doesn't have to defeat him in real life, is the centerpiece of his selfish and melodramatic false insanity.

face to face in society. But there is more than one way to skin a chimera. While we see ourselves like the Minotaur—the repulsively bovine mutant offspring rejected by, but not freed from, our noble parentage*—we see in Bruce Wayne a possible alternative: the successfully democratic reconciliation of our human and animal nature.

For Bruce is a prince—the eldest male heir of a bloodline so moneyed as to be self-sovereign—who becomes a knight, not a knave, by descending to our democratic level. Breaking with his noble lineage, he moves *through* the realm of Tocqueville's "aristocracy of wealth" (which marks the passing of the old age and the onset of our own) into our realm, where the terror of knowing what our world is about leaves us desperate to access a form of pride capable of arming us against that fear. To be sure, Bruce's transformation into Batman bespeaks an ancient aristocratic teaching: "the fable according to which the ancient princes were taught their art by a centaur means nothing other than that princes must be half inhuman." Machiavelli, that last of the ancients, "mentions only one teacher of princes, namely, Chiron the centaur who brought up Achilles and many other ancient princes."[11]

> His model is half beast, half man. He urges princes,
> and especially new princes, first to make use of both

---

*"Proximity begets invidiousness if one's gaze is perpetually directed toward the neighbor *in our face*." Joshua Mitchell, *The Fragility of Freedom* (Chicago: University of Chicago Press, 1995), 187, emphasis in original. "The Bible tells us to love our neighbors," says Chesterton, "and also to love our enemies; probably because they are generally the same people." *The Collected Works of G. K. Chesterton: The Illustrated London News, 1908– 1910*, ed. Lawrence J. Clipper (San Francisco: Ignatius Press, 1987), 563.

natures, the nature of the beast and the nature of the
man . . . ; Machiavelli is our most important witness
to the truth that humanism is not enough. Since man
must understand himself in the light of the whole or
the origin of the whole which is not human, or since
man is the being that must try to transcend humanity, he must try to transcend humanity in the direction of the subhuman if he does not transcend it in
the direction of the superhuman.

Here in our realm, where we are all so traumatized by the
way the no-longer-aristocratic family thrusts us so quickly
and cruelly from innocent childhood into sexual maturity,
Chiron's education is an allegory of how flawed and incomplete princely, aristocratic teachings about death will be
for us. Rousseau, Tocqueville's constant intellectual companion, used the image of Chiron training Achilles to run as a
warning not to break the boundary between the turned-in
household peace of childhood and the turned-out world of
adulthood ruled by the fear of death[12]; we seek a chimera
who shows that our mutant nature, subhuman, human, *and*
superhuman, can shelter us from that fear, not trap us inside it.

That's Batman: the hero we deserve—and the one we
want, after all.

It is *Bruce/Batman* who shows us how to find the pride
that will let us face the fear of death both sanely and actively. In director Christopher Nolan's exceedingly popular
2005 account, *Batman Begins* from Bruce's ordeal in the world
of Rousseau's warning. Child that he was, his innocent curiosity tipped him into his own estate's abandoned well. At

the bottom, figuratively dead and at risk of actually dying, the bats swarmed up and out of the subterranean layer beneath, becoming death's living symbol. Later, spooked by batlike dancers in the swanky opera his parents dragged him to, Bruce returns the false favor, dragging them away mid-show—and into their death at the hands of a mugger. Running from his fear of death only brought death face to face; still later, at the climax of his martial arts training, Bruce discovers that bringing death face to face in the most intimate way allows him to master his terror. "To conquer fear, you must become fear. You must bask in the fear of other men," his trainer tells him.

> And men fear most what they cannot see. You have to become a terrible thought. A wraith. You have to become an idea! Feel terror cloud your senses. Feel its power to distort. To control. And know that this power can be yours. Embrace your worst fear. Become one with the darkness.

At first blush, this sounds all too pat. But it is actually far better counsel than the dubious, insidious, Instagram-famous recommendation endorsed by Emerson: to "always do what you are afraid to do."[13] And it is even more American. "No necessity forced him to leave his country," Tocqueville praises Bruce; "nor was his object . . . to better his position or accumulate wealth; he tore himself away from home comforts in obedience to a purely intellectual craving; in facing the inevitable sufferings of exile he hoped for the triumph of *an idea*."[14] Wait. Sorry, not Bruce—the Puritans. Of course, the Puritans, unlike Bruce, "gave up a desirable social position and assured means of livelihood," just as we are forced to do, or driven to choose, to grasp what we long for today. But that's why we have a hero in *Bruce/Batman*. Although he's a billionaire, he uses his money not just to fight for us, but to *freely be* how we, too, can be.

To accept that death is intimately inherent to our being is no evil. It is necessary to the art of being free—for in our lifelong ping-ponging, ceasing only in death, we need to be freely whether alone or together. And even when we are alone, we are alone together with death.*

By *living out dying* well—in a sense akin to Socrates's claim in the *Phaedo* that philosophy is an intense practice of death†—we escape the humiliation of fleeing or worshiping death. Mastering our fear of death brings a pride of unique authenticity and potency. In an era when the collapse of caste inequality has shown we can't truly master other people, and the collapse of the aristocratic age's majestically slow tempo of change has shown we can no longer master the swiftness of time, we huddled masses thirst for the genuine experience of proper command.‡ Yet we also

---

*"Equality allows every man to be ambitious, and death provides chances for every ambition. Death constantly thins the ranks, creating vacancies, closing and opening careers." Alexis de Tocqueville, *Democracy in America*, ed. J. P. Mayer, trans. George Lawrence (New York: Harper, 2006), 657.

†Recall his suggestion that non-philosophers "are likely not to be aware that those who pursue philosophy aright study nothing but dying and being dead. Now if this is true," he continues, "it would be absurd to be eager for nothing but this all their lives, and then to be troubled when that came for which they had all along been eagerly practicing." Plato, *Phaedo*, Vol. 1, trans. H. N. Fowler (New York: Macmillan, 1913), 223.

‡From a different angle, to be sure, Machiavelli saw this coming. For him, the ideal hierarchical order traces its origins to "a single act" which then must only be conserved; although "this may be difficult, it is nothing compared to the problems" facing people governed by chance and acci-

hunger to know ourselves as free of the illusion of false pride, the pride of our mistaken forbears. In mastering our fear of death, we come fully to embrace death; but we also master our pride, coming fully to embrace pride.

FROM HERE TO ETERNITY

This quintessentially democratic form of pride allows us one more crucial bit of encouragement: it's proof that we, in our humanness, can occasionally master our mere animality.

From the standpoint of nature as a whole—that is, from the standpoint of animals—no personal I achieves or attains anything that stands outside of time. Naturally speaking,

---

dent, episodically. J.G.A. Pocock, *The Machiavellian Moment* (Princeton, NJ: Princeton University Press, 2003), 188. But the difficulty is not insurmountable. "When citizens perfect their own relationships in a context of time, they practice *virtu*, in the sense that they seek superiority over *fortuna*" (189). A people who "escape from *fortuna* by the exertion of a *virtu* which is their own and not that of a superhuman," Machiavelli boldly wagers, can slow time in a way "more durable, and more virtuous, than any attainment open to" a hero (190). In a time when our Bruces become Batmans, not leaders, that may be a consolation. But then the question (which haunts this book) arises: what do we need *ourselves* to be stable enough to take on the task of ordering our relationships in time? Nietzsche worried that "when the 'actors,' *all* kinds of actors, become the real masters," one "human type is disadvantaged more and more and finally made impossible; above all, the great 'architects': the strength to build becomes paralyzed; the courage to make plans that encompass the distant future is discouraged; those with a genius for organization become scarce" (Friedrich Nietzsche, *The Gay Science* [New York: Vintage, 1974], sec. 356)—a jarring echo of Tocqueville's warning that, trapped in the present, our fear of death will shutter us up in our stuffed teddy-bear hearts. Nietzsche accused those who hoped to build a "free society" of peddling an oxymoron. This book supposes that Tocqueville, Nietzsche, and Machiavelli all might at least be right about one thing: a society of people is more likely to learn about the art of being free from an all-too-human Batman than from a superhuman leader.

eternity itself is atemporal—it is, in Tocqueville's eerie sense, *only waiting*. From our human standpoint, however, eternity makes no sense without regard to time. And as we hurtle toward death in time, we oscillate frantically between the inward and the outward, torn between a rest we cannot find and a quest we feel all too unable to complete amid the intimate details of life. Without a sense of accessing the eternal in a fully human way, our natural mortality drives us doubly crazy, trivializing our pleasures even as it whips us into a frenzy of pleasure-seeking. The kind of eternity we can participate in could best be described as *transcendent, yet suffusing*. Surely, a person can partake of experiences that gesture toward natural eternity—gazing at the stars or watching a fire burn. But tapping into eternity *as a person* means partaking of experiences that humans will experience in the same way *for all of eternity*. This, our uniquely human sense of eternity, is bolstered by our reconciliation of our animal nature to our human nature via the properly proud mastery of our fear of death.

But however much solace and spirit we share with our hero, *Bruce/Batman*, he gets us only so far as a fictive symbol of this eternal trope and teaching. A world whose heroes are confined to fiction is a world without real heroes. And a world such as ours—where so much, including our relation with death, is so often experienced as an analogy to war—loses its moorings to reality in the absence of real war.

What? We need war in order to be fully human?

This is a hard idea to bear. Not only do we flee *from* war because it brings us face to face with death; we flee *to* a mutual, egalitarian psychological war wherein perpetual policing of our unstable boundaries vents an otherwise inexpressible fury, even as it distracts us from a still and silent reckoning with our shared mortality. "The collapse of personal life originates not in the spiritual torments of affluence but in a war of all against all. Experiences of inner emptiness, loneliness, and inauthenticity," warns Christopher Lasch, "arise from the warlike conditions that pervade American society, from the dangers and uncertainty that surround us, and from a loss of confidence in the future." Indeed, the "profound shift in our sense of time" induced by the rancor of everyday life forecloses participation in eternity, and augurs the death of the future. "The search for competitive advantage through emotional manipulation" promises "the glorification of the individual" but culminates "in his annihilation,"[15] the war of all against all making us more interchangeably insignificant than ever. Lasch, like Rieff, fears that our craziness has finally blurred the primal boundary between love and hate—that soon an age will have dawned when "the primacy of possibility took over the streets and millions died in them; that was the era of mass-murder therapy, when everyone was an actor, [and] all actors were lovers who . . . read a script that called for killing the thing he loved."[16]

These fears of Gotham City come to life are scary enough, but Tocqueville—always attuned to the way our oscillations make us more like teddy bears even as we grow more like panthers—does not share them. To be sure, our enmity for our neighbor, brought on by the full view they give us of our ugly mutant nature stripped bare, shows forth in a riot of petty feuds. But often we are so disgusted that we simply remain on the move and avert our gaze. Our fear

of death breeds more melancholy than malevolence, privileging the enjoyment of health and safety over the pursuit
of sickness and peril. Tocqueville would rather see our era as
an "age of embarrassment" and largely "unspendable rage"[17]
than an era of mass-produced supervillains. Our dark halves
will characteristically remain runts, weighing in at well
under 50 percent, for the same reason we will prove so apt
to avoid war's irruption into our lives. Though the inbuilt
limits imposed by life today may drive us crazy, they ensure it always seems in our own best interest to cling to
what petty pleasures we can. "The ever-increasing number
of men of property devoted to peace, the growth of personal
property which war so rapidly devours, mildness of mores,
gentleness of heart, that inclination to pity which equality
inspires," and the "cold and calculating spirit" of our democratic age all leave "little room for sensitivity to the poetic
and violent emotions of wartime."[18] Though our resent-
ments be bitter and our envy consuming, our hearts and
minds sooner drive us to go to war against our own neighbors than to join with them in going to war against a larger,
shadowy enemy. For the former conflict promises to safely
bolster our pride; the other poses a secret risk of destroy-
ing it. Unlike our petty feuds, war is a power *over* us—far
grander than we, and more than merely human.

> War reveals dimensions of human nature both above
> and below the acceptable standards for humanity. In
> the end, any study of war must strive to deal with
> gods and devils in the form of man. It is recorded in
> the holy scriptures that there was once war in heaven,

and the nether regions are still supposed to be the scene of incessant strife. Interpreted symbolically, this must mean that the final secrets of why men fight must be sought beyond the human, in the nature of being itself.*

To reckon with the nature of being is to reckon with death in a way not even *Bruce/Batman* can do for us. He is a hero but a fantasy, because he finds his irreducible I in a place we never can: neither in the teddy-bear household nor the den of panthers but in the bat cave. He is a natural sovereign unto himself; free from war because he is a one-man war. In Bruce's and Batman's very mortality and mere humanity, they are supernatural creations drawn to defend us, in collective dread, from the dark truth of true war. It is no accident that *Bruce/Batman* was born just as the Second World War began—or that he arose amid a feeling that we somehow needed to avail ourselves, in that moment, of our stubbornly but incompletely persisting aristocratic inheritance.† In his exile *for us*, he is our ideal improvement on the gentleman-ranker immortalized by Kipling—once born to wealth and privilege, now disgraced and condemned to fight as a common soldier:

---

*These are the closing lines of J. Glenn Gray in *The Warriors: Reflections on Men in Battle* (Lincoln: University of Nebraska Press, 1998), 242.

† "Bruce Wayne's first name came from Robert Bruce, the Scottish patriot, Chief of the Knights Templar. Bruce, being a playboy, was a man of gentry. I searched for a name that would suggest colonialism. I tried Adams, Hancock . . . then I thought of [Revolutionary War hero and General in Chief] Mad Anthony Wayne." Bob Kane with Tom Andrae, *Batman and Me* (Forestville, CA: Eclipse Books, 1989), 44.

When the drunken comrade mutters and the great guard-lantern
gutters
And the horror of our fall is written plain,
Every secret, self-revealing on the aching white-washed ceiling,
Do you wonder that we drug ourselves from pain?

The dark knight, the Batman, finds his sacrificial antecedent:

We're little black sheep who've gone astray,
Baa—aa—aa!
Gentlemen-rankers out on the spree,
Damned from here to Eternity,
God ha' mercy on such as we,
Baa! Yah! Bah!*

Dreams that they are, neither Bruce nor Batman can participate in eternity in a truly human way. Nor, merely dreaming of these heroes, can we. Neither cathartic nor analytic
pastimes can prepare us *through experience* to be surprised
by life's full reality; only a forceful encounter with death can
do that. Our fear of war as a killer of pride may well mask
a deeper and more secret fear—that we kill our time with
petty feuds and relentless restlessness because we are *merely*

---

*Rudyard Kipling, "Gentlemen-Rankers," *Barrack-Room Ballads and Other Verses* (London: Methuen, 1892), 63–65. At a tense moment in *Zulu* (1964), Michael Caine's snooty legacy officer, Lt. Gonville Bromhead, confesses to army engineer Lt. John Chard: "Right now I wish I were a ranker, like Hook or Hitch." "But you're not, are you?" Chard warns him. "You're an officer and a gentleman." Exhausted at film's end, Bromhead turns again to Chard. "Does everyone feel like this afterwards?" "How do you feel?" Chard asks. Bromhead: "Sick." "Well," says Chard, "you have to feel alive to feel sick."

waiting for a conflict grand and superhuman enough to re-awaken the ultimate kind of pride, the kind felt when our irreducible I converges, however fleetingly, with that within us which is both eternal and good.

"You know that I do not love war or want it to return," a French woman under Nazi occupation told an American veteran. "But at least it made me feel alive, as I have not felt alive before or since."[19] "Why is it," Walker Percy asks, "that the only time I ever saw my uncle happy during his entire life was the afternoon of December 7, 1941, when the Japanese bombed Pearl Harbor?"[20] Why is it that my own great uncle, now deep into his nineties, freely admitted his favorite decade was the 1940s? Why did Nikki Sixx thirst to find a real-life experience as intense as being brought back to life after an overdose? And why did his EMT bother to try again when the first attempt to revive him had failed?

When I sat down to figure out how to write this chapter, nothing came. Why is it that I could only see back into this book's future, and my own, when my dearest friend, Christian—who chronicles war and death for a living—admitted that night he wanted to be Bruce Wayne?

> Thus death [says Tocqueville] in some way helped
> life forward, as face to face they seemed to wish to
> mingle and confuse their functions.[21]

Love

What can a friend tell us about love? In suspicion, our standards have dropped. All too vainly we agree with Emerson that "most men are afflicted with a coldness, an incuriosity, as soon as any object does not connect with their self-love. Though they talk of the object before them, they are thinking of themselves, and their vanity is laying little traps for your admiration."[1]

With him, too, we agree—in a similarly subtle, Hamlet-like mix of naïveté and schemery—about what we want from our friends. No, not steadfastness. (Too stolid!) What we think we want is damn near the opposite, a virtual box of chocolates.

> Life is a series of surprises. We do not guess to-day
> the mood, the pleasure, the power of to-morrow,
> when we are building up our being. . . . The one

thing we seek with insatiable desire, is to forget ourselves, to be surprised out of our propriety, to lose our sempiternal memory, and to do something without knowing how or why; in short, to draw a new circle. Nothing great was ever achieved without enthusiasm. The way of life is wonderful; it is by abandonment.[2]

Today we all have heard of the supposedly ultimate love, so strong it lets your lover let you go. What could be more artful and free? But in these circles of romantic openendedness, Rieff, Lasch, Bellah, and the other great critics reacting to the culture that climaxed in 1972 saw how Emerson's spirited New World naïveté was so defenseless in the face of disenchantment. Instead of a newly liberated erotic dispensation, Emerson's cycles of abandon locked many into something more akin to "The Chant of the Ever-Circling Skeletal Family," the closing track of David Bowie's would-be *1984* soundtrack, *Diamond Dogs*. It was his final word on the old totalitarian nightmare summoned forth by black magic into democratic times. ("Shake it up, shake it up," the fallen family sadomasochistically croons to Big Brother—a "frightening paean to the Super God" of total possibility wielded over all by the single "strong man.")* Even for those of us who avoid imprisonment in the worst kinds of broken and breaking families, the possibilities Emerson's

---

*David Buckley, *David Bowie: The Music and the Changes* (London: Omnibus, 2013), 48. The song, the closing track of *Diamond Dogs* (1974), "ends" on a so-called locked groove, Bowie, the family, and we the listeners caught in an infinite loop of arrested invocation. "Beware the savage jaw of 1984," Bowie counsels earlier.

heirs pull us toward turn out to be dark tricks. What advertises itself as a freewheeling, free-loving "human potential movement," our 1970s culture critics feared, leads men and women equally to "reject any language in which permanence could be grounded in something larger than the satisfactions provided by the relationship itself."[3]

> Discussing the possibility that the changes he finds so exciting might be dangerous to their relationship, Fred says, "Intellectually I think I can justify that they might be dangerous, but I feel pretty secure about our relationship, and if one of those changes happens to be something that ends our relationship, then that's probably the way the relationship was headed anyhow. If that happens it's because our relationship didn't have what it takes or took." Marge continues his thought: "Or not that it didn't have what it takes or took, but it's just what the relationship led to."

For the 1970s critical reactionaries, the "therapeutic culture," wherein Marge and Fred learned "I'm O.K." through their "participation in *est* (Erhard Seminars Training)," feeds all too well into the superficially sane but secretly crazy American logic that tells us everything is rationally negotiable. Fred and Marge

> turned to the human potential movement as a way of revitalizing their marriage by doing what Americans have classically done—each, as an individual, making fuller, freer choice of the other based on a

truer, more authentic sense of self . . . because for them, as for most Americans, the only real social bonds are those based on the free choices of authentic selves. Both in hard bargaining over a contract and in the spontaneous sharing of therapeutically sophisticated lovers, the principle is in basic ways the same. No binding obligations and no wider social understanding justify a relationship. It exists only as the expression of the choices of the free selves who make it up. And should it no longer meet their needs, it must end.[4]

If our successions of "conflicting and unrealized selves" stubbornly reveal themselves, even only in secret, to be nothing more than Hamletesque fictions and illusions,[*] we're all too often left *not* to wonder: what other way can we live but through abandonment?[†]

---

[*] "A man is after all himself and no other, and not merely an example of a class of similar selves." Walker Percy, "The Delta Factor," *The Message in the Bottle: How Queer Man Is, How Queer Language Is, and What One Has to Do with the Other* (New York: Farrar Strauss Giroux, 1975), 26. But the "cult of personal relations," according to our reactionary theorists, "conceals a thoroughgoing disenchantment with personal relations," at the root of which is the death of the irreducible, personal I; "the ideology of personal growth, superficially optimistic, radiates a profound despair and resignation. It is the faith of those without faith." Christopher Lasch, *The Culture of Narcissism: American Life in an Age of Diminishing Expectations* (New York: W. W. Norton, 1991), 51.

[†] Philip Rieff, *My Life among the Deathworks: Illustrations of the Aesthetics of Authority,* Vol. 1 of *Sacred Order / Social Order* (Charlottesville: University of Virginia Press, 2006), 10. "It is charitable, now as it never was before, to think all the world a stage. This tragic locution of despair has become the fun place of selves dramatized by those who think of these selves as free at last from all unstaged worlds" (34).

A FATE WORSE THAN DEATH

And what becomes of us in its wake? Thomas Pynchon—who explicitly linked war, technology, sadomasochism, sex, and the worship of all possibility in his crisis-year opus *Gravity's Rainbow* (1973)—today, in the noirish *Inherent Vice*, gives us the tragic figure of stoner private eye Doc Sportello, whose glide path into the premature death of the abandoned life makes him a witness to, and ambassador of, the ravenous anticulture stalking Los Angeles amid the Manson murders. When Shasta, his old flame, lands in trouble of the free-love variety with Mickey Wolfmann—L.A.'s corrupt real estate kingpin, a silver fox and teddy panther who's "technically Jewish but wants to be a Nazi"—she comes to Doc for a kind of help no one else in her life can supply. Only he "never did let [her] down" and was "always true."[5] But there is to be no reunion or reconciliation. "Not that they were even together that long," Doc muses in melancholy.

> Soon enough she was answering casting calls and getting some theater work, onstage and off, and Doc was into his own apprenticeship as a skip tracer, and each, gradually locating a different karmic thermal above the megalopolis, had watched the other glide away into a different fate.[6]

Stoned into a mournful limbo, *merely waiting*, Doc had been too startled by Shasta's appearance—without warning in his house, but also physically transfigured, and not in a good way—to get her story straight: "she was all in flatland gear . . . looking just like she swore she'd never look."[7] In the

1980s, Allan Bloom lamented those whose American minds and hearts had so swiftly been closed up—"men and women at the age of sixteen who have nothing more to learn about the erotic. . . . They may become competent specialists, but they are flat-souled. The world is for them what it presents itself to the senses to be; it is unadorned by imagination and devoid of ideals. This flat soul is what the sexual wisdom of our time conspires to make universal."* In what Rieff calls our "spiritual flatlands," an exhausted honesty is our cold consolation. "What keeps hearts from falsehood in this flat region," he quotes the poet Joseph Brodsky, "is that there is nowhere to hide and plenty of room for vision."[8]

In fact, that grim verdict squares with Percy's more American take on our transitional era—wherein the old theory of being human has failed too much, but we know not enough of a good replacement—that only when there's nothing left to contribute to a broken interpretation are we free to create afresh. Not that creation is anywhere as impulsive as we reflexively believe it to be. In a deeper key, Percy points to Tocqueville's counsel that we "must study means to give men back that interest in the future which neither religion nor social conditions any longer inspire, and without specifically saying so, give daily practical examples" that "nothing of lasting value is achieved without

---

*Allan Bloom, *The Closing of the American Mind* (New York: Simon & Schuster, 2012), 134. At the outset of *The Last Gentleman* (New York: Picador, 1966), epigram, Percy quotes Romano Guardini's *The End of the Modern World*: "the world to come will be filled with animosity and danger, but it will be a world open and clean." Here again is the allure of the desert, tempting us to find salvation in the purification of the will, not the forbearance of grace.

trouble."* Still, if there's one divine lesson we haven't un-learned, it's that creation has a beginning.

As we'll soon see, Percy himself has a great deal to say about finding the beginning of the art of being creative and the art of creating being.

But let's not leave Doc Sportello hanging.

Abandoned yet again, with Shasta scooting off into hiding, Doc muses on the way we let nothing lasting get us in so much trouble.

> He ran through things he hadn't asked, like how much she'd come to depend on Wolfmann's guaranteed level of ease and power, and how ready was she to go back to the bikini and T-shirt lifestyle, and how free of regrets? And least askable of all, how passionately did she really feel about old Mickey? Doc knew the likely reply—"I love him," what else? With the unspoken footnote that the word these days was being way too overused. Anybody with any claim to hipness "loved" anybody, not to mention other useful applications, like hustling people into sex activities they might not, given the choice, much care to engage in.[9]

Our unspendable rage needs this claim to "permissiveness," leading largely—but never exclusively—"to expression of libidinal instincts, not to aggression."[10] *Just how weird can you*

---

*"Thus the same means that, up to a certain point, enable men to manage without religion are perhaps after all the only means we still possess for bringing mankind back, by a long and roundabout path, to a state of faith." Alexis de Tocqueville, *Democracy in America*, ed. J. P. Mayer, trans. George Lawrence (New York: Harper, 2006), 549.

stand it, brother, before your love will crack? If Doc ever finds an answer to Hunter Thompson's beloved koan, we don't see it. Instead of getting back with Shasta, restored to what looks, at least, like her former self, we leave him in the car, moving south at uncertain speed, still waiting: "For whatever would happen. . . . For the fog to burn off, and for something else this time, somehow, to be there instead."[11] Though he knows enough to know his guardian nemesis, pent-up Detective Bigfoot Bjornsen, "sure needs a keeper," Doc somehow can't know, perhaps until the fog of Shasta and the pain of nothing lasting burn away, that what he really needs is a friend.[12]

BETTER CIRCLES

"You don't want love. You want a love experience." For me, there was no more occult an experience than sitting alone in the same nearly empty theater as the one in which I saw *Inherent Vice*, watching Bruce Wayne himself, Christian Bale, play the lost man Bruce might have become in Los Angeles— pinned by little aphorisms like the love-experience one, tracing and retracing my own steps and shuttlings and circles with a precision that erased the line between illusion and reality.* Bale (also a pivotal minor figure in *Glamorama*, of course) plays the titular *Knight of Cups*, a pale yet darkened prince, like Hamlet, who does not know (until the end) whether he is indeed a knight or merely a knave. This is a film divided into chapters named after tarot cards; the final two are Death and—this one not in the tarot deck—Freedom.

---

*Just how much precision, you want to know? Buy me a drink.

Yet I was much more moved by this film as an unintentional warning of abandonment, in its all too familiar particulars, than by its seemingly redemptive conclusion. It certainly stung to read one critic, the *Guardian*'s Peter Bradshaw, sigh that Terrence Malick had taken his talents to "tiresome tinseltown LA, where a screenwriter . . . undergoes what has to be the least interesting spiritual crisis in history."[13] More theologically attuned reviewers have noted instead that the film is intended as a realistic contemporary restatement of the most interesting spiritual crisis recurrent in history—the quest of the man who, like Dante, has found himself in the middle of life astray in a dark wood of panicked paralysis.* For Malick,

---

*"It sounds trite, almost to the point of blasphemy, to call *The Divine Comedy* a self-help book, but that's how Dante himself saw it," Rod Dreher suggests in "The Ultimate Self-Help Book: Dante's 'Divine Comedy,'" *Wall Street Journal*, April 18, 2014. "In a letter to his patron, Can Grande della Scala, the poet said that the goal of his trilogy—*Inferno, Purgatory* and *Paradise*—is 'to remove those living in this life from the state of misery and lead them to the state of bliss.'" Rod recounts his own quest in *How Dante Can Save Your Life: The Life-Changing Wisdom of History's Greatest Poem* (New York: Regan Arts, 2015). Far be it from me to bat an American away from Dante or any European philosopher of the soul in the questing tradition that Malick, too, sets out from within. But the constitutive craziness of our specifically American lives should counsel a specific prudence in accepting that even Europe's grandest visions have a sharply limited role in our quest to ameliorate what maddens us so. We Americans will ever be led astray from our quest by mistaking for our own Europe's ancient longing to manifest a unity of human life and cosmic order in a comprehensive social superstructure. And the utter social failure in Europe of the Reformation and post-Reformation visions that arose in reaction to that project—whether Luther's, Marx's, Kierkegaard's, Nietzsche's, Freud's, Heidegger's, or Arendt's—should remind us that, however gifted we Americans may be at disarming weaponized European words, looking for salvation in either of the Old World's grand dreams—full unity or absolute agency—will lead us, at best, to the most isolated of margins, ceding to craziness, whether through fanatical inwardness or outwardness, the very heart of American life.

as Trevor Logan has noted, it is Kierkegaard's retelling of the quest that animates *Knight of Cups*—from the opening voiceover from *Pilgrim's Progress* to repeated recitations from the ancient eastern Christian text (and gnostic favorite) the Hymn of the Pearl[14]:

> *Then I became single and alone,*
> *to my fellow-lodgers I became a stranger.*
> *But in some way or another,*
> *they perceived that I was not of their country.*
> *So they mingled their deceit with me,*
> *and they made me eat their food.*
> *I forgot that I was a son of kings,*
> *and I served their king.*
> *And I forgot the pearl,*
> *on account of which my parents had sent me.*
> *Because of the burden of their exhortations,*
> *I fell into a deep sleep.*[15]

Sounds about right. But in the hymn, this knight who chose poorly is rescued by a reminder of his identity conveyed by his royal family and all their nobles. In the world of the film, however—our world, Tocqueville's, and, acutely, mine—there are no kings and queens, no knight and no nobles, only broken analogies to an irrecoverable era dangling like chains. In our world, it is *superficially* fulfilling and artistically sound to see Bale awake to his true Freedom through romantic love, as he appears to do in the film—finally breaking his cycle of dead-end erotic experiences to find a woman with whom he starts a family. But it would *secretly* ring hollow and false, another self-flattering fiction, if this were all there was to it.

Knight of Cups ends with rising music and scenes of the Knight with a graceful, angelic woman and a crawling baby in a garden. This woman, unlike the others, is seen only fleetingly, but we do hear her praying Psalm 139 ("the darkness is not dark to you"). How did the Knight meet this woman? What is their life together like? We don't know—but then again, Bunyan didn't give us much detail about life inside the Celestial City.[16]

But again, on the *other* other hand, why is Bale's pale Knight a brother without a keeper, a son without a friend? In addition to his struggle to escape the gravitational pull of his failed father, his troubled biological brothers (one dead, one teetering on the brink of desperation) weigh so heavy on his soul that it seemed beyond doubt to me—partly through inductive reasoning, but all the more through personal experience—that the pale Knight tries to narcotize himself in a haze of sensual encounters *because* no fellow son is acting as his keeper. But then where are his fellow sons? Where did *they* disappear to? Why can't any find him hiding in plain sight? And why doesn't he seem to need their help to snap out of the dream of the senses and find his way out of the woods? How can the Knight experience and know the truth about love without experiencing and learning the truth about friendship?

Malick doesn't explicitly answer these questions. For him, completely keeping with the dramatic narrative inaugurated by Dante, the spiritual crisis of the lost *man* is the most interesting in history because it is resolved through a cosmically correct and complete unification with the *woman*.

As the camera lingers over the back of a woman tattooed with the word *faith*, Logan observes, a voice at a sumptuous/vacuous party intones, "I've always enjoyed the company of women . . . they are closer to the mystery." Without doubt, Tocqueville pointedly avows that women are the guardians of mores, and mores the fruit of faith. But Kierkegaard's belief—"that woman was closer to God, and therefore man must follow her in order to learn the movements of faith, for it is the woman who knows how to live both in sensuousness and spirit, in the ideal and the real"[17]—pushes us, as Malick seems unintentionally to demonstrate, toward the un-Tocquevillean idea that our access point to succor from our craziness is the cosmic unity of romantic love. Let me be the first to tell you, if you haven't heard it already, that the devoted pursuit of this delusion of grandeur leads not to enchantment but disenchantment.

But there is another interpretation. Perhaps the Knight's keeper really does exist, hiding in even plainer sight than Bale's character himself. At this moment I want to create the possibility for us that *Knight of Cups* and Bale's pale Knight are actually redeemed by a secret friendship, invisible on-screen because it develops in the visually imperceptible three-dimensional space beyond its flatness, *between us and it*. By bearing the film to its end, *we* are his friends—and we men among us his fellow sons, bearing the weight of his suffering by bearing its witness, sharing in it silently. Without us, in an ironic way familiar to more than just postmodern philosophers, there "is no film." Earnestly, without us, the pale Knight is *forever* unknowable, even to himself. This idea, quietly crystallized, makes the film what it appears not to be: an allegory of friendship hiding in plain sight—one that *seems* incomplete but in fact *calls us* to see how we were in some sense always, already the ones who could complete it.

Here we draw a far better hermeneutic circle—that is, a theory of interpretation—than Emerson. "Our chief want in life," he blithely, recklessly guessed, "is, somebody who shall make us do what we can. This is the service of a friend. With him we are easily great. There is a sublime attraction in him to whatever virtue is in us."[18] This is scarily half true—again, in the same crazy, half-willful way he ignorantly recommended we do whatever scares us. "Our conversation once and again has apprised us that we belong to better circles than we have yet beheld," Emerson gushes. "In excited conversation, we have glimpses of the Universe, hints of power native to the soul, far-darting lights and shadows of an Andes landscape, such as we can hardly attain in lone meditation." Besotted with the power of the interesting, Emerson risks interpretation in the wrong way. "A tradition comes to life, and can give life, only when we *risk* interpretation, when we are willing to accept uncertainty, when we are willing to be drawn outside of ourselves"—*not* into an imagined cosmic totality of primal possibility, but "into a community of discourse."[19]

Alas, the deck of our days is stacked against us.

LOVE, EXPERIENCED

The constitutive craziness of life, wherein death is always untimely and time is always too short, shuttles us restlessly from the most interchangeably insignificant details to the out-of-reach experience of the encompassing All that we, in our obsession with unity, crave. No wonder Emerson almost admits what Tocqueville prophesies—that in the self-enclosure of the teddy-bear household, friendship reveals itself to be an illusion, one more theatrical act of self-flattery. "New York is a sucked orange," he sighs. "All conversation is at an end, when we have discharged ourselves of a dozen personalities, domestic or imported, which make up our American existence. Nor do we expect anybody to be other than a faint copy of these heroes. Life is very narrow."[20] This unquiet quietude is a far different discharge, marking a far different theory of friendship, than our silent sharing in the pale Knight's suffering.

But friendship, of course, is never carried out only in silence. Its hermeneutic circle demands of friends that they risk one another's interpretations. In a friend's hands, you make yourself vulnerable to transfiguration by their very words. "Feelings and ideas are renewed, the heart enlarged, and the understanding developed only by the reciprocal action of men one upon the other."[21] Without mutually interpreting one another, the fullest form of which is friendship, our irreducible Is remain all too minimal—weakened hosts for a parade of conflicting, unrealized selves.

The key to mutual interpretation is mutual risk: accepting the *dare* to tell the other who he or she is, no less than the dare to be told, by him or her, who we are. Our formidable *linguistic* power we share to declare things into being—ourselves and one another included!—can be used for evil, to be sure. But without it, we are nothing. Transcending and suffusing *Democracy in America* is the insight that our feverish reason must be taught forbearance; still more profoundly, it *can* be taught forbearance because of what supervenes upon reason among us—not just our remembering and imitating animal being but also our uniquely human nature as the language-speaking creature. Our animal brains "create patterns from experience and memory, and we interpret new experiences so as to conform with those patterns," an effort to ensure our survival.[22] When we realize this, our sense of survival is initially threatened by the frightening fact that what *appears* to be our "selves" is actually just the rationalized "upshot of our patterns." But then—*if we are taking on the risk of this inquiry mutually, in a hermeneutic circle safe for friendship*—we swiftly realize we have the ability to master our fear by catching ourselves in the act of fashioning the patterns of survival that seem to lock us into our false selves.

> In an environment where we're not scared—where we can openly and freely share such narrations, for instance—this can even be a startlingly humorous experience. When we realize that we can make the choice not to define ourselves inaccurately as the upshot of our patterns of memory and imitation, we recognize that being human means already and always existing in a condition of radical freedom: the freedom to make fundamental choices about who we are, and promises about who we will be.

This is not an end to fear, however. It takes courage to choose exactly how our irreducible I will be. "It also pertains to embracing others not as objects of fear, but as equally radically free creatures." The courage specific to knowing how to be the particular language-speaking creature we uniquely are gives the "tremendous power" of language its character. "Sure enough, it has a 'super-natural' feel to it because we really are overcoming some of the most basic parts of our biological operating system."

Possessed of that more-than-merely-animal courage, we may come to realize that we have entered fully into our human and personal pride *through love*—and not, like *Bruce/Batman*, through death alone.

To state it formally: the love we have encountered arises constitutively from the experience of:

(a) accepting together our reciprocal vulnerability to
(b) renew our minds, enlarge our hearts, and develop our understanding by
(c) becoming how we choose ourselves and one another to be through
(d) the transfiguring power of authentic declarations.

The more you look, the more you will find evidence for the momentous capacity of love, through the grace of language, to save us from the constitutive craziness of life.* It is in the Bible ("in the beginning was the Word")[23]; it is in Helen Keller's miraculous transfiguration, through her

---

*Though we, as Percy suggests even more directly than Tocqueville, "have been deprived of the language needed to express the longings of real human beings"—to the point of often having lost "the language of the individual" itself—our ability to be moved, touched, and inspired "by both love and death" remains, hiding in plain sight. Peter Augustine Lawler, *Stuck with Virtue* (Wilmington, DE: ISI Books, 2005), 39–40. "If you don't know any grandmasters, it's not because you haven't encountered them, but rather because their art is hidden in plain sight." Peter Thiel with Blake Masters, *Zero to One: Notes on Startups, or How to Build the Future* (New York: Crown Business, 2014), 128.

sudden awareness of language, into an irreducible I who could name, know, and choose freely how to be[24]; it is in the Declaration of Independence, where fellow friends staked their declaration of a new and special kind of country into being on their "sacred honor" as much as on the *integrity* their language could have only among a people who had already prepared the way for such a declaration to be heard and recognized.*

Love arises through the grace of language when we speak as the particular persons we are: persons whose words have meaning because they come out of mouths that are connected, in an integral way, with our knowledge of ourselves as radically free—free from the illusion that we're mere "selves" projected against the walls of our consciousness by flickering, survival-seeking patterns and memories.

THE ART OF BEING FREE

Because we are now at risk of being friends, I can tell you what I had no place to say when I first formulated and published some of these insights about language and love.

I did not learn them from Walker Percy.

Imagine, if you can, how it felt, less than twenty-four hours before I typed this sentence, to discover that Percy discovered how language was the key to a new (yet Tocquevillean) theory of how humans can freely be—by himself

---

*"Beginnings are special. They are qualitatively different from all that comes afterward," says Thiel. "Founders should share a prehistory before they start a company together—otherwise they're just rolling dice." Thiel, *Zero to One*, 109.

discovering Helen Keller's discovery of how language allowed her, and us, to be free.

> For a long time the conviction had been growing upon me that three short paragraphs in Helen Keller's *The Story of My Life* veiled a mystery, a profound secret, and that, if one could fathom it, one could also understand a great deal of what it meant to be . . . man the speaking animal, man the symbol-monger.[25]

"In order to see it," Percy discovered, "one must either be a Martian, or, if an earthling, sufficiently detached, marooned, bemused, wounded, crazy, one-eyed, and lucky enough to become a Martian for a second and catch a glimpse of it." This momentous *it*—the "Helen Keller phenomenon," he calls it—turns out to be something "everyone experiences at the oddest and most unlikely times"—not just in spaces safe for friendship but also in spaces of the greatest danger. Consider "Prince Andrei lying wounded on the field of Borodino and discovering clouds for the first time. Or the Larchmont commuter whose heart attack allows him to see his own hand for the first time."[26] Rather than occurring to ourselves as being *here*, mysteriously somewhere *inside* us, we occur to ourselves as being *there*.

In these moments we also suddenly see ourselves as capable of truly existing in the *there* of the *then*—in *the future*.

In being given a future, we are given life.

We cease to be *imprisoned* in the present moment, which becomes a prison insofar as it is tyrannized by the primary of possibility, and come to recognize who we are as specific beings possessed *of* potential, but not possessed *by* it. To be possessed by potential is to live "in a state of pure possibility, not knowing what sort" of a person you are or what you "must do, and supposing therefore that," in some tyrannizing sense, you are everyone yet no one, capable of anything.* "You have potential," Victor's college love interest tells him in *Glamorama*'s pivotal flashback scene†; Victor's imprisonment in the primacy of possibility will make him witness and ambassador to mass murder in the streets by models, if not actors, reading from scripts where all have to kill who they love. The love of a friend, meanwhile, shared through the grace of language, brings you face to face with the manner in which *you*, specifically, are possessed *of* potential.

Once it does that, it spurs friends, in love, to freely declare how one another, in accordance with their specific potential, will be newly brought to life.

Speaking of the world, G. K. Chesterton said, "The point is that when you do love a thing, its gladness is a reason for loving it, and its sadness a reason for loving it more."[27]

This is as true, if not more so, of the friend.

Imagine, if you can, how it felt to discover these things *not* through Percy in his discovery of Keller's discovery, but through Keller's discovery *as it was presented* at the supposed embodiment and heir of everything wrong with our delusional, illusory therapeutic culture: the Landmark Forum, the flagship educational program produced by the authorized intellectual successors of Werner Erhard himself, creator of *est*. Imagine how it felt to sit in the forum, trying to find

---

*"Lucky is the man who does not secretly believe that every possibility is open to him." Percy, *Last Gentleman*, 4.
†Bret Easton Ellis, *Glamorama* (London: Picador, 1999), 207.

some way to regain control as I knew I was free-falling toward divorce; and then, at free fall's end, packing up my library, moving out, "borrowing" a book that wasn't mine and seemed never to have been read—an anthology of three Walker Percy novels; imagine somehow, for some reason, picking up the anthology while casting about for some way to be during the combination breather periods and terrible doldrums between sessions of writing *The Art of Being Free*.

These serendipities bespeak a more Tocquevillean reality than our culture critic reactionaries have been willing to risk. They take the shape of a gospel: the good news that we are serendipities for one another in the making, suffused with just as much enchantment as the personal pilgrimages of our respective lives.

We are here, each in all our particularity, to declare one another into our fully human pride, mastering fear, through love even more than through death.

This is Tocqueville's open secret, no less than our own.

> I thank you with all my heart for . . . the friendship that unites us. Let us hold onto that feeling with all our might . . . : it alone in this world is firm and stable. As long as we can support ourselves on each other with confidence in this way, we will never be weak; and if one of us falls, he will at least soon be lifted up again. . . . Friendship . . . can conserve its character forever.[28]

For all of you who know who you are and all of you who don't:

The art of being free is the art of being your friend.

Conclusion

The time has come to speak of what has gone un-
said: first, the least personal matter for me in this
book—national politics; second, the most personal of all—
my son.

The two are intimately related. Their secret relation is
found in the mystery of Tocqueville's silence on the two biggest touchstones of American politics: our Founding, and
the practice of representation that Founding brought to
being.

The first mystery is solved, as both *The Art of Being Free*
and *Democracy in America* suggest, in Tocqueville's insight
that the Declaration—and then the Constitution—could
only be spoken into being for a people who had already *been*
waiting for it, prepared *not just through speech* but through the
kinds of anchoring of the heart that come *without, and prior*
to, speech. This single thought runs deep—as he says, to the

cradle. It is in the most natural and primal sense that Tocqueville's quiet, constant emphasis draws us toward the power of the passive, the invisible, and the covert—over the active, the visible, and the overt. The child is *prepared* to receive love through the grace of language *by* that love which needs no language to speak—the love of the mother.

But before we pursue this thought deeper into the realm of life at its most silent and private, let us follow it to its conclusion in life at its most vocal and public. From Tocqueville's vantage, the preeminent need for a new politics, capable of being heard and realized in our new era, is to give the passive, invisible, covert power its due—not to stamp it out by filling every last corner of the world, as we are tempted to do, with word and deed.

In our era, however, we face a dual temptation: to retreat into the dark enclosure of the brooding, bitter heart, possessed by all the worst of passivity and invisibility, and none of the best. Only by the careful, fragile grace of the face-to-face can we fashion a clearing where love may, first, irrupt into our lives through language *and then gain purchase*, commingling *with* us in a truly generative way.

It is the preeminence and urgency of this sheltered, veiled, and gradual process that does double duty against our dual temptations by pulling us *out* of bad passivity, at the same time it draws us *back* from the worst of activity and visibility: the naked, unbuffered linguistic combat of demands and counterdemands that, above all, *we* (as individuals shouting *"Me me me!"*) be recognized, and *our* suffering cured.

For, after all, the political mode in which that rage is spent is the mode of representation.

There we, who demand that the most visible, active, and

overt among us *speak for us*—in a way that, separately, we're too interchangeably insignificant to speak for ourselves—pit each of our gladiator-champions against the other, thrusting endlessly toward dark fantasies of a total victory, a final wholeness, and a complete unity that never comes.

Of this nightmarishly arrested development, *Democracy in America* speaks only covertly—much as I have hung back, so far in this book, from what we are now stuck with in spite of Tocqueville's teaching of the art of being free.

For *only now* that we have prepared each other to speak of it are we able to *occur* to ourselves as having been merely waiting for it to be named.

So let us look together at how what appeared to be such active speech in *The Art of Being Free* has been, all along, in a deeper sense only graspable now, a way to get the spirited part of us to *be patient and wait* for what comes now in the way of political wisdom. Though Tocqueville counted Jean-Jacques Rousseau as one of his three constant intellectual companions, neither Rousseau nor any theory of representation is overtly visible in *Democracy*. Yet, according to J.G.A. Pocock, "Rousseau had already asked whether there was any sense in which one moral being could represent another, and whether one did not consent to one's own corruption in choosing another whose actions should be considered as one's own."[1]

> Representation was in fact a fiction, and the creation of an entirely fictive, and fictitious, system of government might prove incompatible with the notion that one acted as a citizen or a being naturally political.

It was seen as of the essence of modernity that one inhabited a world of fictions in which self and other were creations of the partial encounters between humans in a world of exchanges.

As we have seen and shown and known, today and in this book, our dual temptations toward errant inwardness and errant outwardness manifest madly in false, failed selves and others—unto death. That does *not* mean our salvation is to be found in some revolutionary purification of the (general) will, tearing down the representative superstructure our Founders created in a pogrom of scapegoats and sins. Rousseau was half great: he recognized what would damn us but not what would save us. Rather, politically, we must reach back to what conditions us in love *so that* the language of love may be spoken and understood, to the habits of the anchored heart that teach reason to *forbear* from thrusting at what unaided reason cannot abide.

It may very well be that we ourselves have reached a condition where the knowledge of fictiveness is unsatisfying to the point of being intolerable; in doubting whether the oligarchy of politicians who oblige us to choose between them represents us in any way worth speaking of, we doubt whether we have selves left to be represented. The global economy [that is, the reality spoken and lived into being in our age] finds an ally in that postmodernism which informs us that self and society are alike fictitious and that our only choice is which fiction to buy next.[2]

Alone, the counsel of reason is a counsel of wrath: wrath damned to express itself, enraged at its own impotence, at the very political site where it is forever broken and shattered against the rocks. The mind's instinct is to quench and crush the cycle of false pride and envy toward our phony, failing selves and others by surrendering to the *logic* of a politics of equal servitude—that we reside beneath a vast and central power so immense, so total, that our interchangeable insignificance should offer us all repose, and not rage, in our shared identity.

But, surpassing unaided reason, even "if there seems to be a historical story which leads from the apparently real to the increasingly fictitious, we can return to its study and find there the many ways in which we have been making ourselves and are not yet reduced to the choice between being our own solitary fictions and being the passive material of those always anxious to do our inventing for us."[3] It is the challenge *in* our politics, but not *of* it, to recover the habits of heart contained in this book, which show *through experience* how the constitutive craziness of life can be not destroyed but *ameliorated* in a generative way; "as David Frum once suggested, it is all but impossible for an individual to attend to the imperatives of political and social decay—especially by forging friendships—if he or she is burdened, as so many are, by the personal obligations created by what we call our 'baggage,' our 'issues,' or our 'drama.' "[4] As reality decays, even the false choice between being imprisoned in illusions separately, or together, has fallen away. Today is unreal enough that we may, and often do, choose both. Cops *and* queers, as Marilyn Manson says, make good-looking models.

TO VICTORY

But now that we have successfully risked being friends, I can tell you that Tocqueville has left me stuck with one particular unresolved problem: one he, in real life, conspicuously lacked.

As precious as *Democracy in America* and the art of being free may be, they are ultimately only an education in the patience and stillness required to prepare for the truth that confronts me, alone, at the end of this book.

The *decisive* site where I must attend to the rot that spreads, suffusing us and our world, is not only—or even especially—the site of friendship.

It is the site of fathership.

When my son Nikos was two years old, his favorite book was *The Monster at the End of This Book*, starring *Sesame Street*'s lovable, furry old Grover. Over the course of that book, gripped but not paralyzed with fear, Grover labored crazily to prevent me, the reader, from turning the pages that bring me ever closer to the promised monster at the end of the book. In the final pages, of course, the secret hiding in plain sight is revealed—it's Grover himself who was the prophesied monster.

"And you were so *scared*," he laughs . . .

But on the last page, in a trembly little thought bubble, he admits it.

"Oh, I am so embarrassed."

Who is the monster at the end of this book?

I have been scrambling not to find out for a long time. Listen to me tell my son what happened to the novel,

Iconography, that I started in 1999 and am only now revisiting.*

Back then, as a young lawyer-in-training who had unknowingly moved into Promenade Towers, the building in downtown Los Angeles where Edward Norton's apartment explodes in *Fight Club*,† I wanted to capture the terror, real and imagined, that I faced gazing into the future. I felt tremendously alone. Little did I know, I was already rushing down a path another young lawyer and trader in 1990s Manhattan, Peter Thiel, had already seen coming: "I began to understand why so many become disillusioned after college. The world appears too big a place. Rather than fight the relentless indifference of the universe, many of my saner peers retreated to tending their small gardens."[5] I, like him, could see the "backdrop" behind the glamorous "mania that started in September 1998," when *Mechanical Animals* was released: "a world in which nothing," aside from the sudden explosion of cyberspace, "seemed to be working"—a meatspace rotten enough to be kicked over and ugly enough to be scourged in suddenly spendable rage. In my novel of rock stars and terrorists, I wanted to show how a boy with no real adolescence came suddenly of age, thrust into the rot by scourges both gorgeous and hideous.

It was a Tocquevillean plot, but in ways I did not understand and Tocqueville could not have imagined. Not only was Tocqueville's problem that the world of *Glamorama* and

---

*For that you have Braxton Pope to thank.

† In the movie it's called Pearson Towers, "A Place to Be Somebody." He lived on the fifteenth floor of what he truthfully called "a filing cabinet for widows and young professionals," with walls of "solid concrete," a few doors east of my place on the thirteenth floor.

Iconography existed only in an unrealized haze beyond the horizon of his imagination. What's more, to his sadness, he also never had a son. And more still, although not even I could see it at the time, *Iconography* was about a boy thrust into manhood without the protection of a father.

It was, in that way, yet another retelling of the ultimate L.A. story, *Rebel without a Cause*. In that film, "Jim's own search for love is a desertion from his assigned role of authority and fatal to its assigner: the smallest boy, who can scarcely entrust his empty gun to so young and untried a father surrogate."[6] But in *Iconography*, that smallest boy was so small he did not yet exist: my would-be hero's own yet-to-be-conceived son. Without a father's protection, my would-be hero, whose given name I've forgotten, became a premature man incapable of imagining himself into being as a father.

It was my teddy panther nightmare—a boy therapeutically allowing himself to drift half-knowingly into a realm of transgression so enabling, yet unforgiving, that its vastness and terrible sublimity masked the truth. It was actually the smallest of small gardens—the only one the boy, in his pride, would allow himself to want to tend.

At the end of *Glamorama*, imprisoned in the present and unimaginably alone, no one and nowhere, Victor finds himself "drinking a glass of water in the empty hotel bar at the Principe di Savoia and staring at the mural bar," where a giant illustrated mountain pulls him in to a place where the unimaginable and the real converge: "surging forward, ascending, sailing through dark clouds, rising up, a fiery wind propelling me, and soon it's night and stars hang in the sky above the mountain, revolving as they burn. The stars are real. The future is that mountain."[7] *Glamorama*, it was later revealed, was a book about a father who wanted to get rid of his son. My book, I finally understood, was a book about a son ridding himself of the imaginability of being a father.

Even now, with you, Nikos, it is impossible to expunge what's left of that fear. For the world around us is busily, frantically dis-imagining fatherhood, declaring it out of being, disintegrating the habits of heart that place boys in patient waiting to hear and speak for themselves the language of fatherly love.

Now having a family is just seen as one of many choices, and not necessarily a benign one. Who asked *you* to have a boy, "they" say. Nobody gave *you* the right to care more about *this* boy than any other person. It's not so much that some diligent group of wrong people or evildoers are hard at work assassinating, as Nietzsche put it, the future of man.* It's that the logic of our age, the programming language knitting and reknitting the fabric of everyday life, is structured to transform you and I into people dispossessed of our inborn capacity to make and fulfill the promises of fathership and sonship.

Without that capacity, a man is a slave.

Without it, he "has lost even the memory of his homeland; he no longer understands the language his fathers spoke; he has abjured their religion and forgotten their mores"; without it, "he is left in suspense between two societies and isolated between two peoples."[8]

---

*This is the guy, I told you when you asked, who refused to admit that evil is what you find beyond good and evil. See Friedrich Nietzsche, *Genealogy of Morals* (New York: Vintage, 1989), second essay, sec. 11.

Deprived of that capacity, "in the whole world there is nothing but his master's hearth to provide him with some semblance of a homeland."

Thus dispossessed, he has "no family; for him a woman is no more than the passing companion of his pleasures, and from their birth his sons are his equals."

Who today can say this? Who dares? Who can be coaxed into stillness and friendship long enough to grow ears to hear?

People at least are willing to hear and know how apt we are, and why, to see one another as a nation of Minotaurs, a humbled, bitter herd in a labyrinth of mirrors.

People at least remember the ancient metaphor upon which that message depends—the mutant son sent to scourge the father for his sins, but locked away in the father's endless maze.

But who today can hear, much less understand, the way I, for so long, have struck myself—as a mutant who, because of the special relationship to the aristocratic and democratic ages he inherited from his father, cannot even be banished to a labyrinth, but must seek refuge in one of his own creation?

> The prospect of being lonely but right—dedicating your life to something that no one else believes in— is already hard. The prospect of being lonely and *wrong* can be unbearable.[9]

When my novel about a son's dispossession was itself taken away from me (made impossible to imagine finishing by the terror of September 11, 2001, which not only screwed up the plot but made the whole future unknowable), I retreated into music. Here was a garden I could tend, that I had learned to tend in years of labyrinthine seclusion. Here was a field of villagers where I could celebrate safely at the base of the mountain. But there was no future in it, not to mention no money. There was the freedom of forgetfulness, passing pleasures, and primal wordless languages. Eventually there was no choice but to remember the pearl: you.

But if the pale Knight of Cups was brought back to true freedom, memoriousness and the pearl of his own, by romantic love, was he ever prepared to prevail when the world, or circumstance, or providence dispossessed him of *that?* Who could prepare him—or save him as he slipped back toward tending a false and barren Eden?

Who could forgive him the humiliation of being the monster at the end of his own book?

Not the father, I felt sure, being too aristocratic.

Not even fellow fathers, now too democratic.

But what about a fellow son, trapped, too, in this labyrinthine world? Desperate, too, to truthfully hear he was *not* doomed to life as a living dangling chain, *equally* unable either to fall freely into a future negating who he is *or* to cling fruitfully to a past keeping him who he is?

Yes. He could know how to rescue. The stamp on this book of my dearest friend and fellow son testifies to that.

And yet.

Here at the end of my book, beyond Tocqueville's horizon, it is not an end in itself to successfully cope with the constitutive craziness of the world. It is not enough to master the art of being free. It is not even enough to be friends, not even with fellow sons.

All these things must look beyond and above themselves—in our case, to you.

To a world where you are free from an enclosed and universal economy of lies.

A world where my protection is great enough to prepare you for that freedom, but not so great that it makes you ashamed to live and freely speak through it.

A world where you are free to be fatherly no less than sonly.

Where you can show the people what your name says you, and all fellow sons, truly are.

A victory.

To suffer woes which Hope thinks infinite;
To forgive wrongs darker than death or night;
To defy Power, which seems omnipotent;
To love, and bear; to hope till Hope creates
From its own wreck the thing it contemplates;
Neither to change, nor falter, nor repent;
This, like thy glory, Titan, is to be
Good, great and joyous, beautiful and free;
This is alone Life, Joy, Empire, and Victory.[10]

Notes

Introduction

1   Mark Reinhardt, *The Art of Being Free: Taking Liberties with Tocqueville, Marx, and Arendt* (Ithaca, NY: Cornell University Press, 1997).

2   Wendy McElroy, *The Art of Being Free: Politics Versus the Everyman and Woman* (Baltimore, MD: Laissez Faire Books, 2012).

3   Alexis de Tocqueville, *Democracy in America*, ed. J. P. Mayer, trans. George Lawrence (New York: Harper, 2006), 240.

4   Quoted in Christian Smith, *The Sacred Project of American Sociology* (Oxford: Oxford University Press, 2014), 61.

5   *Hamlet*, act 5, scene 2.

6   G. K. Chesterton, *Orthodoxy* (Chicago: Moody Classics, 2009), 34.

7   Tocqueville, *Democracy*, bk. II, chap. 13.

8   "He is best not at seeming to be such / but being so." The *Seven against Thebes*, in *Aeschylus I*, ed. David Grene and Richmond Lattimore, trans. David Grene (Chicago: University of Chicago Press, 2013).

9   See Walter Isaacson, *Benjamin Franklin: An American Life* (New York: Simon and Schuster, 2004), 338.

10 Laura Kipnis, "Sexual Paranoia Strikes Academe," *The Chronicle of Higher Education*, February 27, 2015, http://chronicle.com/article /Sexual-Paranoia-Strikes/190351/.

11 See *The Tragedy of Macbeth,* act 5, scene 5.
12 See Jean-Jacques Rousseau, "The Social Contract," bk. 1, chap. 1, *The Social Contract and Other Later Political Writings,* trans. Victor Gourevitch (Cambridge: Cambridge University Press, 1997).
13 See *Macbeth,* act 3, scene 1.
14 Karl Marx and Frederick Engels, *The Communist Manifesto: A Modern Edition* (New York: Verso, 2012), 33–34.
15 Jacques Derrida, *Specters of Marx: The State of Debt, the Work of Mourning and the New International* (London: Routledge Classics, 2006).
16 Jules Levallois, quoted in Françoise Mélonio, *Tocqueville and the French,* trans. Beth G. Raps (Charlottesville: University Press of Virginia, 1998), 127.

Change

1 Alexis de Tocqueville, *Democracy in America,* ed. J. P. Mayer, trans. George Lawrence (New York: Harper, 2006), 631.
2 Ibid., 9.
3 Ibid., 13.
4 Ibid., 12.
5 Ibid., 630–31.
6 Richard John Neuhaus, *The Naked Public Square: Religion and Democracy in American Life* (Grand Rapids, MI: Eerdmans, 1984).
7 Horace Mann, Twelfth Annual Report as Secretary of Massachusetts State Board of Education, 1848.
8 Tocqueville, *Democracy,* 12.
9 David Singer, "Bush Adds Troops in Bid to Secure Iraq," *New York Times,* January 10, 2007.
10 Tocqueville, *Democracy,* 645.
11 See Doug Stone, "The Coens Speak (Reluctantly)," *Indiewire,* March 9, 1998, http://www.indiewire.com/1998/03/the-coens-speak-reluctantly-83037/.
12 Tocqueville, *Democracy,* 691–92.
13 Ibid., 533.
14 Ibid.
15 Ibid.
16 Ibid.
17 Ibid., 49.
18 Ibid., 32, 508.

19 Plato, *Republic*, bk. 7, 516c–e., 195.
20 See ibid., bk. 8.
21 Tocqueville, *Democracy*, 43.
22 Ibid., 44.
23 Ibid., 46–47.
24 Ibid., 474.
25 Joshua Mitchell, "The Trajectories of Religious Renewal in America: Tocquevillean Thoughts," *A Nation under God: Essays on the Future of Religion in American Public Life*, ed. R. Bruce Douglass and Joshua Mitchell (New York: Rowman & Littlefield, 2000), 41n56.

Faith

1   Richard Rorty, "Religion in the Public Square: A Reconsideration," *The Rorty Reader*, ed. Christopher J. Voparil and Richard J. Bernstein (Hoboken, NJ: Wiley-Blackwell, 2010), 462.
2   Alexis de Tocqueville, *Democracy in America*, ed. J. P. Mayer, trans. George Lawrence (New York: Harper, 2006), 243.
3   Ross Douthat, *Bad Religion: How We Became a Nation of Heretics* (New York: Free Press, 2012), 277.
4   Tocqueville, *Democracy*, 444.
5   Douthat, *Bad Religion*, 12.
6   Ibid., 234.
7   Tocqueville, *Democracy*, 614.
8   Ibid., 615.
9   Ibid., 535.
10 See Matthew 27:46.
11 In the tenth episode of *Cosmos*, "The Edge of Forever."
12 Tocqueville, *Democracy*, 443.
13 Ibid.
14 Ibid., 451–52.
15 Ibid.
16 Ibid., 453.
17 Ibid., 483.
18 Ibid., 454.
19 Philip Rieff, *Fellow Teachers* (New York: Harper & Row, 1973), 185.
20 Philip Rieff, *Charisma: The Gift of Grace, and How It Has Been Taken Away from Us* (New York: Pantheon Books, 2007), 2.
21 See Peter Thiel with Blake Masters, *Zero to One: Notes on Startups, or How to Build the Future* (New York: Crown Business, 2014), 62.

22 Max Weber, *The Protestant Ethic and the Spirit of Capitalism*, trans. Talcott Parsons (Mineola, NY: Dover Publications), 182.

23 Thiel, *Zero to One*, 81.

24 Tocqueville, *Democracy*, 292, 312, 313, 314.

25 Ibid., 695, 703, 702.

26 Ibid., 287.

27 Ibid., 446.

28 Ibid., 450, 450–51.

29 Ibid., 450, 458.

30 See 1 Corinthians 12 (KJV).

31 Tocqueville, *Democracy*, appendix 1, 735nY.

32 Ibid., 445.

33 See ibid., appendix 1, 735nBB. See also Bret Easton Ellis, *Lunar Park* (New York: Alfred A. Knopf, 2005), esp. 5, 10, 12.

34 *Macbeth*, act 5, scene 5.

35 Tocqueville, *Democracy*, 642

36 Ibid., 296, 535.

37 Ibid., 544.

38 Ibid., 487.

Money

1 Alexis de Tocqueville, *Democracy in America*, ed. J. P. Mayer, trans. George Lawrence (New York: Harper, 2006), 551.

2 Ibid., 551–52.

3 Bret Easton Ellis, *American Psycho* (New York: Vintage, 1991), 276.

4 Ibid., 261.

5 Peter Thiel with Blake Masters, *Zero to One* (New York: Crown Business, 2014), 97. See also my "Competing to Conform," *The New Atlantis*, no. 45 (Spring 2015): 99–110.

6 Tocqueville, *Democracy*, 730, 557, 730.

7 Ibid., 557.

8 Ibid., 511.

9 Ibid., 512.

10 Ibid., 532.

11 Ibid., 535.

12 Ibid., 467.

13 Ibid., 221.

14 Ibid., 630.

15 Ibid., 537.

16 Calvin Coolidge, Address to the American Society of Newspaper Editors, Washington, DC, January 17, 1925.

17 Tocqueville, *Democracy*, 453.

18 See ibid., vol. 1, chap. 2.

19 Ibid., 47.

20 Ibid., 243–44.

21 Ibid., 645.

22 Ibid., 630–31, 631.

Play

1 Ralph Waldo Emerson, "Illusions," *Essays and Lectures* (New York: Library of America, 1983), 1115–16.

2 Alexis de Tocqueville, *Democracy in America*, ed. J. P. Mayer, trans. George Lawrence (New York: Harper, 2006), 255–56.

3 Ibid., 284.

4 Ibid., 462, 460.

5 Rob Markman, "2 Chainz's *Me Time* Will Be Music to 'Let Your Hair Down' to," *MTV News*, July 17, 2013, http://www.mtv.com /news/1709153/2-chainz-me-time-new-album/.

6 C. Vernon Coleman II, "2 Chainz's 'B.O.A.T.S. II: Me Time' Will Come with a Cookbook," *XXL*, July 20, 2013, http://www.xxlmag .com/news/2013/07/2-chainzs-b-o-a-t-s-ii-me-time-will-come -with-a-cookbook/.

7 David Riesman, *Individualism Reconsidered* (New York: Free Press, 1954), 204, 538.

8 Ibid., 202–3.

9 Ibid., 203.

10 Tocqueville, *Democracy*, 467.

11 Ibid., 468, 614.

12 *Hamlet*, act 1, scene 4.

13 Tocqueville, *Democracy*, 645, 507.

14 Ibid., 506.

15 Ibid., 507.

16 *Hamlet*, act 2, scene 2.

17 See Plato, *Republic*, trans. Allan Bloom (New York: Basic Books, 1991), bk. 1, 330e–331c.

18 Tocqueville, *Democracy*, 546.

19 Ibid., 440.

20 Ibid., 538.

21 Ibid., 539.

22 David Brooks, *Bobos in Paradise: The New Upper Class and How They Got There* (New York: Simon & Schuster, 2000), 170, 203.

23 On moral kitsch, see Avishai Margalit, "Human Dignity between Kitsch and Deification," *Hedgehog Review* 9, no. 3 (Fall 2007); on the abyss, Friedrich Nietzsche, *Beyond Good and Evil* (New York: Vintage, 1989), epigram, sec. 146.

24 Riesman, *Individualism*, 218.

25 See the "LifeList" Andrew "made in 2001 and probably looked at . . . every day until around 2008." Phillip Crandall, *Andrew W.K.'s I Get Wet* (33 1/3) (New York: Bloomsbury, 2014), 155.

26 "Erich Fromm's *Escape from Freedom* finds American specification in David Riesman's *The Lonely Crowd*." Philip Rieff, *Freud: The Mind of the Moralist*, 3rd ed. (Chicago: University of Chicago Press, 1979), 339.

27 Tocqueville, *Democracy*, 441.

28 Ibid., 533.

29 Ibid., 534.

30 Ibid., 605.

31 Ibid., 644, 530, 631, 645, 630–31.

32 Ibid., 548.

33 Emerson, "Illusions," 1117.

Sex

1 See Joshua Mitchell, *Plato's Fable* (Princeton, NJ: Princeton University Press, 2006), 113–14.

2 See, e.g., Philip Rieff, *My Life among the Deathworks: Illustrations of the Aesthetics of Authority*, Vol. 1 of *Sacred Order / Social Order* (Charlottesville: University of Virginia Press, 2006), 9–11.

3 Alexis de Tocqueville, *Democracy in America*, ed. J. P. Mayer, trans. George Lawrence (New York: Harper, 2006), 598.

4 Ibid., 538.

5 Ibid., 615.

6 Ibid., 16.

7 Ibid., 734–35.

8 Rachel Lowry, "Meet the Lonely Japanese Men in Love with Virtual Girlfriends," *Time*, September 15, 2005, http://time.com/3998563/virtual-love-japan/.

9 Zadie Smith, "Windows on the Will," *New York Review of Books*,

vol. 63, no. 4, March 10, 2016, http://www.nybooks.com/articles
/2016/03/10/windows-on-the-will/.

10   Tocqueville, *Democracy*, 735.

11   Ibid., 622.

12   Quoted in Philip Rieff, *Triumph of the Therapeutic* (New York:
Harper & Row, 1968), 24n17.

13   Andrew Polsky, *The Rise of the Therapeutic State* (Princeton, NJ:
Princeton University Press, 1991); Katie Wright, *The Rise of the Therapeutic Society* (Washington, DC: New Academia, 2011).

14   Tocqueville, *Democracy*, 291.

15   Ibid., 506, 507–8.

16   Philip Rieff, *Fellow Teachers* (New York: Harper & Row, 1973), 122.

17   See Vladimir Nabokov, *King, Queen, Knave* (New York: Alfred A.
Knopf, 2011), 172.

18   Tocqueville, *Democracy*, 585, 587, 585.

19   Ibid., 591.

20   Amy Nicholson, *Tom Cruise: Anatomy of an Actor* (New York:
Phaidon, 2014), 114, 116.

21   Tocqueville, *Democracy*, 590, 585.

22   Ibid., 291.

23   Ibid., 595, 602.

24   Ibid., 598.

25   Ibid.

26   Ibid., 291.

Death

1   Alexis de Tocqueville, *Democracy in America*, ed. J. P. Mayer, trans.
George Lawrence (New York: Harper, 2006), 531, 536, 536–37.

2   Ibid., 296.

3   Ibid., 297.

4   Ibid., 547, 527, 529, 548, 537.

5   David Riesman, *Individualism Reconsidered* (New York: Free Press,
1954), 217.

6   Sigmund Freud, "Beyond the Pleasure Principle," *The Freud Reader*,
ed. Peter Gay (New York: W. W. Norton, 1989), 601.

7   Philip Rieff, *Freud: The Mind of the Moralist*, 3rd ed. (Chicago, University of Chicago Press, 1979), 346–47, 348.

8   Tocqueville, *Democracy*, 548.

9   Rieff, *Freud*, 349.

10 Tocqueville, *Democracy*, 528.

11 Leo Strauss, *Thoughts on Machiavelli* (Chicago: University of Chicago Press, 1978), 51, 78.

12 See Joshua Mitchell, *The Fragility of Freedom* (Chicago: University of Chicago Press, 1995), 14 n132.

13 Ralph Waldo Emerson, "Heroism," *Essays and Lectures* (New York: Library of America, 1983), 379.

14 Tocqueville, *Democracy*, 36 (emphasis in original).

15 Christopher Lasch, *The Culture of Narcissism: American Life in an Age of Diminishing Expectations* (New York: W. W. Norton, 1991), 26–27, 53, 65, 70.

16 Philip Rieff, *Crisis of the Officer Class: Illustrations of the Aesthetics of Authority*, Vol. 2 of *Sacred Order / Social Order* (Charlottesville: University of Virginia Press, 2007), 167.

17 Walker Percy, *The Last Gentleman* (New York: Picador, 1966), 148.

18 Tocqueville, *Democracy*, 646.

19   J. Glenn Gray, *The Warriors: Reflections on Men in Battle* (Lincoln: University of Nebraska Press, 1998), 216.

20 Walker Percy, "The Delta Factor," *The Message in the Bottle: How Queer Man Is, How Queer Language Is, and What One Has to Do with the Other* (New York: Farrar Strauss Giroux, 1975), 4.

21 Tocqueville, *Democracy*, 27.

Love

1 Ralph Waldo Emerson, "Culture," *Essays and Lectures* (New York: Library of America, 1983), 1017.

2 Ralph Waldo Emerson, "Circles," *The Essential Writings of Ralph Waldo Emerson* (New York: Random House, 2000), 261–62, quoted in Philip Rieff, *Crisis of the Officer Class: Illustrations of the Aesthetics of Authority*, Vol. 2 of *Sacred Order / Social Order* (Charlottesville: University of Virginia Press, 2007), 74–75.

3 Robert Bellah et al., *Habits of the Heart: Individualism and Commitment in American Life* (Berkeley: University of California Press, 2008), 107.

4 Ibid., 106, 107.

5 Thomas Pynchon, *Inherent Vice* (New York: Penguin, 2009), 5.

6 Ibid., 11.

7 Ibid., 1.

8 Rieff, *Crisis of the Officer Class*, 76, 78.

9   Pynchon, *Inherent Vice*, 5.

10 Christopher Lasch, *The Culture of Narcissism: American Life in an Age of Diminishing Expectations* (New York: W. W. Norton, 1991), 179.

11 Pynchon, *Inherent Vice*, 369.

12 Ibid., 350.

13 Peter Bradshaw, "*Knight of Cups* Review: Malick's Back!" *Guardian*, Sunday, February 8, 2015.

14 See Trevor Logan, "Kierkegaard in L.A.: Terrence Malick's *Knight of Cups*," *Curator*, March 4, 2016, http://www.curatormagazine.com /trevor-logan/kierkegaard-in-l-a-terrence-malicks-knight-of -cups/.

15 See *The Acts of Thomas*, ed. Julian Victor Hills, trans. Harold W. Attridge (Farmington, MN: Polebridge Press, 2010).

16 William Randolph Brafford, "Terrence Malick's Openness to Life," *First Things*, March 17, 2016.

17 Logan, "Kierkegaard in L.A."

18 Ralph Waldo Emerson, "Considerations by the Way," *The Conduct of Life, Essays and Lectures* (New York: Library of America, 1983), 1093.

19 Joshua Mitchell, *The Fragility of Freedom* (Chicago: University of Chicago Press, 1995), 217n9.

20 Emerson, "Culture," 1017.

21 Alexis de Tocqueville, *Democracy in America*, ed. J. P. Mayer, trans. George Lawrence (New York: Harper, 2006), 515.

22 I'm quoting henceforth from my "Pink Police State: An Anatomy of the New American Regime," *Society* 51, no. 3 (May/June 2014): 274–81.

23 John 1:1.

24 Helen Keller and Annie Sullivan, *The Story of My Life* (New York: Cosimo, 2009), 10–12.

25 Walker Percy, "The Delta Factor," *The Message in the Bottle: How Queer Man Is, How Queer Language Is, and What One Has to Do with the Other* (New York: Farrar Strauss Giroux, 1975), 30.

26 Ibid.

27 G. K. Chesterton, *Orthodoxy*, quoted in Patrick Deneen, *Democratic Faith* (Princeton, NJ: Princeton University Press, 2005), 239.

28 Tocqueville to Louis de Kergorlay, March 27, 1828, in *Alexis de Tocqueville: Selected Letters on Politics and Society*, ed. Roger Boesche, trans. James Toupin (Berkeley: University of California Press, 1986), 35.

Conclusion

1   J.G.A. Pocock, "Afterword," *The Machiavellian Moment* (Princeton, NJ: Princeton University Press, 2003), 582.

2   Ibid.

3   Ibid., 583.

4   See my "Freedom and Friendship," *National Affairs*, no. 22 (Winter 2015): 163.

5   Peter Thiel, "The Education of a Libertarian," *Cato Unbound*, April 13, 2009.

6   Philip Rieff, "By What Authority?" in *The Feeling Intellect*, ed. Jonathan Imber (Chicago: University of Chicago Press, 1990), 342. See also my "Fellow Sons," in *The Anthem Companion to Phillip Rieff*, ed. Jonathan Imber (London: Anthem Press, 2017).

7   Bret Easton Ellis, *Glamorama* (London: Picador, 1998), 546.

8   Alexis de Tocqueville, *Democracy in America*, ed. J. P. Mayer, trans. George Lawrence (New York: Harper, 2006), 317.

9   Peter Thiel with Blake Masters, *Zero to One: Notes on Startups, or How to Build the Future* (New York: Crown Business, 2014), 98.

10   Percy Bysshe Shelley, *Prometheus Unbound*.

Index